TASTES
OF SOUTHERN ITALY

Rediscovering Mediterranean Cuisine

by Rita and Mariano Pane

VILLA TRITONE
www.villatritone.it
© Rita and Mariano Pane

ISBN 978-1-84753-695-2

Tastes of Southern Italy by Rita and Mariano Pane
First edition: Villa Tritone Editore - October 2005
Second edition: Villa Tritone Editore - June 2007
Third edition: Lulu.com -- September 2007

English translation of **_I sapori del Sud_** by Rita and Mariano Pane
First edition: Rizzoli - November 1991
Second edition: BUR - June 1993
Third edition: BUR - January 1994
Fourth edition: BUR - September 1998
Fifth edition: BUR - March 1999
Sixth edition: Villa Tritone Editore - July 2005

English translation by John Cullen
The photographs by Katia Kissov and Francine Reculez are on the Appendix (ISBN: 978-1-84799-011-2).

TASTES
OF SOUTHERN ITALY

To Amelia, Paola, Giuseppe,
Matteo, Alessandro

PRESENTATION

The great cellist Mstislav Rostropovich, while dining with us one evening, called for no fewer than three encores: The title of the symphony: Linguine with Sea-urchins and Shellfish. Thirty years ago, when Rita and I got married, she had just graduated from a classical preparatory school, and she knew more about Greek and Latin than she did about even the simplest way to cook an egg. Had someone told me then that one day the largest publishing house in Europe would publish a learned cookbook written by my wife, I wouldn't have stopped laughing for a week.

From early childhood I had been accustomed to cooking that was, to say the least, extraordinary, and when my happy marriage began, I left behind in my parents' home ten superb cooks. That's right, ten: my grandmother, my mother, and eight sisters. I was initiated into the art of fine cuisine as a little boy, and by the age of twelve I was already making turnovers that were quite respectable. My father was seriously concerned about this culinary vocation of mine, and he ordered me to stay away from the cooking stoves. He was hoping, properly enough, for better things from his only son. It took twenty years and the force of circumstances for me to rediscover my former vocation. I convinced Rita by example that cooking is a joy, and that gastronomy is one of the most civilized of mankind's pleasures.

Deluding ourselves with ideas of easy success, we began with the simplest things and discovered that exactly those are the most difficult. If you blunder while preparing a dish of spaghetti, garlic, and oil, it's a catastrophe beyond redemption, whereas a mistake in an extremely complicated sauce is easily made good. We tried all kinds of cuisines, from Austrian to Russian, Indian, Chinese, and French. But in recent years we've determined that there's nothing in the world better than our southern Italian and Mediterranean cuisine.

There are many reasons for this assertion: ours is not only a healthy way of eating, but also, by turns, refined, erotic, light-hearted, multifarious, stimulating, evocative. Southern Italian cooking has always been aristocratic or plebeian, and sometimes both. The advent of higher standards of living has had the unfortunate but inexorable result of importing into southern Italy the middleclass cuisine of the richer, more prestigious North.

This is a frenchified cuisine, native to Piedmont (like the members of the House of Savoy who were Kings of Italy), a rich cuisine loaded with butter, cream, and elaborate sauces. And despite all the talk about it, Mediterranean cuisine is invaded daily by Interlopers that have nothing to do with it. Almost every recipe that we have sought out and included here provides not only gastronomic delight but also a veritable lesson in proper nutrition. Our cuisine is the discovery of a rigorous science obedient to chemical, physical, dietary, and hygienic laws in the kind of harmonious balance one finds only in true works of art.

We've expended considerable effort in tracking down old, lost recipes, and we have scrupulously tested every one of them. In these years of work on this project, the most gratifying surprise has been that we have both regained the trim figures of days gone by, and our blood pressure and cholestorol level are exactly what the doctor ordered!

We've found recipes copied and recopied by nuns, old aunts, grandmothers, cooking enthusiasts. We've read hundreds of books and recipe-collections, Italian and foreign, and we've discovered, to our amazement, some true literature. One interesting and sometimes amusing observation we've made is that many recipes were dictated by people who had no intention of revealing their secrets. And there's nothing worse than altering a recipe or changing the strict order of its prescribed steps. In some cases, the results can be devastating. If you change an E-flat for a B-sharp in a music score, dissonance will result, and if you change basil for sage, that will be a dissonance too!

Cooking combines art and mathematics; art, because all the senses are involved, and mathematics, because there are rigorous rules.

A recipe is indeed like a score, and it should be read like music, with no possibility of changing notes. On occasion, it can be interpreted, passionately, discreetly, philologically, romantically, and (why not?)conveniently, but ingredients cannot be changed.

From Gesualdo of Venosa to Stravinsky: between these names lies all the classical music we know and love. From the Medicis, Gonzagas, and Bourbons to Escoffier: all modern Occidental cuisine takes shape in this period. After the void, we soon come perilously close to the absolute.

Cooking, like music, rests on three fundamental pillars: tone, timbre, and rhythm. The ingredients indicate the tone or key that produces the notes in the kitchen; the timbre, which in music ranges from the harpsichord to the most modest wooden flute, extends in the kitchen from the big copper pot to the humble strainer; and the rhythm that gives the beat translates into heat intensity and cooking time!

Few cooks can permit themselves the luxury of invention, and were those few well-informed, they would discover that their original inventions are generally old news. So let's ignore our creative impulses and dedicate ourselves passionately to the kind of sensitive, evocative interpretation that always gives delight and brings back, if only unconsciously, "remembrance of things past." Our research has so emphasized this principle that we almost called our project "the past recaptured."

The south of Italy was poor, but like all poor lands it gave its people a great gift: free time for meditating, testing, inventing foods with simple ingredients which, lovingly treated, become sophisticated dishes. We've learned that arriving at brilliant and sometimes even genial culinary solutions requires the labor of generations.

Normans, Arabs, Angevins, Swedes, Aragonese, Spaniards, French - all have left on our land marks that time may have rendered unrecognizable but are nevertheless still present, like DNA strands, offering sublime delights in infinite combinations.

There was a time when automobiles and elevators didn't exist, when room temperature was very hot or very cold, according to the season, and work of whatever kind required great physical effort; the body burned a quantity of calories enormously higher than what is usual today.

With this in mind, we have lightened most of the recipes presented here by removing the excess fats which, in the past, provided necessary fuel for the body, but which today have nothing better to do than deposit themselves serenely on our flanks, requiring drastic diets and debilitating slimming programs.

The cuisine of the 18th century has taught us the art of miniaturization, which allows foods to cook rapidly and preserves all their organoleptic characteristics - their tastes and aromas - while the shorter cooking time consumes less energy. We have not discussed wines, because this topic, as everyone knows, would require more than twice the space allotted us here. We can say only that our southern Italian region has some incredible surprises in store, in the form of wines as good as the best produced on the planet Earth.

Every day we see more and more people discovering the joys of good cooking and dedicating themselves to it with passionate enthusiasm. We're moving farther and farther away from Orwell's prophecy of a uniform, insipid cuisine; indeed, dining is becoming increasingly less formal, and seems even more delightful when one can drink and converse in a relaxed, civilized atmosphere.

Writing this book has given us a great deal of pleasure. We hope as much for our readers, not just from reading it, but, above all, from using it.

MARIANO PANE

GLUTTONY: A CAPITAL PLEASURE

«Prima digestio fit in ore»
«Nutrit quod sapit»
«Quod appetit, prodest».
(School of Salerno, 13th cent.)

«I hate people who are not serious
about meals. It is so shallow of them».
(Oscar Wilde,The Importance of Being Earnest)

Some of the latest cooks are students of the fanciful and modern nouvelle cuisine, which had its beginnings in that gastronomical gymnasium of the ephemeral known as Futurism. Futurism desired to break with the past in all areas of art and culture, and the resulting chasm left the imagination deliriously, dangerously free. But the attempt to inflict a debacle upon the Mediterranean diet by bringing together incompatible ingredients and upsetting the order of courses failed to make people forget home-made pasta, the flavors and images of tradition, the aroma of a turkey raised for a year and then cooked with love and with the help of simple but genuine ingredients.

The new school of cooking, born at the same time as culinary cubism, which reached its greatest expressive heights with the *bouillon cube*, revealed itself in 1912 at the table of the French poet Guillaume Apollinaire, who relates in *Le poète assassiné* (published. 1916) the birth of gastroastronomy.

Named thus in memory of the astronomer Lalande (1737-1807), an eccentric type who was reputed to munch on frogs and caterpillars, this cuisine did not in any way purport to appease hunger. Here's the menu of the first gastro-astronomical dinner:
- Stemless fresh violets seasoned with lemon juice
- Angler-fish with eucalyptus leaves
- Loin steak with tobacco (Faux filet lattaignan, in memory of Gabriel Charles de L'attaignan [1697-1779], abbot, libertine, and author of frivolous, satirical poetry, including *J'ai du bon tabac*)
- Quails in licorice juice
- Walnut oil and brandy salad
- Savoyard cheese with grated nutmeg

The condiments demonstrate rare culinary audacity and certainly go beyond the usual limits of gastronomy. Thus "Futurist cooks will march vigorously in the tracks of their *successors*."[1]

So we can see that the history of gastronomy is an endless struggle between tradition and innovation. Apicius, citizen of imperial Rome, wrote a treatise on cooking wherein he recommends covering natural products with gravies, jellies, and complicated sauces, thus rendering them unrecognizable. Good cooking preserves the tastes of foods. Our happiness, our abilities, our actions are subject to the influences of the barometer, but also to that marvelous creature, the creature who cook. It is not heresy, but simply acknowledgment of how firmly our roots are bound to the earth, to say that every one of us absorbs everything our senses detect: what we see, what we hear, what we touch, what we smell, and, above all, what we eat. Some molecules of the odors that we sense enter into us through our olfactory organs, but, when we taste, our organism possesses the food entirely, with all its characteristics.

We are, therefore, what our senses encompass: what we look at, what we listen to, and (why not?) what we eat.

"Man is what he eats,"[2] Feuerbach asserted polemically, attempting to focus the interests of philosophical reflection upon man and maintaining that the human body, the world of the senses, is the foundation of reason. Rabelais knew this well. Gargantua and Pantagruel, with its interminable lists of dishes, satiates all the senses and invites the reader to consume its contents in a burlesque verbal delirium that delights in sheer quantity. The gourmand of tradition smacks his lips, whoops, raves: "Divine!" He feels a hedonistic, almost orgasmic pleasure in savoring, tasting, chewing, swallowing, like Petronius's Trimalchio or a character in Rabelais.

It is rare to meet such a person today. In our world flavors are often impersonal, cold, indefinable, and emotions are internalized. Sophisticated, international foods may claim to be scientific, but they don't speak to the soul, they remind us of nothing. Everyone has the "madeleine" that he deserves! What's a flavor, or a taste? It doesn't stop at the instant when the tongue receives the food as it enters the mouth; tastes evoke memories, nostalgia, as Proust's madeleine does. Thanks to gluttony, which arouses what the trouble de la mémoire had kept hidden, we can be certain that, in spite of forgetting, nothing gets destroyed in the unconscious. There can occur a moment of bewilderment, a kind of loss of consciousness, when your eyes don't see the room you're in and your mouth is savoring a taste that was there before, preserved in a corner of the memory.

But let's pass, now, to humbler topics. We don't want this book that we're getting ready to write to be a pretentious cooking treatise. You won't find anything in here about sophisticated sauces, complicated dishes, or ironclad rules. Just common sense, love for the oral traditions, for the dear, good, old dishes our grandmothers prepared, and the desire to recapture the tastes of days gone by have persuaded us to compile this collection of recipes.

The art of cooking has a language that speaks through images and is therefore perfect even for our society, dominated as it is by what Jeari Baudrillard calls "the ecstasy of communication."[3]

Thus the laden table becomes the place where man, as a social being, ratifies a contract, the place of solidarity, of relationships. There we satisfy our natural needs and restore our spirit, where Mediterranean people, as we are, honor the cult of hospitality, where flavors and textures harmonize, as words and sounds harmonize in other languages, the music, where we display attractive foods and dishes in all their variety, where the theme of natural, elemental beauty is wedded to the fragile human elaborations. Our work has delighted us and has taken us on a winding, rich journey through the gastronomical marvels of the South. We've been gathering material for some time, and we're certain that the pleasures of the table have an influence on our happiness and even in our business affairs. An aphorism that we find particularly congenial comes from Anthelme Brillat-Savarin is Physiology of Taste: "To invite any one, implies that we charge ourselves with his happiness all the time that he is under our roof."[4]

The success of a dish - and therefore its flawless execution - presupposes the knowledge of a suitable recipe, not a list of arcane sorceries, but a guide to a logical series of rational operations, as in a successful mathematical equation. Since we must nourish ourselves, and since we spend on average several hours a day at table, let's try to do so in the best way possible, with discernment and delight. We like to agree with Leibniz: this could be the best of all possible worlds. No rule states that good cooking must be plain or elaborate; there's great plain cooking and great elaborate cooking, just as there's bad plain cooking and bad elaborate cooking.

When you prepare food, your mind wanders and your hands work; it's like a creative drug. It's a kind of priority check, allowing us to rediscover the enjoyment of working with our hands, and the pleasure of knowing that we can reawaken nostalgia for what we loved as children. The necessity of working, cultural standards, the evolution of tastes, the factors of climate and religion constitute a patrimony of rooted traditions.

Nevertheless it's proper for the exceptional to cohabit with the commonplace, and for the palate to savor the simplest dish along with the one concocted out of many distinct, identifiable elements.

A meal where each dish tastes delicious and cheerful conversation regales and uplifts the mind is a luxury and a delight. Let your table companions be no fewer than the Graces, and no more than the Muses! Septem convivium, novem convicium. ("Seven make a feast, and nine a confused noise," says the Roman poet Varro in a fragment from his Menippean Satires.)

Marvels of the Roman Banquets

Fine dining was unknown to the Romans as long as they were struggling to subjugate their neighbours; they ate most frugally. But when their conquests had extended to Greece, whose civilization was more advanced, exciting dishes were introduced in Rome. From the Greeks the Romans learned letters and philosophy; their customs grew more refined, and they discovered the delights of the banquet. Their extravagance reached incredible heights. The most varied foods were imported from all over the known world: guinea-fowl and truffles from Africa, pheasants from Greece, rabbits from Spain, peacocks from Asia, peaches from Persia, cherries from Greece, apricots (which began to be cultivated in Roman gardens) from Armenia; fish were transported in vases filled with honey; aromas, flowers, and spices were infused into wine. The number of courses served grew considerably. The emperor Geta, brother of Caracalla, gave a notable luncheon that lasted three days and included thousands of exquisite dishes. Elioagabalus astonished his guests with rice, truffles, and pearls, or fava beans in shells of gold. Such luxury and the desire to satisfy the guests' sensual desires degenerated into gross extravagance, into jaded exhaustion, as described by Horace, Tibullus, and Petronius Arbiter.

From Petronius Arbiter's Satyricon

"What's eating you?" he asked. "Have you forgotten where you're going tonight? Trimalchio's giving the meal. He's real swank. Got a great big clock₅ in his dining room so the old man won't forget how fast his time is slipping away"... On a large tray stood a donkey made of rare Corinthian bronze; on the donkey's back were two panniers, one holding green olives, the other, black... in dishes shaped to resemble little bridges there were dormice,₆ all dipped in honey and rolled in poppyseed.₇

Nearby, on a silver grill, piping hot, lay small sausages, while beneath the grill black damsons and red pomegranates had been sliced up.

"Friends," he said, "I ordered peahen eggs to be set under that hen,₈ but I'm half afraid they may have hatched already. Still, let's see if we can suck them." We were handed spoons - weighing at least half a pound apiece - and cracked open the eggs, which turned out to be baked from rich pastry. To tell the truth, I had almost tossed my share away, thinking the eggs were really addled. But I heard one of the guests, obviously a veteran of these dinners, say, "I wonder what little surprise we've got in here." So I cracked the shell with my hand and found inside a fine fat oriole, nicely seasoned with pepper. Spaced around a circular tray were the twelve signs of the zodiac, and over each sign the chef had put the most appropriate food. Thus, over the sign of Aries were chickpeas, over Taurus a slice of beef, a pair of testicles and kidneys over Gemini, a wreath of flowers over Cancer, over Leo an African fig, virgin sowbelly on Virgo, over Libra a pair of scales with a tartlet in one pan and a cheesecake in the other, over Scorpio a crawfish, a lobster on Capricorn, on Aquarius a goose, and two mullets over the sign of the Pisces. Servants came with a tray on which we saw a wild sow of absolutely enormous size. Perched rakishly on the sow's head was the cap of freedom which newly freed slaves wear in token of their liberty,₉ and from her tusks hung two baskets woven from palm leaves: one was filled with dry Egyptian dates, the other held sweet Syrian dates.

Clustered around her teats were little suckling pigs made of hard pastry, gifts for the guests to take home as it turned out, but intended to show that ours was a brood-sow...

The servants came in with an immense hog on a tray almost the size of the table... The cook... drew out his knife with a shaking hand and then slashed at the pig's belly with crisscross cuts. The slits widened out under the pressure from inside, and suddenly out poured, not the pig's bowels and guts, but link upon link of tumbling sausages and blood puddings...

"First off we had some roast pork garnished with loops of sausage and flanked with more sausages and some giblets done to a turn. And there were pickled beets and some wholewheat bread made without bleach. Then came a course of cold tart with a mixture af some wonderful Spanish wine and hot honey...chickpeas and lupins, no end of filberts, a roast of bearmeat some soft cheese steeped in fresh wine some tripe hash, liver in pastry boats and eggs topped with more pastry and turnips and mustard a dish of olives pickled in caraway. This deadly entertainment would never have ended if the servants had not brought on another course, consisting of pastry thrushes with raisin and nut stuffing, followed by quinches with thorns stuck in them to resemble sea urchins.[10]

The history of ostentatious dining preserves memories of frenzied trenchermen, of superb banquets, such as the one organized by Domenico Grimani, Patriarch of Aquileia, member of a most ancient Venetian family, son of a doge, friend of Pope Julius II and of Lorenzo de' Medici, and a munificent patron of the arts. His fabled banquets included 90 courses, ending with pies from which, after they were sliced open, birds took flight.

This was a case for saying with Boileau:

Chaque acte dans sa pièce est une pièce entière.

Starting from gluttony, memory, and Nature's grace
to approach the Italian South

At the end of the 18th century, Charles Maurice Talleyrand- Périgord discoursed eloquently upon food, with as much interest and seriousness as if he were discussing an important political problem. This intellectualization of gluttony gave birth to gastronomy, an expressive neologism that has its roots in two Greek words and says clearly what it means. Gastrolatry (from - gastri latreuo - meaning "stomach-worship"), on the other hand, is a more rarely used term, defined by Balzac as follows: "Digestion engages human capacities in an internal struggle which, among gastrolators, is equivalent to the profoundest joys of love."[11]

In the Roman time the era of temperance engendered the era of curiosity and with it the experiments that led to sensuality and corruption. Persian excess influenced the Greeks, and the Romans, once they were rich and powerful, abandoned their frugal ways and indulged in high living that reached new levels of culinary depravity. Thus Trimalchio and his cooks served meat shaped to resemble fish, and Apicius, a notable culinary degenerate who lived at the time of the emperor Trajan, discovered ways of preserving many foods and turned every meal into a spectacle offering such dishes as peahens' eggs containing warblers stuffed with the spiced yolks of chickens' eggs.

Man has always sought out food with elective affinities to that marvelous machine, the human body, the perfect, complex, unfathomable result of creation. Without flinching, we gulp down not only junk food, but also tons of questionable, obscure more than harmful medicaments, we subject ourselves to brutal cosmetics and expose our epidermis to the piercing, malignant light of the quartz lamp; so we can't allow ourselves to contemplate the black-magic pharmacopeia of the past with ironic haughtiness and complacent disdain.[12]

Instead of a culinary primitivism in the guise of energy-dispensing alchemical transformations, we have opted for recipes where different tastes act together in harmony, producing the kind of unity in diversity that painters give to their colors. Why encourage the anesthesia of the city-dweller's palate, accustomed as it already is to fast food, preservatives, chemical additives, and frozen dinners?

Gluttony, a sin that every good Christian of former times struggled against with lenten fasts and frugal meals, is regarded today even by good Catholics as a metaphor, although it remains one of the seven capital vices.

But only gluttony can put food back in its rightful place and revive the joys of the table and the link between cooking and love. The excesses of epic tragedy (as in the case of the progenitors of humankind, whose historic greediness led them to ruin for the sake of an apple) are, however, unnecessary. From Christ to Luther, from Plato to Kant, a great deal of culture has taken shape around a loaded table; in fact, as Lévi-Strauss writes in the Raw and the Cooked, once people have abandoned the animal stage of tearing at uncooked food with their teeth and begun to cook, gradually discovering the correct proportions, culture is underway. The cooking process transforms raw, unprepared food, a natural object never subjected to human elaboration, into a cultural object. The implicit equivalence of two oppositions, that between nature and culture and that between the raw and the cooked, is emphatically manifest in the figurative use of the word cru ("raw") to indicate the absence of normal cultural intermediaries between the body and things.

In the 17th century, danser à cru could mean to dance barefoot, just as today, in English, to sleep "raw" means to sleep without clothes.[13]

Strangely enough, a supporter of rawness, the Cynic philosopher Diogenes, although he rejected the cooking-fire because it implied civilization, was the first to eat publicly in the market-place. Until that period (4th century B.C.), model citizens habitually took their meals in enclosed places, fairly to ritual taboo.[14]

Prepared food, therefore, can be understood as cultural evolution or as ostentatious display, almost like fireworks, as in the case of a meal described by the Sicilian writer Tommasi di Lampedusa in his historical novel *The*

Leopard. When food is linked to the theme of time, it can signify growing up, reaching adulthood, with the inevitable loss of innocence; when linked to greediness, it can imply guilt complexes and their consequent punishment, as Lewis Carroll - emphasizing the negative aspects of growing up-demonstrates in Alice in Wonderland.[15] Food can stimulate memory, as in Proust's Recherche, in which the author, dunking little cakes into his tea, evokes hidden sensations that furnish him with the key to understanding his life. *"I raised to my lips a spoonful of the tea in which I had soaked a morsel of the cake. No sooner had the warm liquid and the crumbs with it touched my palate than a shudder ran through my whole body, and I stopped, intent upon the extraordinary changes that were taking place. An exquisite pleasure had invaded my senses, but individual, detached, with no suggestion of its origin. And at once the vicissitudes of life had become indifferent to me, its disasters innocuous, its brevity illusory - this new sensation having had on me the effect which love has."* [16]

Also evocative of love are the cream and chocolate pastries coveted by the pretty misses to whom Guido Gozzano dedicates his insinuating poem "Greedy Girls":

> *I'm in love with all the women*
> *who eat pastries in the sweet-shops.*
>
> *Ladies and young ladies*
> *with ungloved hands*
> *choose their pastries. And*
> *become little girls again!*
>
> *Among those heady, strange,*
> *cloying fragrances -*
> *citron, syrup,*
> *creams, custards,*
>
> *Parisian essences,*
> *sweet violet, scented hair -*
> *Oh! these women, they*

become little girls again!

Why does an inconvenient law
forbid my drawing near
and kissing you,
one by one,

O beautiful fresh mouths
of young women,
kissing you where you taste
of chocolate and cream?

I'm in love with all the women
who eat pastries in the sweet-shops.[17]

What joy, what tastes, what delight! It would be a real sin to renounce certain charms, certain pleasures! Yet people's approach to food is unfocused, mechanical.

The collective madness, the frenzy of the modern era has precipitated a crisis in the age-old cradle of good cooking, the lands of Mediterranean Europe, the cultural traditions of the Latin countries.

On the other hand, the civilization of the countryside, which has always respected the rhythms of Nature and promoted good nutrition through agricultural methods consistent with biology, enjoys a calm and tolerant relationship to food. Horace, in his Art of Poetry, writes: *Omne tulit punctum qui miscuit utile dulci* ("He who mingle usefulness with delight gains everyone's approval")[18] .

And Jean-Jacques Rousseau, in Emile: *"If I might have cherries when it's freezing and golden cantaloupes in the dead of winter, how could I delight in their taste when my palate has no need of being moistened or cooled? In the dog-days of summer, would I take pleasure in heavy roasted chestnuts?*
Should I prefer them, fresh from the skillet, to gooseberries, to strawberries, to the many thirst quenching fruits that the earth offers me with such solicitude?" [19]

Mediterranean cuisine is deserving because of using fresh foods, particularly seafood, to their fullest advantage, flavouring everything with virgin olive oil, one of Nature's greatest gifts, which promotes rather than impedes the digestive process. If we follow the principles of this cuisine, we can recover those whole foods - fibers, cereals, wheat - recommended by Hippocrates as early as the 4th century B.C. Pythagoras too, as Ovid tells us in his Metamorphoses, taught men to nourish themselves with grains, with the fruits that flexed the branches with their weight and the grapes that swelled on the vines, with tender, pleasant herbs, with milk, with honey. The ancient age, called golden, was content with the fruits of trees and herbs and did not pollute its mouth with blood.[20] This according to Pythagoras, but also according to the principles of Mediterranean cuisine, which gives pride of place to pasta, legumes, and vegetables.

By the same token, it bends all its efforts to arouse even the most dormant appetite with foods that caress it instead of assaulting it. Some types of cuisine seem to favour an ideal, ever-enticing image at the expense of the food, all of which tastes the same. Mediterranean cuisine evokes more than any mere illusion, no matter how attractive.

Our cuisine restores hearty eating to its proper eminence, no longer to be humiliated by the rigors of chronic dieting.

The attributes that delight our sense of taste are order, variety, proportion, and surprise. Without going so far as Vatel, maître d'hôtel to the Prince of Condé, Louis XIV's cousin, who gained eternal fame in 1671 by falling upon his sword because a shipment of fish from Boulogne failed to arrive in time for a banquet,[21] nor so far as Brillat-Savarin, who expected his guests to burst into tears of joy before the inimitable culinary art of certain gastronomical preparations, the Mediterranean diet proposes the recovery of a genuine approach to pleasurable nutrition, the discovery of the power that certain ingredients have to recall familiar, beloved tastes, and a just balance between tradition and the new rules of lighter eating.

The Mediterranean Sea bathes the shores of many countries and has witnessed the passage of many eras and people – Minoans, Ancient Egyptians, Phoenicians, Romans and Greeks, to name a few.

Wars, trade, and cultural exchanges among the Mediterranean lands have fostered gastronomical exchanges as well, and it is for this reason that many foods show little variation from Spain to Yugoslavia to Morocco to Greece to Italy. But among all the Mediterranean lands, it is Campania which Pliny the Elder, in Book III of his Natural History, singles out for an ampler description: *"Campania...[is] so blest with natural beauties and opulence, that it is evident that when nature formed it she took a delight in accumulating all her blessings in a single spot - how am I to do justice to it? And then the climate, with its eternal freshness and so replete with health and vitality, the sereneness of the weather so enchanting, the fields so fertile, the hill sides so sunny, the thickets so free from every danger, the groves so cool and shady, the forests with a vegetation so varying and so luxuriant, the breezes descending from so many a mountain, the fruitfulness of its grain, its vines, and its olives so transcendent; its flocks with fleeces so noble, its bulls with necks so sinewy, its lakes recurring in never-ending succession, its numerous rivers and springs which refresh it with their waters on every side, its seas so many in number, its havens and the bosom of its lands opening everywhere tothe commerce of all the world, and as it were eagerly stretching forth into the very midst of the waves, for the purpose of aiding as it were the endeavours of mortals! For the present I forbear to speak of its genius, its manners, its men, and the nations whom it has conquered by eloquence and force of arms."*

The very Greeks themselves, a race fond in the extreme of expatiating on their own praises, have aptly given judgment in its favour, when they named but a small part of it *Magna Graecia"*.[22]

And Goethe, who came to Italy in 1786 and stayed for a long time in Naples, remarked in his *Italian Journey* upon the Neapolitans, who, discontentedly rumbling because of their economic straits, wait like Vesuvius for the right moment and meanwhile release steam through sarcasm, satire, and lavish banquets.

"There is no season when one is not surrounded on all sides by victuals. The Neapolitan not only enjoys his food, but insists that it be attractively displayed for sale. In Santa Lucia the fish are placed on a layer of green leaves, and each category - rock lobsters, oysters, clams and small mussels - has a clean, pretty basket to itself. But nothing is more carefully planned than the display of meat, which, since their appetite is stimulated by the periodic

fast day, is particularly coveted by the common people. In the butchers'stalls, quarters of beef, veal or mutton are never hung up without having the unfatty parts of the flanks and legs heavily gilded".[23]

Several days in the year and especially the Christmas holidays are famous for their orgies of gluttony. The Toledo and other streets and squares are decorated most appetizingly; vegetables, raisins, melons and figs are piled high in their stalls; huge paternosters of gilded sausages, tied with red ribbons, and capons with little red flags stuck in their rumps are suspended in festoons across the streets overhead. I was assured that, not counting those which people had fattened in their own homes, thirty thousand of them had been sold. Crowds of donkeys laden with vegetables, capons and young lambs are driven to market, and never in my life have I seen so many eggs in one pile as I have seen here in several places. Not only is all this eaten, but every year a policeman, accompanied by a trumpeter, rides through the city and announces in every square and at every crossroad how many thousand oxen, calves, lambs, pigs, etc., the Neapolitans have consumed. The crowd show tremendous joy at the high figures, and each of them recalls with pleasure his share in this consumption.

So far as flour-and-milk dishes are concerned, which our cooks prepare so excellently and in so many different ways, though people here lack our well-equipped kitchens and like to make short work of their cooking, they are catered for in two ways. The macaroni, the dough of which is made from a very fine flour, kneaded into various shapes and then boiled, can be bought everywhere and in all the shops for very little money.

As a rule, it is simply cooked in water and seasoned with grated cheese. Then, at almost every corner of the main streets, there are pastry-cooks with their frying pans. The octopus-and-mussel-vendor occupied a very choreographic space: upon benches painted in the liveliest hues were large copper jars filled with gaudy paper flowers. In the middle the vendor would cook huge octopuses in plain seawater. The skillets in the fried-food stand turned out the most incredible variety of fritters with fish, greens, and fruit. The stall selling the "head-and-tripe-pork" was framed by ivy vines; a calf's head was fastened to the center by large nails and surrounded by pigs' trotters, and the whole was garnished with lemons, halved or entire.

The Importance of Regional Cuisine

In the Age of Enlightenment, Italian cuisine was still the most significant in Europe, even if French cooking had by then won over many royal courts (including that of the Bourbons at Naples). Anonymous works included the *Piedmontese Cook, Perfected in Paris* (1766) and *The Tasteful Sweet-Maker* (1790).

Vincenzo Corrado, author of *The Amorous Cook* (Naples, 1786) provides many recipes that use ingredients from the New World: tomatoes, beans, corn flour, and chocolate and vanilla for sweets. Francesco Leonardi, cook to Catherine II, Empress of All the Russias, wrote *The Modern Apicius* (1790) and may be considered one of the first to codify Italian regional cuisines in his *Gianina, or the Alpine Cookbook.*

Vincenzo Agnoletti, Marie Louise of Austria's cook, also gives Italian regional recipes a great deal of importance in his *Cook and Pastry-Maker's Manual*. Later, Ippolito Cavalcanti, Duke of Buonvicino, compiled a collection of Neapolitan recipes, remarkable for its delicious, colorful language and the amount of space it dedicates to a sauce that he calls *culì*, which seems to be a type of glaze to be poured over "whatever you want."

In the sixteenth century the virtuous doctor Leonardo Fioravanti, a tireless truth-seeker who learned from everyone he met, from a "woman of low custom" and from a "stupid, uneducated greengrocer, who showed us his wares one by one", believed in "knowledge through science" as well as "knowledge through experience"[24] and published his findings in his *Medicinal Fancies*. While living with Sicilian peasants, he elaborated the theory he called "food mutation," according to which one must not change diets too casually; the consequences can be lethal. The learned balladsinger Giulio Cesare Croce illustrated this point with his story of the death of Bertoldo, the peasant hero, defender of the defeated and oppressed, fount of irrefutable wisdom ("Keep the scales true, for the poor man as for the rich man"; "Never pass judgment on anyone in anger"; "Spurn flatterers as well as slanderers").[25] This pius agricola, forced to be untrue to his natural diet, perishes inexorably.

The complex of food, life, death, health, and disease justifies the search for that regimen sanitatis which must be suitable to the individual's physiological structure and equilibrium, so that the assimilation and metabolizing of food, thanks to the cook's knowledge of nutrition, may be healthy, coherent, and restorative of lost energy.

Michel Foucault, in *L'usage des plaisirs*, writes that diet "characterizes the way we conduct our own existence and allows us to establish a complex of rules for behavior... Diet is an art of living."[26]

Rita Vessichelli Pane

FOOTNOTES

1. Guillaume Apollinaire, Le poète assassiné, Gallimard, 1979, pp.256-260.
2. Ludwig Feuerbach, Advertisement to Moleschott, Lehre der Nahrungsmittel: Für das Volk (1850).
3. Jean Baudrillard, L'altro visto da sé, Edizioni Costa & Nolan, 1987.
4. Jean Anthelme Brillat-Savarin, La physiologie du goût, Julliard. English translation: The Physiology of Taste, Liveright Publishing Corporation, 1948, p. xxxv.
5. In Roman times, possessing a clock was a luxury almost unheard of.
6. The Romans considered dormice a luxury.
7. Poppyseed was a frequent ingredient in Roman cuisine and was used in various sauces.
8. Peacock was a luxury dish.
9. The wild pig had been designated as to be the last dish of the dinner the previous day, but the satiated guests had passed it up; now it comes back to the table dressed like one of the freed slaves, who wore a "freedom cap" as a sign of their new social condition.
10. Petronius, The Satyricon, translated by William Arrowsmith, New American Library, 1959, pp. 38-75.
11. Honoré de Balzac, Grand Dictionnaire Universel Larousse du XIXe siècle.
12. Piero Camporesi, I balsame di Venere, Garzanti 1989, p.75.
13. Claude Lévi-Strauss, Il crudo e il cotto (The Raw and the Cooked) .
14. Diogenes Laertius, Lives of the Philosophers, Loeb Classical Library.
15. Lewis Carroll, Alice's Adventures in Wonderland.
16. Marcel Proust, A la recherche du ternps perdu, Grasset, 1913. English translation by C. K. Scott Moncrief, Remembrance of Things Past, vol. 1, Swann's Way, pp. 54-55.
17. Guido Gozzano, Poesie, Rizzoli, 1977.
18. Horace, Ars Poetica, line 343.
19. Jean-Jacques Rousseau, Emile.
20. See Ovid, The Metamorphoses, Book XV, lines 75-98.
21. Georges Bernier, Antonin Carême. La sensualité Gourmande en Europe, Grasset, 1989, p. 16.
22. Pliny the Elder, Natural History, Book V, translated by John Bostock and H. T. Riley, London, Bohn's Classical Library (1855), Vol. 1, pp.182-183.
23. Johann Wolfgang Goethe, Italienische Reise translated as Italian Journey, 1786-1788 by W. H. Auden and Elizabeth Mayer, San Francisco: North Point Press, 1982, pp. 319-321.
24. Piero Camporesi, La miniera del mondo, Il Saggiatore 1990, pp. 10 –11.
25. Giulio Cesare Croce, Le sottilissime astuzie di Bertoldo, Einaudi, passim.
26. Michel Foucault, L'usage des plaisirs, Gallimard.

BREAD

Il pane (Bread)
(serves 8-10)

7 cups flour - 1 level tbsp. salt - 3 cups water -
1 ounce brewer's yeast or natural yeast - 3 tbsp.
vegetable or seed oil

Writers often use the image of bread in their work to represent such conceptions as the commonplace, the good qualities of human nature, or age-old wisdom.

Homer called mankind "bread-eaters." The history of bread provides the basic nucleus of the history of man's survival in connection with his primary need: food. Leavening was first discovered by the Chinese around 2000 B.C., followed by the Egyptians in the Mediterranean Basin. According to the reliable descriptions of Giovanni Michele Savonarola of Ferrara, the 15th century author of the Book of Nature, and of the Properties of Things that Nourish, and of Unnatural Things, bread was made with every kind of grain: barley, millet, and rye, as well as flour made from fava beans and other legumes, and even with chestnuts and pears. Poppy and sesame seeds, which had narcotic powers, were sometimes mixed in. But wheat was the most prized ingredient of all.

In order to make the bread easier to digest, aniseed or fennel (good for the eyes) or saffron was added to the dough. Bread is essential to our culture, and it is no exaggeration to suggest that bread was probably responsible for the origin of our industrial society, simply because it required us to invent machines to grind grain and to harness power (wind, water, etc.) to make the mills work. Wasn't the mill, perhaps, the first mechanical instrument?

Bread is also a presence in the life of the spirit. Every religion has made use of it, and Christ himself identified his body with bread. The symmetry of the grains in an ear of wheat is an emblem of harmony and equality. No other food incorporates such a sense of the brotherhood of man. In his Last Judgement, Michelangelo painted the image of a woman who, crouching and desperate, clasps something very precious in her arms: yeast! In fact, it's easier to make yogurt at home than yeast. That's the reason why women used to preserve it from day to day and hand it down within the family lest it get lost.

Yeast is a substance composed of microorganisms that can provoke the fermentation process. In bread-making, a bit of dough is fermented, then mixed in with other dough so that that will ferment too; this is natural yeast. Artificial or brewer's yeast, on the other hand, contains microorganisms obtained during the process of making beer. We aren't far from believing that the pleasure of making bread at home is comparable to an act of creation.

Dissolve the yeast in a cup of lukewarm water. Put aside for ten minutes. Mix into the flour with the salt, working the dough well for ten minutes in order to liberate the gluten. Add the olive oil and sufficient water to obtain a smooth dough, not too stiff and not too soft. Knead into a ball, then place in a bowl. Cover with a teatowel and put the bowl in a warm place away from draughts. When the dough has doubled in volume (around one hour), cut into small pieces, shape them as you wish, and place them on a greased baking-pan.

After around 45 minutes, the loaves will have doubled in size. Bake them at 400°for about a half-hour or until the bread has reached a nice golden color.

Pane al latte
(Bread with milk)
(serves 8-10)

7 cups flour - 2 eggs - 1 ounce brewer's or natural
yeast - 2 tbsp vegetable or seed oil - 1 cup milk - 1
cup of water - 1 tbsp butter - 1 tbsp sugar - 1 tbs salt
- 1 tsp pepper - 1 tbsp fennel seed
to colour the bread before cooking: 1 egg yolk - 1 tsp
honey - 2 tsp milk

Mound the sifted flour on the working surface, make a well in the center, and put in the well the eggs, oil, butter, sugar, salt, pepper, fennel seeds, and the yeast, which you will have dissolved in one cup of lukewarm milk. Begin to blend all these ingredients, starting from the middle, using a fork with one hand and the fingertips of the other. Eventually you'll have to put the fork aside and knead the mixture well.

You should obtain a rather soft dough; if there's not enough liquid, you can add some water. After the dough has become soft and smooth, place it in a bowl, cover it with a towel, and let it rise until doubled in size (about 1 hour) in a closed place away from air currents. After the rising, turn out the dough again, and very delicately tear off pieces and shape them as you wish: ring-shaped buns, plaited rolls, croissants, etc. Place these small loaves on a greased baking-pan and let the loaves rise again until double in size, brush them with a mixture of the beaten egg yolk, the honey, and 2 tsp. milk, then cook in a pre heated oven at 400°for about half an hour, or until they appear puffed up and golden. If the operation has been successful, the fragrance will be your first reward.

Time eats life, history eats itself, and men eats what remains,
and everything finishes and then starts again, etcetera, etcetera,
then...why do we eat what we eat?
"Because we're hungry!" would answer a restless duodena, a greedy
stomach,an anxious colon.
We eat and we drink for more complex cultural and human reasons.
Food – sweet, salty – has a huge importance in our life.
Leo Longanesi said: "Italian unification is linguistic and culinary".
Nowadays only some regional tastes keep us together.
[...]
Food is a consolation, a tranquilliser, a language.
We need it to love ourselves (sometimes to hate ourselves if we exaggerate)
and to make the others love us: when we invite them for lunch.
First of all, eating together, in good company
- the "agape" for Ancient Greeks –
makes possible that anything you bite with the teeth and move with the
tongue becomes tasty, merry, joyful, different from simple nutrition.
Only Saints can eat alone, all the others must sit at Rita Pane's table.
Her diabolic cuisine is worth a quote from Joyce's Ulisse:
"God makes the food, Devil the cooks".
As" a name is a destiny", Rita Pane or "Bread", provokes in us a jerk whilst
the yeast rises in her bread.
Stomach doesn't care to ask the hand what it is offering.

Roberto d'Agostino

APPETIZERS

Acciughe aceto e olio
(Anchovies in oil and vinegar)
(serves 6)

1 lb salted anchovies - 1 cup vinegar - 1 cup olive
oil

One of the most traditional preparations served as an appetizer along the Amalfi coast on holidays or their vigils (Christmas Eve, Ash Wednesday, Good Friday) is anchovies in vinegar and olive oil.

This mixture probably descends from the Roman garum, which was a sauce ("Apicius's Sauce") obtained by seasoning anchovies, sardines, or herring with salt and aromatic herbs and fermenting them (according to Apicius) in a mixture of sweet honey and sour vinegar. Carefully bone and wash the salted anchovies in cold water, being certain to remove all traces of salt. Arrange on a plate and cover with vinegar. Let stand at least 2 hours.

Pour off the vinegar while holding back the anchovies with a fork, then cover them again with the olive oil. After about an hour the flavors will have married wonderfully, and the anchovies will be ready for serving, accompanied by country-style bread and delicate, pale yellow unsalted butter.

Alici marinate
(Marinated anchovies)
(serves 6)

1 lb anchovies - 2 lemons - 1/3 cup olive oil - 1 clove
garlic - parsley - a few mint leaves - salt

Extremely simple to prepare, marinated raw fish makes a tasty cold appetizer. The indispensable prerequisite for success: the fish must be perfectly fresh (ça va sans dire). Remove head and bones from fish. Wash fish repeatedly under cold running water to remove all impurities and traces of blood. Arrange on a plate and cover with lemon juice. Marinate for about 2 hours, until a superficial color change shows that the juice has begun to cook the fish but has not impregnated it completely.

This procedure brings out the natural flavor of the fish, which is enriched but not overwhelmed by the lemon. Some find that vinegar produces a more harmonious effect and therefore prefer it; it's equally effective.

After two hours, pour off the liquid and replace it with a mixture of very finely minced parsley, chopped garlic, two or three mint leaves, olive oil, and salt.

Caciottine
(Fresh cheese in the basket)

For 12 portions, placed in small reed baskets: 1
gallon milk - 2 tsps rennet

These are little tidbits, light and barely moist, delights fit for a cardinal. As the principal ingredient, it's imperative to use milk fresh from the cow and still warm, into which you mix 1 tsp. of rennet (the same procedure is followed in preparing junket).

Cover the container with a linen cloth and let stand for at least two hours. At this point, the milk will have set and you can make cuts in it with a knife. Pour a cup of boiling water into the center of the container. This step allows the whey to separate completely from the milk. Spoon the curdled milk into the little baskets; as the whey continues to separate and drain off, continue to add curdled milk until the baskets are full. After about an hour, the caciottine will be ready te eat. Place them as they are on fig, grape, or lemon leaves and serve without salt; simple, but extremely delightful.

A similar cheese was the fresh, boiled cacio that the Romans called manu pressus, a favorite of Augustus Caesar. When the milk began to coagulate, it was divided into portions and immersed in boiling water, then worked by hand into various shapes and pressed into wooden molds. After the milk had set in salted water, it was colored by smoking with applewood.

Our modern smoked provola (a fresh soft cheese) is derived from this ancient cheese.

Carciofi arrostiti
(Roasted artichokes)
(serves 6)

12 artichokes (use young, tender artichokes, Italian
if possible) - 4 cloves garlic - lots of parsley - 1
tbsp. lard - salt - pepper - 1/3 cup olive oil

A stupendous, fragrant dish, this requires, for best results, the use of coals burned almost white, so that the cooking process will be slow, gradually penetrating the artichoke's center, that heart filled with a thousand tastes, not the least of which comes from being cooked over live coals. Procure artichokes of the first quality, the ones that first appear on the stem, not the lateral growths. Wash them well, but don't cut away the hard outer leaves, which will protect the artichokes from heat that's too aggressive.

Finely mince garlic and parsley together, season generously with salt and pepper, mix in a tbsp. of lard. Put a tsp. of this mixture into the center of each artichoke. Place the artichokes on the coals and cover them with aluminum foil. Every five minutes or so, uncover and sprinkle them with a solution of salt and water. Dribble oil into them at the last minute; avoid dripping oil onto the coals, because this can give the artichokes a bad odor. They'll be cooked just right after about an hour. Take off the unpresentable outer leaves, put the artichokes on a serving dish, and, if necessary, add more olive oil.

Cozze au gratin
(Mussels au gratin)
(serves 4)

2 lbs. mussels - 4 tbsp. olive oil - 4 cloves garlic - parsley - 4 tbsp. finely grated breadcrumbs - salt - pepper

Ideal for beginning a meal, wonderful by the seashore.
Wash the mussels and immerse them in lightly salted water for about an hour to eliminate the sand. Drain and scrape off any algal incrustations. Put mussels in a large skillet with a little olive oil and two crushed garlic cloves. Cover and cook over medium-high heat, shaking the skillet from time to time, until the shells open. Be wary of those that remain closed, and don't use them. Drain the open shells but save the liquid, passing it through a fine sieve to eliminate sand particles. Put this liquid aside to cool. Heat oven to 350°. Finely mince 2 garlic cloves and a bunch of fresh parsley, add olive oil, breadcrumbs, and a few tbsp. of mussel juice, and make a thin paste. Adjust seasoning with salt and pepper. Line up mussels on a baking-pan, having thrown away the empty half-shells, and cover the halves containing the molluscs with the sauce you've prepared. Bake for 8 minutes and serve hot or cold.

Fagottini di formaggio fresco al profumo di limone
(Lemon-scented fresh cheese parcels)
(serves 4)

½ lb fresh cheese (mozzarella) - 16 lemon-tree leaves - salt - pepper - a lemon.

Cut the mozzarella into eight slices. Wash the lemon leaves well and place them two at a time on the work surface so that they form little crosses. Put a mozzarella slice in the center of each cross and season with salt and pepper and a little lemon zest. Wrap the leaves around the cheese and fasten each "parcel" with two toothpicks. Place on a baking-pan and put them quickly into a 400°oven for 5 minutes. Serve immediately.

Giuncata
(Junket)
(serves 4)

1 qt. milk - 1 tsp rennet - lemon leaves - 1 fresh lemon - salt - pepper

This recipe is for those fortunate ones who can obtain fresh milk straight from the cow, and lemons and lemon-tree leaves right from the garden. If you have these few but rare ingredients, you're in business!
Parmi toccar giuncata e fiutar rose ("I seem to touch junket, and inhale roses"): Mozart's Don Giovanni, enraptured by Zerlina, thus describes his ecstatic feelings in the words of Da Ponte's libretto. Junket offers absolute softness to the touch; smooth as velvet, it dissolves tenderly in the mouth, caressing the gullet with chaste sensations.

Pour the fresh milk, preferably still warm, into a large saucepan. If the milk has already cooled, heat it over a very low flame to about 100°. Remove from heat, add ½ tsp. of rennet (available commercially), mix with a wooden spoon, and cover with a cotton cloth. Let the mixture stand for about 2 hours. Rennet contains the enzyme rennin, a substance used to curdle milk in cheese-making. Rennet is extracted from the abomasum, the fourth or true digestive stomach of ruminants. In calves, this stomach secretes an acidic liquid, namely rennet. After the 2 hours have passed, prepare the little reed baskets (you can find pretty ones in Chinese import shops). Wash the lemon leaves well, then arrange them artfully in the baskets. Using a skimmer or perforated spoon, scoop the milk out of the saucepan (the milk will have set) and gently transfer it to the baskets. Place these on a tray and refrigerate for about an hour; from time to time, pour from the tray the whey or milk serum which will continue to separate from the milk. Before serving, sprinkle with grated lemon rind. Invite your guests to season their junket with salt and freshly ground pepper.

Insalata di mare (Seafood salad)
(serves 8)

4 small octopuses, about ½ lb. each - 2 squids - 4
cuttlefish - 8 prawns - 1 lb. shelled shrimps
For the "bouillon": 2 carrots - 1 onion - 2 stalks
celery - 2 tomatoes - 4 white peppercorns - ½ cup
vinegar - salt - parsley
For the dressing: 1 clove crushed garlic - ½ cup
olive oil -1 lemon - parsley

Squid - elegant swimmers, almost transparently pink when alive;cuttlefish - from the sandy ocean-floor, with wings that wave like plumes; octopuses - lazy residents of rock fissures.

Mediterranean prawns - languid, they let themselves be captured in trawling nets; shrimps - other rose-colored crustaceans, unfortunately often secondclass citizens, but sometimes marvelous when caught along our coasts: this confederation produces an harmonious union where tyrants don't exist.

Prepare a rich "bouillon" in a large saucepan with about 3 qts. of water, the grated carrots, the whole onion, the rinsed celery stalks, the halved tomatoes, the peppercorns, the vinegar, the parsley, and salt to taste. Boil for twenty minutes. Strain the bouillon. Add peeled shrimp, and cook these for three minutes. Take out shrimps and set aside. Remove the eyes and ink pouches from the octopuses, wash them, and boil whole in stock for 15 minutes. Remove, set aside, and boil squid and cuttlefish for 10 minutes. Finally, boil the prawns in the bouillon; they will be ready in five minutes. Rub a fine white platter with crushed garlic, and place one whole octopus in the center. Cut up the other octopus, along with the squid and cuttlefish; arrange attractively with prawns and shrimps around the centerpiece.

Dress with lemon juice, olive oil, and finely minced parsley. Good when served cold.

Olive ripiene alla siciliana
(Sicilian-style stuffed olives)
(serves 6)

24 large olives - ½ cup breadcrumbs - 1 tbsp. grated pecorino cheese - 1 clove garlic - parsley - vinegar - 1 tbsp. olive oil - flour as required - 1 cup vegetable oil for frying

Large Sicilian olives, swollen with sunshine and flavors, can be stuffed and fried like sardines a *beccaficu* (see Fish section).
Mince a handful of parsley very finely with one garlic clove .
Mix in a bowl with the breadcrumbs, cheese, olive oil, and vinegar.

Stuff the stoned olives with this mixture, dust lightly with flour, and fry them in plenty of hot cooking oil. Serve them hot as tasty tidbits before dinner.

Pomodorini gratinati
(Stuffed and baked cherry tomatoes)
(serves 6)

2 lbs. cherry tomatoes - 1 cup breadcrumbs - 4 anchovies - 1 tbsp. capers - salt - olive oil

Cut off a cap from the top of each tomato and remove central portion with pulp and seeds. Rub pulp through a sieve and add enough breadcrumbs to obtain a thick, creamy mixture. Wash and bone the anchovies, break them into small pieces, and add to the mixture with capers and a thin ribbon of oil. Stuff the tomatoes with this mixture, line them up in a baking-pan, season with salt and a dribble of oil, and bake them in a moderate oven for about twenty minutes or until they begin to shrivel.

Sauté di frutti di mare
(Shellfish sauté)
(serves 6)

l lb. cockles - 2/3 lb. razor-clams - 1 lb. clams - 1 lb. mussels - 5 tbsp. olive oil - 2 cloves garlic - 1 hot pepper - parsley - sliced bread

Wash all the shellfish well, brushing them and removing the beards from the mussels. Leave them 10 minutes in salted water.
Heat the oil in a skillet and lightly fry the pepper and the crushed garlic. As soon as the garlic begins to brown, remove it, and add the other ingredients in order of size and resistance to cooking: first the cockles, the aerodynamic

razor-clams, and finally, together, the clams and the mussels. Wait one minute before adding each successive kind of shellfish. Cover the skillet and shake it now and then so the heat reaches every side of every shell; they'll all be open after a few minutes. Turn off the heat. Strain the liquid released by the molluscs through a fine cloth. Return the liquid to the skillet and bring everything back to the boil. Arrange the molluscs on a heated servingplatter, pour the hot cooking liquid over them, and strew them with plenty of minced parsley. Accompany with toasted bread slices.

Terrina di fegato
(Liver terrines)
(serves 6)

*2/3 lb. calves' liver - 3 ½ ounces chicken livers - 1
onion - 7 tbsp. olive oil - 2 tbsp. butter - salt - pepper
- 1 bay leaf - 1/2 cup marsala
For the béchamel sauce: 1 ounces butter - 2 tbsp.
flour - 1 cup milk - salt – pepper*

Terrines, originally a way of using up scraps and leftovers, have reached a high level of refinement.
Heat the olive oil and half the butter in a frying pan; add a small, thinly-sliced onion. When this becomes soft and transparent, add the chicken livers (first remove any greenish traces with a damp cloth), and then the calves' livers cut up small. Season with salt, pepper, and bay leaf. Sautè over low heat until liver is cooked through, but don't brown it (otherwise it will become tough). Pour in marsala; after it evaporates, remove pan from heat. Let cool a little. Finely chop livers and onions (remove bay leaf) on a cutting board.
The béchamel or cream sauce, which you will have prepared earlier, should now be dense and cold; add to liver mixture with the other half of the butter. Mix and pass through a sieve or food mill.

Place in lightly-buttered terrines (small earthenware dishes) and cover these with lids or plastic wrap to avoid discoloration. Let the patés set in the refrigerator for a few hours before serving. Remove them from their containers, place on a bed of bay leaves, and garnish with parsley sprigs or radish slices. Serve with oven-toasted bread.

STOCKS AND SOUPS

Brodo
(Broth or Stock)
(serves 8-10)

4 lbs. beef - 2 lb. chicken - 7 qts. water - celery -
parsley - onion - 4 carrots - 2 tomatoes - 6 cloves -
½ cinnamon stick - 2 eggs - 3 peppercorns - 1
shotglass Sherry - salt

A good stock is often needed for cooking.

The most flavorful cuts of beef for making a broth are the shanks, rump, shoulder, ribs, and brisket. Capons, hens, and doves add excellent flavor to the stock when used with beef. For every pound of meat, you need about 1 ½ quarts of water. If you want the best flavor from the stock, put the meat into ice-cold water and then light the gas. Slowly the heat will dissolve the "osmazoma" that Brillat-Savarin talks about. This is the exceptionally flavorful substance extracted principally from red-meat animals.

The "osmazoma" gives good soups their quality, and their particular fragrance is released through its presence. If you're having ten for dinner, boil 4 lbs. of beef and a hen in a large, heavy pot. Before the neurotic "mad cow" started to complicate our shopping in the butcher's shop, a white bone was always added to the stock to enrich the flavor. When it was cooked and cut, a wonderful, white soft delicious marrow could be spread on bread for the happiness of the guests.

Furthermore the bones are composed largely of gelatine and calcium phosphate and were used in preparing rich galantines. Before boiling (at about 150°or so) remove the impurities or scum that will rise to the surface of the stock; this is the albumin contained in meat and blood. Then season the stock with salt and a bunch of aromatic vegetables - celery, parsley, onion, carrots, tomatoes - few cloves, cinnamon, some peppercorns. Cover the pot and simmer for three hours or more over a low heat; the pot should "smile," so that the stock does not boil vigorously.

When the meat is well cooked, pass the stock through a fine sieve covered with a tight cloth which will absorb the rest of the impurities. Although this stock is quite good, you can refine it by cooling it and removing from the surface as much fat as you can. To do so beat two egg whites till stiff and mix into the stock when it is lukewarm. Bring it again to simmer. All the impurities will be drawn into a foam, like a syrup, which can then be removed. Now pass the stock again through a sieve or fine cloth. Finally add a shot of Sherry and let it evaporate.

This stock, which cheers the stomach and prepares it to receive and digest food, is called fond in French and brodo in Italian. The secret of its success lies in moderation, in a careful balance of ingredients, so that the flavors will not be concealed, but heightened.

Brodo della nonna Speranza
(Grandmother Speranza's stock)
(serves 6)

2 ½ qts. meat stock - 2 lbs. zucchini - ½ lb ground meat - grated Parmesan cheese - 1 egg - parsley - stale bread - ½ cup milk – salt

Add peeled, sliced zucchini to a good boiling stock, along with meatballs made from a mixture of the ground meat, egg, chopped parsley, salt, and some stale bread crumbs, softened in the milk and then squeezed. The meatballs and zucchini will cook in the broth; serve hot with plenty of grated Parmesan.

Benedetto pasquale
(Easter benedict)
(serves 8)

1 lb lean beef - half a chicken, about 1 lb. - 1 lb lamb - 2 onions - 4 tbsp. olive oil - water - salt - pepper - parsley - 6 eggs - grated Parmesan and Pecorino cheese

In some small villages on the Bay of Naples, the traditional Easter dinner begins with benedetto, a very special type of stock.

Cut up the various meats (beef, chicken, lamb) into small pieces and brown in a little oil. Then add the whole onions, and, after a few minutes, when everything is taking on a golden color, pour water into the pot, about three ladlefuls for each diner. Season with salt and pepper and cook slowly for about two hours. After cooking, strain the broth, then add chopped parsley and the eggs, beaten with grated Parmesan and a little grated pecorino.

All these flavors, well combined and heralded by exciting fragrances, will surely find hospitable stomachs more than happy to participate in the ceremony of the squaresima or end of Lent, when, after the period of fasting (now rarely observed), taste organs mortified by abstinence can again rejoice.

La Squaresima
("The end of Lent")

Fasting is a voluntary abstention from food for some moral or religious purpose ... it dates from the highest antiquity...

Let us now glance at what was done on fasting-days. Meat could not be eaten; people had no breakfast; and consequently were more hungry than usual.

At the regular hour they dined as heartily as they could, but fish and vegetables are soon digested, and before five o'clock everyone was ravenous; some were looking at their watches and did their best to be patient; others were working themselves into a passion, even whilst securing their salvation.

About eight o'clock they had not a good supper, but a "collation," a word borrowed from the convent, and so called because at the end of the day the monks assembled to hold conferences on the fathers of the Church; after which they were allowed a glass of wine. At the "collation," neither butter, eggs, nor anything that had been alive, was served. They were obliged to be satisfied with salads, preserves, and fruits, - food, alas! not very suitable for the appetites people had in those times; but patience was practised for the love of Heaven, they went to bed, and began again the same programme every day during Lent...

The strict observance of the Lenten fast gave rise to a pleasure unknown at present - namely, that of breaking our fast by breakfasting on Easter Day.

(From *The Physiology of Taste* by Anthelme Brillat- Savarin)

Fondi
(Bases)

Little virtues, or using things in the kitchen that would otherwise get lost.

Let's get to know some kitchen "bases," so-called because they are basic ingredients in many elaborate, structured dishes, whose characters are determined by the presence of these "distilled" flavors.

Meat base is a brown, very concentrated stock made from veal knee-bones broken up into small pieces, oven-toasted, and hen enriched by savory vegetables (onions, carrots, celery, parsley, tomato) in small quantities, since they are to be confederates and not tyrants in the final taste.

When making meat base, you must keep the water level high enough to cover the bones; keep a pot of water boiling on the stove so that you can add water to the base without changing its temperature. Before adding the vegetables, skim the stock well so that it is free of impurities.

The cooking process will take about five hours, over a very weak, lazy flame; at the end of this period, filter the stock through a fine strainer. Chill the stock so that the fat can be skimmed off easily; after you skim it, the stock will be ready for use.

For fumet or fish stock, instead of the veal bones used in the meat base, we resort to fish heads. Make sure they're very fresh, remove the gills, and wash thoroughly to eliminate blood and impurities. Put a small amount of oil in a saucepan and "sweat" a finely chopped onion - that is, let it cook slowly, until the water it contains evaporates. Add the fish heads, washed and broken up, and let them also give off their liquid content. Then cover completely with water, savory vegetables - parsley, celery, carrot - a tablespoon of vinegar, and one, two, or three peppercorns. Simmer for about 20 minutes, skimming frequently, then filter the stock through a fine strainer. Add salt sparingly, because cooking reduces the liquid.

The best fish for fumet are those that are used in soups, for example, red snapper, turbot, halibut, sea perch, and red mullets. Fumet is different from the clear fish broth you can obtain by the following procedure. Heat a generous amount of water (2 qts. for every ¾ lb. of fish) in a saucepan with a celery stalk, a green onion, a carrot, a handful of parsley, 1/2 tsp. of pepper, a tomato, and salt. Boil vegetables for 20 minutes, add small fish and cook for 10 minutes more. Once this broth is strained, it's perfect for dishes containing rice and seafood.

Shellfish fumet, made with prawns, shrimp, crawfish, or lobster, has a more pronounced taste. Toast the shells in a pan, add savory vegetables, and "sweat" these with the shells; pour in some white wine, let it evaporate, and then cover shells and vegetables with water. Cook over low heat for about half an hour. Don't forget to skim off the scum that rises to the surface from time to time. Filter the stock through a fine strainer.

Shellfish fumet, or *coulis*, can be properly used in making dishes such as "risotto alla pescatora".

Cardone di Natale
(Christmas cardoons)
(serves 10)

For the stock: 1 capon - 2 onions - 1 full celery - 2 carrots - parsley - 1 tomato - cloves - cinnamon - salt
For the little meatballs: 2 lbs. ground beef - 3 eggs - 4 tbsp. grated Parmesan - 2 slices of white bread softened with water - minced parsley - nutmeg - salt -
To finish: 5 eggs - 6 tbsp. grated Parmesan - ¾ cup pine nuts - 1 ½ lb. cardoons - 3 lemons - pepper - salt

Benevento, an austere town with narrow medieval streets, where modernity makes its presence felt without causing excessive havoc, where the past is respected, where the passage of the seasons is observed, where winter really comes, is the birthplace of this soup. At Christmas-time it is prepared with cardoons, which are similar to artichokes. Wild cardoons must be cleaned of their leaves, tufts, and outer fibers. Cut them into ½ inch lengths and soak them overnight in water and lemon juice. Boil them in fresh water and lemon juice, then refrigerate them immediately so that they do not turn black. Prepare a rich stock with a good-looking capon and the vegetables. Shape tiny meatballs from a mixture of finely ground veal, 3 eggs, plenty of grated Parmesan, the bread, salt, finely minced parsley, and nutmeg. Cook the stock over very low heat for about four hours and strain. When the stock looks clear and pure, put it back on the heat. Beat 5 eggs with grated Parmesan, salt, and pepper. After drying the cardoons well with a dishcloth, add them to the stock, along with one or two handfuls of pine nuts, and then the egg-and-Parmesan mixture. Cook for a few minutes, stirring with a whisk, and let stand for a while before serving.

"Ciambotta" calabrese
(Calabrian vegetable stew)
(serves 6)

2 green peppers - 3 Italian eggplants - 2 lbs. potatoes - 2/3 lb. ripe tomatoes - olive oil - 1 onion - salt

In Calabria, as in all the regions of southern Italy, tomatoes, onions, and peppers have a very special taste and scent, and are widely cultivated, profiting from the sunny warmth that is vital to their success. This superb recipe produces a uniquely "southern" dish.
Blanch the tomatoes for a few seconds in boiling water, peel them immediately, and remove their seeds. Cut the peppers in half and remove their seeds, too. Peel the potatoes and eggplants and cut into pieces.

Use a cooking-pot with an ample diameter so that the vegetables won't clump together and produce a steam that will smother them; they should be first brown. Heat the oil sufficiently to sauté the thinly-sliced onion; don't burn it or it will be indigestible. Add the potatoes, stirring from time to time; then add a cup of warm water. Cut the tomatoes into pieces and add them.

In two separate skillets, fry the peppers and the eggplants. Then add them to the stew, allowing the flavors to marry. Adjust with salt. This dish can be served lukewarm.

"Cianfotta" sorrentina
(Sorrento style summer "ratatouille")
(serves 6)

1/3 cup olive oil - 1 hot pepper - 1 onion - 1 clove garlic - 1 lb. plum tomatoes - 1 lb. potatoes - ½ lb. carrots - 1 lb. zucchini - ½ lb. yellow summer squash - 1 Italian eggplant - 1 lb. white summer squash - 6 dried prunes - 6 small tart pears - basil - salt

A sunny dish, bursting with summer colors and flavors, cianfotta contains all the savor and elegance of our vegetarian cuisine. The vegetables are fresh and distinct when they reach the palate; each one maintains all its individuality, yields all its taste, yet joins in the delicate mutual harmony.

The result is a thick summer soup, thrifty but gay, rich in colors and fragrances. Thinly slice the onion and sauté in oil with the hot pepper and the garlic clove. Remove garlic when it turns golden. Peel tomatoes and cut into pieces, add them, and cook for 10 minutes before adding the cubed potatoes and carrots and two cups of water. Meanwhile peel the yellow squash, zucchini, white squash, and eggplant, and chop into equal pieces. Put them all into the pot.

Add more water if necessary to cover the vegetables. (Add salt only at the end, so that the vegetables do not lose their bright colors.) Let cook over moderate heat for about an hour. Without too much stirring, add the pitted dried prunes and the pears (not too ripe) cut into pieces.

After 15 more minutes the cianfotta will be ready. Adjust the salt and complete the dish with fresh basil.

Cicoria maritata
(Married chicory)
(serves 6)

1 lb. chicory - 2 qts. meat stock
For the little meatballs: 1 lb. beef - ½ lb. pork - 1
slice of bread softened with water - 2 eggs - salt - 7
oz. scamorza or mozzarella cheese - 3 tbsp. grated
Parmesan

Simple traditional dish of the extreme south, Puglia. Wild chicory is tender and particularly tasty. Cook in boiling water until half done, allowing it to give off the bitter liquid it contains. Finish cooking the chicory in the meat stock. Prepare the little meatballs by mixing together the ground meats, stale breadcrumbs soaked in warm milk, eggs, and salt; form into tiny balls, which will cook in a few minutes in the stock.

Remove meatballs and chicory from stock. In a heat-resistant baking dish, arrange a layer of meatballs, then the sliced scamorza, and finally the chicory; sprinkle with grated Parmesan cheese.

Bake under moderate heat so that the chicory becomes dry and blends together with the cheeses.

Fagioli alla montanara
(Mountain-style beans)
(serves 10)

2 lbs white beans - 3 carrots - 3 celery stalks - salt
- 7 tbsp olive oil - 3 cloves garlic - 1 hot pepper - 1
lb onion - 7 oz. prosciutto - ½ lb ripe tomatoes - ½
lb potatoes - 1 lb short pasta - nutmeg

Apart from its seacoast, Calabria is essentially mountain country, whose people use every part of the pig and love the old days style of cooking it - on a spit, over a wood fire. Theirs is a frugal, rugged cuisine that emphasizes only authentic flavors: a cuisine of few words. To prepare this soup, soak the beans overnight in cold water (rainwater is the best). In the morning, drain the beans and add fresh water of the same temperature. Fill the pot so that the water level is a palm's width higher than the beans. Add a pinch of salt, the carrots and the celery stalks, and set to cook over a low heat for three hours. Sauté a hot pepper and three garlic cloves in a generous amount of olive oil. When the garlic becomes golden, remove it, and replace it with the coarsely-chopped onions. When these are almost cooked, add the lean prosciutto, cut into cubes. Sizzle this a little, then add the ripe tomatoes, cut into pieces. When the beans are about half done, take out the carrot and celery and replace them with the fried mixture, continuing to cook over low heat. When the beans are done, remove the pot from the heat and add the cubed potatoes and the pasta. Let stand covered for about 2 hours.
In this time, the steam will cook the last two ingredients to perfection. Powder with grated nutmeg and serve.

Favata
(Broad bean soup)
(serves 6-8)

2 lb fava beans, dried in their pods - ½ lb pork
meat - ½ lb Italian sausage - 1 tbsp. lard - 4 tbsp
oil - 1 bunch fresh fennel - 1 onion - parsley - 1 stalk
celery - salt - pepper

A typical dish of the Barbagia region in Sardinia, traditionally prepared for the last day of Carnival.
Soak the beans overnight in tepid water. Next day replace with fresh lukewarm water. Boil beans until they swell up nicely, cool and peel them. Mince the lard, onion, parsley, and celery, and put them in a saucepan with the oil, pork, and coarsely-sliced sausage.
Cover with plenty of water and cook over low heat. Add shelled beans and fennel cut into little strips. Cook until done, season with salt and pepper.
Serve this soup hot with toasted homemade bread.

Fave e foglie
(Beans and leaves)
(serves 8)

2 lbs chicory - 1 ½ lb dried fava, broad, or lima
beans - 6 tbsp. olive oil - 1 onion - 1 small pepper
- salt

A pastoral recipe whose origins are lost in the distant past, but which has been violated in recent years by additions as harmful as they are useless.
The only "innovation" we allow here is the small pepper, which arrived only in the 17th century from the Americas.

Soak the dried beans overnight. If rainwater is available, you're lucky. The next day, shell the beans and put them in a pot (earthenware is best) with the onion; cover them with water and add salt to taste.

Cook them until they become mushy. If you want them creamy and smooth, pass them through a food mill. In a separate pot, boil and salt the chicory. Sauté it in a little oil with the hot pepper.

Add the bean purée to the chicory and season with oil and more chilli pepper. Serve.

Fave e zucchine
(Beans and zucchini)
(serves 4-6)

1 lb fresh shelled fava broad, or lima beans - 4 tbsp. olive oil - 1 onion- 1 celery rib - basil - 1 tomato - 1 lb. zucchini - salt

This typical Apulian dish requires beans not yet completely dried in their pods, because they need to cook with zucchini, which in the old days were available only from May to August.

Choose beans of good quality, snip off any black tips, and soak the beans overnight. Next morning wash them, pour them into a pot, cover them with water, add salt, put a lid on the pot and cook the beans over low heat. In a separate pan, put the oil, sliced onions, chopped celery, plenty of basil, chopped tomato, and chopped zucchini; cover and cook.

At the end of the cooking period, mix in the cooked beans and flavor everything with extra-virgin olive oil.

Stir gently so that the beans will stay in their pods, and serve with toasted bread.

"Guazzetto"
(Seafood stew)
(serves 6)

*2 lbs. small octopus - 1 lb. small squid - 1 lb. small
cuttlefish - ¼ cup olive oil - 2 cloves garlic - 1 hot
pepper - 1 cup dry white wine - 1 lb. peeled and
sieved tomatoes - salt*

Explosions of colours, tastes full of character: the proud red of the tomatoes,
the purple veining of the octopus, the tenderness of the small squid and
cuttlefish, which melt in your mouth, and the vigor of the hot pepper. This
guazzetto modulates its ingredients well, manages to combine them and
preserve their identity at the same time.
Crush the garlic, sauté in oil until golden; remove and substitute with hot
pepper and octopus. Cook for 10 minutes until the latter becomes bright red,
then add the cleaned squid and cuttlefish. Pour white wine over all and let it
evaporate. Now add tomatoes and salt. Cook for about 30 minutes, or until
the oil separates from the tomatoes. Heat should be very low. Finish this soup
with the ubiquitous minced parsley, and serve it with little slices of oven-
toasted bread.

La signora con i riccioli
(The Lady with curls)
(serves 6)

*2 lbs. broccoli - ¼ cup olive oil - 1 clove garlic - hot
pepper - 3 cups semolina flour - Parmesan cheese –
salt*

Ringlets, waves and curls almost always complement a woman's face more
than straight hair. When this dish is ready, it has the effect of an allusion to a
female face by Arcimboldo, a parody not of language but of image.
The pale yellow color of the semolina recalls skin, sometimes taut,
sometimes wizened, as in a wrinkled human face. The tangled broccoli leaves
evoke a curly hairdo.

This is a Neapolitan dish, probably French-inspired, but echoed in the frascatela, a rustic soup typical of the town of Sperlinga, in central Sicily. Sperlinga, together with Nicosia, another town nearby, remained faithful to the French during the war known as the Sicilian Vespers in 1282. The long French domination has left many identifiable traces in the local dialect.

To produce this dish and its unique look, proceed as follows: boil the broccoli, then put it in a pot where the hot pepper and garlic have been sautéed in olive oil and then removed. Pour in enough water to cover the vegetables, salt to taste, add the semolina. Stir constantly, adding boiling water only if necessary to achieve a consistent texture. Just at the end, add cubes of hard cheese such as the outermost part of a Parmesan cheese.

Lenticchie con scarole
(Lentils with escarole)
(serves 10)

1 lb. lentils - 4 escaroles - 2 carrots - 1 celery rib - 1 onion - 8 tbsp. olive oil - 1 clove garlic - hot pepper - salt

While the ancient Greeks, the Homeric heroes, were dining happily on bread, wine, roast meat, and animal entrails loaded with blood and fat - these latter were regarded as first-class fare - the Hebrews, having sojourned long in Egypt, were more advanced in cooking matters.

They had fire-resistant cooking vessels, and in one such was prepared the lentil soup that Jacob made Esau pay for so dearly.

Because they contain significant amounts of protein and iron, lentils provide nourishment of fine quality. Highly nutritious and more easily digestible than other legumes, they're delicious when prepared according to this recipe and accompanied at table with crisp grain biscuits or cubes of toasted bread.

Wash the lentils well and cook them in a pot with plenty of water (double the volume of the lentils), salt, tomato, celery, carrot, and onion, all chopped very small.

Celery has a special flavor and deserves a place of honor in the kitchen; it is especially valuable in stocks and soups. The best type has full, hard, whitish ribs. Let the lentils cook, covered, over a low heat for about an hour until they are slightly soft, not mushy or watery. If you need to add water to them while cooking, use boiling water so as not to interrupt the process. Meanwhile, brown garlic cloves in a goodly amount of olive oil; remove them when they turn golden. Clean, wash, and smother the escaroles in a pot. The escaroles should cook with the lid on the pot; when they become faded and soft, they're ready. Drain them. In a saucepan sauté the garlic, remove it, add the escarole, the chilli pepper, let them dry a bit and then add the lentils. Mix together for a few minutes and serve with toasted bread.

Le virtù
(Virtues)
(serves 8/10)

3 ½ oz. dried beans - 3 ½ oz. dried lentils - 3 ½ oz. dried chickpeas - 3 ½ oz. dried fava or broad beans - 3 ½ oz. dried peas - 3 ½ oz. cracked wheat - 3 ½ oz. dried corn kernels - 1 tbsp. lard - 5 tbsp. olive oil - 2 cloves garlic - parsley – salt

A most ancient, ritual dish, whose origins are a matter of contention among Basilicata, the region of Cilento in southern Campania, and the province of Syracuse. It is prepared on the first of May or in Sicily on the 19th of March and is meant to celebrate the prosperity that comes from hard work. This is a soup made from various legumes cooked together, thus solving the problem of what to do with the remains of the winter stores when there's no longer enough of them for individual dishes. In Sicily this dish is dedicated to St. Joseph and called maccu. In addition to the listed ingredients, it contains two bunches of mountain fennel. Inland-dwelling Sicilians begin the meal on their saint's day with a legume soup like this; in accordance with hospitable custom, as a sign that every family is ready to receive any guest, however unexpected, they leave their house-doors open. The evening before cooking, place in separate containers equal portions of all the listed ingredients. Soak in warm water (about 105°) with a tbsp. of salt. According to tradition, in the morning fires were laid in the countryside with wood from the pruning - olive, fig, and ilex. The people built an enclosure of stones, open to the east and equal in number to the principal ingredients of the soup; the firewood was placed in the center. Then salted spring water was poured into a large copper or clay pot and the ingredients boiled in this order: wheat, corn, chickpeas, favas, beans, lentils, peas. A separate mixture of lard, extra-virgin olive oil, garlic, parsley, and salt was prepared and added to the pot; the cooking was completed over a slow flame.

At table the soup was ladled into plates, where pieces of darkgrain biscuits awaited it.

Minestra di cardoni
(Cardoon soup)
(serves 6/8)

3 qts. meat stock - 2 lbs. cardoons - 6 egg yolks -
3 lemons - parsley – salt

The cardoon is a giant among vegetables; the adult plant can reach a height of six feet. We use the stalks of this plant, and the central spines of the leaves. Cardoons have properties similar to those of artichokes. Both stimulate the functions of the hepatic cells, are rich in minerals and raw fiber, and have a delicate taste. Discard the hard outside stems of the cardoons and soak them in water with lemon juice so that they will remain white. Now cut the tender inner stalks of the cardoons lengthwise into 2 inch strips, remove stringy fibers, and boil in water and lemon juice until half done. Place in cold water and add the juice of another lemon. Then put them in a pot, along with parsley sprigs, season with salt, and add the broth. Cook until done.

Before serving this soup, add 6 egg yolks, with a few drops of lemon juice. Blend briefly over a slow fire and serve.

Minestra di verza e riso
(Savoy cabbage and rice soup)
(serves 6)

*4 tbsp.olive oil - 1 clove garlic - onion - hot
pepper - ½ lb.tomatoes - 1 savoy cabbage - 2
carrots - 2 zucchinis - 3 ½ oz. snap beans - 1
Italian eggplant - 1 lb. rice - 1 cup grated
Parmesan - basil - salt*

Cauliflowers and white, yellow, curly, or green cabbages, thriving produce
of the cold season, are basic ingredients in many thick soups and can be
decorative as well. They originated in Europe, and the Romans used them
extensively. Savoy cabbage has wrinkled, open leaves and a distinct aroma.
Cut it into thin strips and boil them in plenty of salted water for a few
minutes, then drain and put aside. Sauté garlic in a saucepan with olive oil;
when barely golden, remove it and then sautè an onion in the oil.
When the onion becomes transparent, add the peeled, seeded tomatoes and
the pepper and cook for 15 minutes. Now put in the cabbage, the chopped
carrots, and the zucchini; then the boiled and chopped snap beans.
Let this all cook for 20 minutes on a very low heat, then add the eggplant,
chopped into chunks. After 15 minutes, add the rice and let it cook, adding, if
necessary, some boiling water. When the rice is done, add cheese and basil.

Minestra di zucchine
(Zucchini soup)
(serves 6)

*4 lbs. zucchini - 4 tbsp. olive oil - 2 cloves garlic -
basil - salt*

Wash the zucchini and cut them into small chunks. Sauté the crushed garlic
in the oil; remove the garlic, add the zucchini, stir and sauté for 5 minutes
over a lively fire. Lower the heat, add a cup of boiling water, cover and let

the soup cook for 15 minutes or until the zucchini are tender. Season with salt and garnish with basil leaves.

Minestra di zucchine con le uova
(Zucchini and egg soup)
(serves 6)

3 ½ lbs. zucchini - 4 tbsp. olive oil - 1 onion - 3 eggs - 3 tbsp. grated Parmesan - basil - salt & pepper

Wash the zucchini and cut into small chunks. Saute the sliced onions in the olive oil until barely golden; add zucchini and ½ cup water. Cover and cook slowly for around 15 minutes. Add the salt when almost done.

Beat eggs with grated Parmesan, salt, and pepper; stir briefly into the zucchini (until the eggs set). Complete the dish with fresh basil leaves.

Minestra maritata
(Married soup)
(serves 8/10)

4 lbs. pork meat (peeled Italian pork sausage, spareribs, rib chops) - 1 ham bone - 4 lbs. various green vegetables (broccoli, beet greens, purslane or portulaca oleracea, cabbage, chicory, savoy cabbage, rucola or arugula) - 1/3 lb. various cheeses (pecorino romano, dry caciocavallo, caciotta, Parmesan) - hot pepper

Pork is, by common consent, so useful an element in cooking that all praise of it is superfluous. Any gourmet would blanch at the prospect of having to banish it from his table. Juvenal called the pig animal *propter convivia natum* ("an animal born for banquets"). And Trimalchio in the Satyricon ordered for his banquet a "Trojan Pig," stuffed with all manner of tasty delights. But the earliest surviving pork recipe is Chinese, dating from the Chou dynasty, that is, before 500 B.C.: suckling pig stuffed with fruit and cooked in a pit lined with red-hot stones. The generous pig, who gives himself entirely, is a source of unequaled gastronomic delight: marbled pressed sausages, pink bacon; bologna, zampone, cotechino, and other pork sausages; salami and ham; chops, cutlets, chines, and loins. And yet, paradoxically, the fat pig follows the law of opposites and is extremely compatible with lean green vegetables.

Select from the greengrocer's inviting display head cabbage, beet greens, purslane, rucola (arugula), broccoli "trees", chicory, savoy cabbage. For the Neapolitans, who until the 17th century were believed to eat essentially leaves, the "married pot", containing meat in proportion to a family's economic condition, was the popular daily meal. Put the "husband", that is to say the meat which will give the soup its flavour, into an earthenware pot with plenty of water and bring to simmer. Use different types of pork in modest proportions for an excellent soup. Remove scum and fat from the stock and strain it. It should become clear and amber-colored.

Clean and wash the green vegetables, plunge each briefly into boiling water (use a different pot for each), and add to the stock. Even when there's no meat, the most authentic "married" soup can be quite tasty, with its greens cooked in broth made from pork bones and maybe some tiny scraps. Originally, this soup was the result of using the medley of pork parts left over after the salting process. Add cubes of country cheese at the end of the cooking time; for example, seasoned caciotta or pecorino or Parmesan (the outermost part, close to the rind). A little hot pepper will enhance the flavours. This soup must be tasted when positively steaming.

Minestrone delicato
(Light minestrone)
(serves 6)

2/3 lb. carrots - 1 onion - 2/3 lb. zucchini - 2/3 lb. potatoes - 3 ½ oz. shelled peas - 1/3 lb. snap beans - ½ lb. spinach - 2 celery ribs - ½ lb. ripe tomatoes - minced parsley - 2 qts. water - 3 tbsp. olive oil - pepper - salt

The substances that the human organism most needs are present in vegetables: vitamins, mineral salts, vegetal protein, and sugars. Carrots and celery are roots that provide a precious resource in winter, because they can be kept a long time. Eaten raw or cooked, carrots are very digestible and constitute an excellent intestinal regulator.

In order to preserve all the nutritives contained in vegetables, it's best to boil them briefly in salted water and, if possible, to use the same water as a broth.

Clean, wash, and chop the vegetables. Barely cover them with water in a pan, and bring to simmer. Then lower the heat, cover, and cook slowly for about 1 hour. Season with salt (and pepper if desired), add olive oil, and remove from heat. Add minced parsley or a few spoons of pesto. The soup should be rather thin. Stir and serve.

Pasta e ceci
(Pasta and chickpeas)
(serves 8/10)

1 lb. chickpeas - parsley - 2 cloves garlic - 1 small bunch celery - 1 onion - 4 carrots - 1 lb. tube shaped pasta or fine lasagna - hot pepper - 6 tbsp. olive oil - salt.

Chickpeas are hard to cook, but a little stratagem can help you avoid unpleasant surprises. The evening before you cook them, soak them in warm water (about 150°) with a few dashes of salt. Change the water in the morning; the new water should also be warm and should take up twice or more the volume that the chickpeas do. Heat. Just before boiling-point, you will notice that a light foam floats to the surface. Remove this and add a fragrant bunch of parsley, garlic, celery, a large onion, and the carrots, all chopped small. Salt to taste. Cover and simmer gently. If you've let too much water evaporate, add more boiling water.

The chickpeas will take about 4 hours to cook, but it's possible more time will be required, depending on the quality of the legumes. When the chickpeas are completely cooked, you can rub some of the vegetables through a sieve, then add olive oil to taste. Cook the pasta so that it's still quite *al dente* and add to the chickpeas; it will finish cooking in the soup.

Add the hot pepper; mix for two minutes. If the soup is too thick, dilute it with some of the pasta water. Pour into a soup tureen and add finely minced fresh parsley.

As an optional you can accompany this soup with crispy pasta butterflies; this must surely be an original idea - a type of pasta usually condemned to broths is granted a kind of reprieve. Cook the butterflies in water (they should be *al dente*). Dry them, and, at the moment when the soup is to be served, fry them in plenty of hot vegetable oil and add to the soup.

Pasta e fagioli
(Pasta and beans)
(serves 8/10)

1 lb. white beans - 1 lb. any small grooved pasta -
1 onion - 3 celery ribs - 3 carrots - 6 tbsp. olive
oil - salt - hot pepper - parsley

Thus Horace, in one of his letters, invites his friend Torquatus to a frugal dinner, bare of all luxury, where he will be offered humble vegetables. The Roman phaselus was surely not the same as ours, which came to Europe in the Spanish galleys only in the 16th century. It was the *dolichos*, of which Varro was so fond and which the Greek merchants imported from Africa. It was eaten fresh in its bright green pod, or shelled, and was quite similar to a kind of snap bean.

For our recipe we use large "American" beans. Wash and put them in a pot with plenty of water; they should occupy 1/3 of the water volume. Add the chopped onion, carrots, and celery. Cover and cook on a very low heat for about 3 hours. Then add olive oil, salt and chilli pepper. If necessary, add boiling water, which you'll keep on the stove just in case. Select with a skimmer the vegetables and filter through the vegetable mill.

Mix with the beans. Partially cook the pasta, then let it finish cooking with the beans. Before serving this delicious soup, sprinkle it with minced fresh parsley.

Polenta gratinata
(Polenta au gratin)
(serves 8)

3 cups finely ground cornmeal or corn flour - 3 qts.
water - 2 tbsp. butter - salt
For the béchamel or cream sauce: 2 oz. butter - 1/3
cup flour - 2 ½ cups milk - salt - pepper - 7 oz.
mozzarella - ½ cup grated Parmesan

"To have the world so bravely dominated,
to be so feared, to be so celebrated,
what boots it, Roland? Far from glory's center
your famous life was ended by polenta."

According to this anonymous 17th-century poet from Treviso, it seems that
the glorious Roland did not end his days in the battle of Roncesvalles in 778,
but was instead, disappointingly, struck down by fatal indigestion after eating
too much polenta. Evidently a poetic joke, since corn (granturco or "Turkish
grain" in Italian) arrived in Venice from America via Turkey.

Polenta was much beloved from the 17th to 19th centuries, especially in the
Venetian region, whence it was no doubt imported to Naples in 1768 by
Maria Carolina of Austria, who in that year married the Bourbon Ferdinand I,
King of the Two Sicilies. Let's hope no ignominious fate lies in store for us
as we begin our polenta recipe.

Put the water in a pot with a handful of salt; when it boils, add the cornmeal
in a steady stream, stirring continuously throughout the cooking period to
avoid lumping. This will require about half an hour. The polenta will be
ready when you can remove it from the pan in one whole piece. Add the
butter and turn onto a lightly-oiled work surface, marble if possible. Spread
polenta with a spatula and allow it to cool.

Meanwhile prepare the béchamel sauce as usual: melt butter over low heat,
remove from heat and add flour. Stir. Add warm milk a little at a time,

stirring constantly. Season with salt and pepper and return to heat; continue to stir until the sauce thickens. Now cut the polenta into finger-thick slices and the mozzarella into little cubes. Pour some sauce onto the bottom of a baking-pan, then alternate layers of polenta, mozzarella, and grated Parmesan, ending with a layer of béchamel. Bake at 400°for half an hour.

Purea di fave con cicorie
(Chicory with mashed broad beans)
(serves 6)

2 cups dried fava or broad beans - 4 tbsp. olive oil - 1 onion - 1 lb. potatoes - 2 lbs. chicory (preferibly wild) – salt

This delicious and simple concoction is considered a speciality in Apulia and Basilicata. For this dish you can use favas dried in their pods (snip off the black tips) or already shelled and dried. In either case, soak them in salted water overnight. In the morning, wash and shell them (if necessary), and begin cooking them in a saucepan, covering them with water, sliced onion, and diced potatoes. As soon as they begin to simmer, lower the heat, salt to taste, add olive oil and cook slowly, mixing often.
When the beans are well cooked, mash or beat them with the potatoes and pour onto a large platter. Accompany with previously boiled chicory, and dress with extra-virgin olive oil.

Tagliatelle e fagioli
(Tagliatelle and beans)
(serves 10)

2 lbs. shelled fresh beans - 1 onion - ½ lb. raw prosciutto - 6 tbsp. olive oil - 1 cup white wine - 2 tbsp. fresh tomato - 2 cups stock - 1 lb. tagliatelle (thin, flat ribbon pasta)

We're talking here about true beans, those of the humble genus Phaseolus, leguminous plants that have always been part of popular cuisine.

Humble but prized, healthy and nutritious, the bean has been in domestic use since ancient times.

So the case of Bertoldo, the peasant born from Giulio Cesare Croce's pen, should come as no surprise. Thanks to his talents and wisdom, Bertoldo became the advisor of Alboin in 570, king of the Lombards, but soon "died in bitter torment, because he couldn't eat turnips and beans." The cause of his sickness, in fact, was "genteel and delicate viands."

Slice the onions and mince the prosciutto; cook in olive oil until all becomes soft and clear.

Pour freshly-shelled beans into the pot, stir, pour in wine, add fresh tomato and some water, and cook over low heat for about 2 hours. When the beans are soft, rub half of them through a sieve or food mill, then put both bean mixtures into the pot with the stock. Bring to simmer. Cook the pasta al dente and add to the bean soup.

<h2 style="text-align:center">Tiella pugliese
(Apulian mussel and rice casserole)
(serves 6)</h2>

1 lb. rice - 2 lbs. mussels - 6 ripe tomatoes - 2 cloves garlic - parsley - salt - pepper - 3 tbsp. olive oil - 1 lb. potatoes - 1 cup grated pecorino - 1 cup grated stale bread

Yellow, bright red, brilliant green, deep black with perhaps some traces of gray-blue: the colors of this dish remind us of canvases by Picasso or Mirò, of imaginary arenas where a toreador, whirling his long red-lined cape, performs before a group of notables dressed in ceremonious black.

Chop the tomatoes on the bottom of a baking-pan, along with the garlic and parsley; add salt and oil, then a layer of rather thicklysliced potatoes. Cover with pieces of tomato, garlic, parsley, grated pecorino cheese, oil, and salt.

Wash and brush the mussels in running water to remove algae and incrustations.

Open them with a sharp knife, leaving them on the half-shell and saving their water with its flavor of the sea. Arrange a layer of mussels in their half-shells on top of the potatoes. Season with oil, garlic, and parsley.

At this point add the uncooked rice, which has been soaking in the mussel water, seasoned with oil, salt, and pepper. Then add, as before, oil, tomato pieces, garlic, parsley, salt, and cheese. End with another layer of sliced potatoes, season with the usual ingredients, and top with a little grated bread. Pour a cup of water into a corner of the pan.

Bake in the oven at 350°for about an hour.

Vellutata di gamberi o bisque
(Shrimps or lobster bisque)
(serves 8)

1 lb. shrimps or prawns or lobster - 3 lbs tomatoes –
½ cup Sherry - ½ cup olive oil - 1 onion - 4 carrots -
1 bay leaf - parsley - 3 ribs celery - hot pepper - salt
- pepper - Angostura - Tabasco - Worcestershire
sauce - 1 cup fresh cream .

In a large saucepan sauté the onion until it colors, add the chopped carrots, the celery, a bay leaf, parsley, and hot pepper. After 8 minutes add the tomatoes and let them cook for 20 minutes. Clean the crustaceans, removing the black juices. Mix them in the sauce. They'll become quite red in 5 minutes. Let the soup get a little cooler, remove the bay leaves, than liquidize everything, including the carapaces, in the mixer. Pass everything through a "Chinese" (cone-shaped) sieve. Put it back in the saucepan, add the Sherry and the different sauces, salt, chilli pepper.

Finally, add the cream and some very finely chopped parsley. Serve immediately with small toasted bread. This soup should be rather peppery, so add more hot pepper if it seems necessary.

Zuppa di cannellini
(White bean soup)
(serves 6)

1 lb. dried white kidney beans (cannellini) - 3 celery ribs - 1 large onion - 2 carrots - hot pepper - 3 cloves - salt - 5 tbsp. olive oil

Since we're preaching the virtues of simplicity, we can't forget bean soup. Soup, originally a humble peasant dish, is making a well-deserved comeback upon today's dinner-tables. In the old days, one made soup in the morning before going to the fields. The legumes cooked in rain-water, simmering in earthenware pots, unwatched, over weak flames. Today - why not? - we too can let the soup cook slowly, unattended, while we're caught up in the "whirlwind of modern life." But knowledge of a few secrets can help us avoid problems.

We use cannellini beans (long, white kidney beans) in this soup. The evening before leave the beans to soak in water. In the morning wash them and cover with water to a palm's width above their level. Add celery, carrot, onion, - all finely chopped - and a piece of hot pepper and the cloves. Simmer, covered, over very low heat. Near the end, add salt and olive oil. It will take about three hours to complete this fine soup. The beans have to be cooked but not mushy, so that the vegetables will have given up all their earthy flavours to the harmony of the whole. Serve with pieces of toasted bread.

Zuppa di fave fresche
(Fresh fava or broad bean soup)
(serves 6)

4 lbs. fresh shelled fava or broad beans - ½ lb. green or young onions - 3 ½ oz. bacon - salt & pepper - 4 tbsp. olive oil - parsley

Shell the beans, removing their tips. Wash and drain beans.

Mince bacon coarsely and sauté in oil with chopped onions. When these begin to soften add beans and a cup of water (later, if necessary, you can add boiling water). Cook uncovered over low heat for about an hour. Cooking time varies, depending on the size and tenderness of the fava beans. Just before the end of the cooking time, add salt and pepper.
When you serve the soup, sprinkle it with minced parsley.

Zuppa di patate con carne
(Potato soup with meat)
(serves 6)

3 lbs. potatoes - 3 tbsp. olive oil - ½ lb. peeled tomatoes - 1 onion - parsley - salt - 2 lbs. beef (rump or round) – ½ cup white wine

Mince the onion and brown it in olive oil; chop meat into big chunks and add them. Let meat brown, then pour wine over it. When this has evaporated, add the peeled, seeded tomatoes and cook covered over low heat for an hour. Then add the cubed potatoes, stir, salt, cover, and cook for 25 more minutes. Finish with minced parsley.

Zuppa di piselli
(Peas soup)
(serves 6)

2 lbs. shelled peas - ½ lb. green onions - 3 ½ oz. pancetta (bacon) - 4 tbsps. olive oil - parsley - salt - pepper.

Cook the chopped onions in the olive oil, add the pancetta, cut into cubes, heat should be low. When these are soft, but not yet golden, add the shelled peas, pour in 1 ½ cups of water, cover the saucepan, and cook slowly for about an hour.
The time will vary according to the size and tenderness of the peas.
Complete the soup with salt, pepper and fresh chopped parsley.

This soup is delicious by itself, but can also be served with pasta (use about a pound of tubed pasta). Cook pasta (not too soft) and add to peas. If you want a thinner soup, add some of the pasta cooking water.

Zuppa di "spolichini"
(Fresh bean soup)
(serves 6)

4 lbs. fresh beans in their pods - 6 celery ribs - 1 onion - 2 carrots - 2 lb. fresh tomatoes for salad - salt - 4 tbsp. olive oil

Summer brings us the wonderful *spolichini*, the fresh beans beloved by the Neapolitans, which have a distinct flavour and can be prepared just by simple boiling. They gladly accept the company of tomatoes; try serving soup and tomato salad side by side on separate plates.
A tomato salad, in fact, flavored with a crushed garlic clove, two or three small sweet green peppers cut into little strips, a celery rib, basil, salt, olive oil, and oregano - this seems to be the best way to bring out the flavour of this particular soup.
Shell the beans and put them in a pot with twice their volume of water. Chop and add all vegetables. Cover and cook over very low heat for two hours or until soft. Towards the end, add salt and olive oil.

Zuppa di verdure
(Vegetable soup)
(serves 6)

4 tbsp. olive oil - 1 clove garlic - 1 onion - 6 juicy tomatoes - ½ savoy cabbage - 1 ½ cup boiled beans - 2 carrots - 2 celery ribs - ½ lb. snap beans - ½ lb.

zucchini - 1 Italian eggplant - 1 green pepper - 1 ½
cups rice - ½ cup cubes of cheese - basil – salt

Brown garlic in oil; remove garlic and substitute with minced onion. Since the onion fries lightly, add chopped tomatoes and cook for 10 minutes. Fill a separate pot with water and boil the cabbage, chopped into little strips, until partially cooked. Drain and add to tomatoes the boiled beans and the chopped carrots and celery. Let all this blend for a while, then chop and add snap beans, zucchini, Italian eggplant, and green pepper.

When the vegetables are almost ready, pour in the rice and enough boiling water to keep the soup from becoming too dry. Season with salt and pieces of various cheeses: Pecorino Romano, Parmesan, cacio, etc. Finish with some fresh basil.

Zuppa primavera
(Springtime soup)
(serves 8)

1 lb. small young onions or spring onions - 4 lbs.
fresh fava or broad beans in their pods (a little
more than 1 lb shelled) - 10 small artichokes
(Italian if possible) - 3 ½ oz. pancetta (bacon) - 2
lbs. new potatoes - 6 ½ lbs. peas, unshelled (about
2 lbs shelled) - 5 tbsp. olive oil - parsley - salt.

This is the market-gardener's triumph, a miracle of fragrance and exuberant freshness. The little artichokes open up like spring flowers, the peas burst from their pods, the fava beans contribute their distinctive flavor, the young potatoes add their velvety softness, the onions grow transparent and then dissolve into the blend. Fava beans are among the oldest food plants.

They were already widely known in China 5000 years ago, and they have always been one of the most common foods in the Mediterranean Basin.

The Romans esteemed favas highly and called them fabae after the name of a noble family, the Fabi. As is the case with legumes in general, fava beans are an excellent source of vegetable protein - "green protein" - and thus provide an alternative to meat.

The artichoke (Cynara scolymus), inside its prickly jacket, hides a tender, tasty heart, a food for connoisseurs. It contains cynarin and enzymatic substances that stimulate the secretion of bile, help gallbladder contractions, stimulate hepatic cell function, and reduce blood glucose and cholestorol.

Shell beans and peas (Pisum sativum); clean the small artichokes and keep them in lemon juice and water so they won't turn black. Thinly slice the onions, dice the potatoes, and cut the bacon into small pieces. Use a large pot to fry the bacon and onions in olive oil. When these are barely transparent, add all the other ingredients: first the beans, then the artichokes, the potatoes and the peas. A capacious pot will keep the vegetables from smothering. Add about 2 cups of water, cover the pot, and cook slowly for about an hour. Just before the end, add salt. Before serving this soup, sprinkle it with very fresh minced parsley.

SAUCES AND PASTAS

SAUCES

The Tomato

"Tomato" is the common name for Solanum lycopersicum, an annual herbaceous plant of the family Solanaceae, order Tubiflores; originally from South America, it is cultivated almost everywhere in the world for its edible fruit, which appears in the form of large, usually red berries containing numerous seeds rich in vitamin E and a phosphorous laden substance called phytin used in medicine as a tonic for the nervous system. Next to citrus fruits, the tomato is the food richest in vitamins C, A, and B.

At the time of its arrival in Europe, however, this fruit was regarded most suspiciously. Defined in 1600 as *alimentum perexigium* et *vitiosum* ("deficient, base sustenance"), it was sold mysteriously and only for aphrodisiac potions or magic philtres. The Neapolitans were the first to mix oil and tomato, fragrance and flavour, thus giving birth (assisted by basil) to the most aromatic of all sauces. But the tomato excited everyone's imagination and interest: the French called it pomme d'amour, the Spanish tomata (from a Mexican and Peruvian root, the tomato having originated in Mexico), and the Germans *Liebesapfel*.

Without the tomato, Neapolitan cuisine would be *anemic*!

Every September tomato-love occupies a large proportion of the population of Naples; the idea is to preserve this precious resource in the larder, as the provident ants do.

The craft of preparing San Marzano tomatoes for domestic storage occupies many people: somebody cleans the jars, somebody washes the tomatoes somebody slices and bottles them, somebody seals the containers hermetically to make them pressure-resistant when they are boiling.

Another type of tomato, the *spugnilli*, is harvested in bunches and stored in a cool, dry place. A tiny amount of these little fruits suffices to add colour to the vivacious sauce that is the proper condiment for pasta.

Salsa di pomodori freschi alla Siciliana
(Sicilian-style fresh tomato sauce)
(serves 6)

2 lbs. ripe tomatoes - 1 big red onion - basil
– 6 tbsp. olive oil - 1 tsp. sugar – salt

Maybe it's the Sicilian sun that makes everything more alive, more colorful and vivid, but also more overwhelming and stupefying, like the fragrance of orange-blossom and jasmine! The tomatoes here are likewise denser, tastier, and even the simplest way of cooking them produces excellent results. And so: wash the tomatoes, chop them coarsely, and cook them in a pan (earthenware is best) with a whole onion, fragrant basil, a pinch of sugar and salt. The heat should be moderate and steady. When everything has at first softened, then thickened, rub through a sieve or food mill; add olive oil and cook for a few minutes more. It goes without saying that the oil must be of the finest quality, made from unadulterated olives, and fresh. As they say in Sicily, "New oil, old wine."

Full-bodied wines can age and grow better with time; oil, on the other hand, is short-lived; it reaches its peak in its sixth month, and alters after a year. This delicious and healthy sauce is a marvelous condiment for pasta, which is particularly good in Sicily, and it's not necessary to enrich it with grated cheese; should you do so, pecorino cheese, fresh or aged, is a good choice.

Il ragù con le braciole
(Ragout with meat rolls)
(serves 8)

6 tbsps. olive oil - 1 tbsp. lard - 1 lb. pork rib meat (or other lean pork) - 2 lbs. beef or veal - 1 big carrot - 2 celery stalks - parsley – ½ cup sultana raisins - 2 tbsps. pine nuts (pinoli) - 4 cloves garlic - 2 large onions – 4 ½ lbs. tomatoes, passed through a food mill - 1 cup white wine – basil - salt – pepper

The Cavalier De Jaucourt, indefatigable author of many entries in the last volumes of the great French Encyclopédie, though he remained in Diderot's shadow, thus defines ragout under the rubric *cuisine: sausse ou assaisonnement pour chatouiller ou exciter l'appétit quand il est émoussé* ("sauce or seasoning for titillating or exciting dulled appetites").

The most literary ragout is the one Giuseppe Marotta describes in *Oro di Napoli* (Gold of Naples): "it's not a sauce, but the history, the novel, the poem of a sauce."

It's the fragrance of Naples and its narrow streets; a ceremony, performed every Sunday, arousing your appetite with its enveloping aromas. As Ferdinand II, King of the Two Sicilies, maintained, ragù must be cooked in an earthenware pot over very low heat.

You need a piece of meat from the tip of the pork ribs and sliced pieces of beef and veal chops (not necessarily of the highest grade), pounded thin as for cutlet dishes like involtini, stuffed with finely crushed garlic, fresh parsley, raisins, pine nuts, salt, and pepper, and then tied shut with cotton thread or held together with toothpicks. Melt the lard in olive oil and brown the meat slowly and attentively; then add a good amount of thinly sliced onions, and, next, the celery stalks and a carrot, both chopped small.

When these ingredients have blended and their juices married, add a cup of white wine, wait until it evaporates, and then pour in the sieved tomatoes and basil (fresh, if in season).

The cooking should be slow, "pensive," languid; it should last about 2 hours. Every time you stir gently with a wooden spoon, the meat will give up its juices to the sauce and assure a better result. Ragout prepared in this way is the ideal condiment for good pasta of the large, tubular type, such as penne, ziti, or candele spezzate ("broken candles"). At table it's proper to sprinkle this steaming dish with lots of freshly grated Parmesan cheese (unless you have some dried caciottina).

We, vagrants in love with the god Dionisus,
and grateful to our mother that gave us birth
in a country full of ugly flaw, but also, of a beauty and pleasures,
we once entered an enchanted garden
and don't think l am exaggerating:
it is less than the fabulous reality of Villa Tritone in Sorrento
passing through the dancing palms,
waving the arms as in Maometto's paradise,
through the wind scented by the sea,
which must still host sirens in these surroundings,
once we bumped into a bewitching scent and went on
attracted by this fascination,
following our noses through the air.
This is how in the enchanted castle,
we found a little witch, or better:.. a little fairy,
with cheerful eyes shining underneath a forest of a black hair,
which trapped us in that scent spiral,
and, on a marvellous terrace in between the blue of the sky and the sea,
enchanted us.

Yes Gentlemen: a ragout... help me to explain:
it was the quinteessence of all delights.
There, whilst lost in that pleasure, we recalled how in all those dishes from
Sorrento and it's region, one can find the signs of the ancient roots, the
history':
Greeks, Romans, Saracens, French, Spanish...
Rita's ragout is one of those precious jewels.
I asked for the recipe, but l am sure that the mysterious element is art, divine
Inspiration... it would be easy otherwise.

Lina Wertmuller

Ragù alla siciliana
(Sicilian Ragout)
(serves 8)

2 lbs. veal – ½ lb. ground meat - parsley or basil –
3 ½ oz. mortadella sausage - 2 hard boiled eggs – 4
½ lbs. ripe tomatoes - 6 tbsps. olive oil - 1 onion -
salt

Sicilian Ragout requires lean, pink veal (sirloin or cutlet) cut into very thin slices that can be rolled up and stuffed with various ingredients.
The Sicilian name to the preferred cut of veal is falsimagro, from the French farce ("stuffing"), and refers to stuffed meat. This is a linguistic memory of French cooking, which lives on in certain popular dishes.
Spread out the thinly-sliced veal on your working surface. Cover it as evenly as you can with a mixture off ground meat, minced parsley or basil, and salt.
Then add a layer of thinly-sliced mortadella, and over that a layer of sliced hard-boiled eggs.

Roll up the meat - make sure all the ingredients stay inside - and sauté it evenly on all sides in olive oil, along with a sliced onion. Pass the ripe tomatoes through a food mill. When the onion is quite golden, add the passed tomato, and (as in any self-respecting ragout) cook the whole very slowly, stirring from time to time, for about 2 hours. The juicy liquid is excellent over pasta, and the meat can be cut into slices and be served.

Genovese
(Genoese stew)
(serves 8)

3 lbs beef - 1/3 lb bacon - 7 tbsps olive oil - 3
celery ribs - 5 carrots - 1 ½ lb. onions - bunch
of parsley - 4 tomatoes - 1 cup white wine - salt

This type of dish, well-known in Naples, has nothing to do with Genoa. Ippolito Cavalcanti, Duke of Buonvicino, famous Neapolitan food writer in the eighteenth hundred, makes mention of it, though he uses a smaller amount of onions. To tell the truth, it seems that some Genoan restaurateurs active in Naples in the 17th century had the ability to cook meat in this way. But it was surely the Neapolitans who discovered the merit of this sauce when served over large types of pasta, such as penne, rigatoni, or maltagliati. The best kind of meat for this preparation comes from the rump or loin.
Wrap the bacon around the meat, tie it together with thread or twine, and put it in a pot with all the minced vegetables. Add oil and salt, brown the meat, and pour white wine over it; when this has evaporated, add 1 ½ cups of water. Cover and cook over very low heat, stirring from time to time, so that the meat slowly transfers its essence, its "feeling," to the liquid. After about 3 hours you'll have a beautiful, thick, bright, amber-colored sauce, ready to be passed through a food mill, and thoroughly cooked, very tender meat.

Pesto con basilico napoletano
(Pesto with Neapolitan basil)
(serves 6)

1 cup basil - ½ clove garlic - 3 tbsp grated Parmesan - 3 tbsp grated pecorino - 1/3 cup pine nuts or freshly shelled walnuts - ½ cup olive oil

The divine poet Vergil tells the story of the good villager who diligently pounds pungent garlic in his mortar after scattering the useless husks on the ground and washing the garlic thoroughly in pure water; he pounds the garlic in a hollow stone with salt and herbs, grinding it until the fragrant clove loses their own odor and color and shape, intimately blending garlic and herbs with heavy blows; then he adds white cheese to improve the color, to make the garlic lose the last of its sharpness, and to merge the flavors.

Although pesto is Genoan, we Neapolitans, by right of our reputation as "leaf-eaters," have allowed ourselves to borrow this recipe and adapt it to the leaves of our basil, which are broader and more aromatic than those of Genoan basil (the best Genovese basil comes from Prà).

Basil: Ocymum basilicum, a plant native to Africa and tropical Asia, from whose leaves is extracted an essential oil used in adding fragrance to liqueurs, particularly in the preparation of chartreuse.

Personally, I follow the "school of thought" that recommends 1 garlic clove for six persons, about 8 basil leaves per person, sufficient salt, many pine nuts or freshly-shelled walnuts, equal amounts of grated pecorino and grated Parmesan, and plenty of extra-virgin olive oil.

This sauce may accompany lasagna, linguine, or vegetable soup.

PASTAS

Spaghetti and Pastas

Spaghetti, macaroni, and other pasta are the blessing of the Neapolitan people, who offer it on every occasion, secure in the knowledge that it will appeal to every stomach and arouse even the laziest appetite. It's not known for certain whether pasta originated in China or Italy, but it is certainly mentioned in Boccaccio's Decameron (written around 1350); when Calandrino inquires about the miraculous heliotrope, Maso replies that most of them can be found in Shangri- La, where the Basques live, in the region called Cockaigne. They tie up the vines with sausages there, and a goose costs a dime, and they throw in a gosling for nothing. And there's a mountain made entirely of grated Parmesan cheese, and on it there are people who do nothing but make macaroni and ravioli and cook them in capon broth, and then they throw them away, and the more you can grab, the more you have. And nearby there's a rivulet of Vernaccia wine, the best anyone ever drank, without so much as a single drop of water. Various regions of Italy lay claim to having been the birthplace of macaroni: Campania, Liguria, Sardinia, Romagna, Sicily; but it seems that honor is due to the last-named, whose claim dates back to the time of the powerful ruler Federico II of Aragon, King of Sicily from 1296 to 1337.

However, the prestige of having built in 1500 the first draw-plate machine, which, when pressing the pasta, ingeniously gave it the desired shape, owns to Naples. We can say, moreover, as a corrective to the stereotype according to which Neapolitans are "macaroni-gobblers" and nothing more, that during the Bourbon period Naples reached, in the judgment of Goethe, Stendhal, and Dumas père, a level of artistic refinement and technological development more advanced than London or Paris had reached at that moment in history.

Naples, restored by the Bourbons to its rank of supreme capital, was the ultimate and most exalting travel experience of the day.

There was an ideal compromise between nature, art, history, society, culture, tradition, folklore, enlightenment, and superstition, the variety and contradictions of life. But everything was imbued with an optimistic faith in progress and comforted by the unique light and proverbial climate.

Naples was a kaleidoscope of complete human experience.

Bucatini neri
(Black bucatini)
(serves 6)

1 lb bucatini (rather large, hollow spaghetti) - 7 oz black olives - 3 salted anchovies - 1 tbsp capers - 1 clove garlic - 3 tbsp olive oil - hot pepper

Wash and bone the anchovies; then, using a mezzaluna (twohanded knife), chop them together with the garlic, chili pepper, capers, and pitted olives, until everything is reduced to a kind of homogeneous paste. Sauté this lightly in olive oil. After all the tastes have mingled, add the bucatini (previously cooked al dente) and stir rapidly to distribute the flavors.

Cannelloni alla sorrentina
(Sorrento-style cannelloni)
(serves 12)

For the pasta: 2 cups white flour - 2 cups semolina flour - 5 eggs
For the filling: 8 eggs - 10 tbsp grated Parmesan -

*1 ½ lb. mozzarella - 7 oz ground meat - 1 tbsp oil
or butter*

"It's divine!" exclaimed Don Alfredo Vezzi, owner of the Cappuccini Hotel in Amalfi, when in 1924 he tasted those pasta tubes lined up by his chef, Salvatore Colletta, who had invented them and named them cannelloni ("big pipes").

But they required the opinion of the town's other connoisseur, Don Andrea Barbaro, who owned the Hotel Luna, a man renowned for his formidable appetite and discerning palate. And such was Don Andrea's enthusiasm that he had the holiday bells rung.

Now, it's not far from Amalfi to Sorrento, so we'll try to describe the *cannelloni* recipe that was handed down in our family.

The first thing you must do is make a good ragout sauce. Then turn your attention to the pasta, which is the home-made kind with flour and eggs (see *Lasagna* recipe)

The only difference is that here the pasta sheets are cut into 1 ½ inch squares. Cook as for lasagna - that is, put a few squares at a time into plenty of boiling salted water and cook for several minutes, removing them while they still offer some resistance to the tooth (al dente). Place in cold water, drain, and arrange on a towel, making sure no water remains.

For the filling, beat the eggs with a pinch of salt, then add generous amounts of grated Parmesan and cubed mozzarella to obtain a creamy mixture. Cook the meat in a skillet with a little oil or butter, break it up with a fork, and add to the egg mixture.

Now layer the filling onto the pasta squares and close them by rolling them up.

Put a few tablespoons of ragout sauce in a bakingpan, and arrange therein the cannelloni you've just stuffed. Pour some more sauce over them, and then some grated Parmesan.

Cover the pan with aluminum foil and bake for 20 minutes at 400°. When the baking is almost over, take off the foil and let the cannelloni brown for another 10 minutes.

Gnocchetti verdi Caruso
(Green dumplings Caruso)
(serves 6)

*1 lb spinach - 1 lb potatoes - 4 ½ cups flour -
1 egg - salt - pepper - nutmeg - 4 tbsp. grated
Parmesan. For the sauce: ragout - 1 cup cream
- basil - grated Parmesan*

The famous neapolitan tenor Enrico Caruso proudly asserted his Neapolitan origins and, despite the adulation America bestowed on him, always nostalgically recalled the cuisine of Naples and the fragrances of its Bay. These little dumplings, dedicated to him, are a very special delicacy enhanced by the perfume of basil and the exuberance of tomato. This recipe is from an excellent restaurant in Sorrento.
Steam the spinach, drain well, pressing it with a wooden spoon so that it loses all its water. Chop it finely and blend with the potatoes already boiled, peeled, and mashed into a very fine purée. Add the flour, egg, salt, pepper, nutmeg, and about 4 tbsp. of grated Parmesan cheese. When you have mixed all the ingredients well and obtained a dough that's quite soft, divide it into lemon-sized pieces and roll them on a flat surface with the palm of your hand so that they form little round sticks using more flour if necessary.
Cut these into 1/2 inch pieces. Lightly powder them with flour and let them dry on a towel.
Then cook them in plenty of boiling salted water for 5 minutes; remove them with a skimmer or slotted spoon, drain them, and dress them with the following sauce: warm the cream and add it to an amount of

ragout sufficient to produce a lovely deep pink mixture; add a lot of basil and grated Parmesan, and spoon the sauce onto the dumplings.

Gnocchi di patate
(Potato dumplings)
(serves 6)

2 lbs potatoes - 4 cups flour - 2 eggs - 1 tbsp olive oil or butter - pinch of salt

The Treaty ot Campoformio (1797), with which Napoleon sold Venice to Austria, introduced into our cuisine new habits: beer, sausage, Prague-style ham, and, especially, the use of potatoes in making dumplings.
Boil and mash the potatoes. Mix in the flour, eggs, oil or butter, and a pinch of salt. When you have a thoroughly blended dough, shape it into finger-thick rolls and cut these into small, equal pieces, denting them with the prongs of a fork so that the hollows formed will be able to hold more sauce and thus more flavor. Boil the dumplings in salted water. They'll be cooked when they rise back to the surface, that is to say very quickly. These are very good if simply served with a sauce of melted butter, sage, and grated Parmesan. If served Sorrento-style, as follows, they're superb. Place them in a baking-pan or in individual clay pots. Dress them with a tasty sauce made from tomatoes, plenty of grated Parmesan, and diced mozzarella. Put them into the oven to form a crust, and garnish them with very fresh basil as you serve them.

Involtini di foglie di verza con il riso
(Stuffed savoy cabbage with rice)
(serves 4-6)

1 savoy cabbage - 1 ½ cup rice - 2 tbsp olive oil - 1 clove garlic - ½ lb ground meat - ½ lb ripe tomatoes - 1 tsp. sugar - salt - ¼ cup grated Parmesan - 3 ½ oz mozzarella - nutmeg - parsley - basil

Strip the leaves from the savoy cabbage, wash them, and blanch them very briefly, a few at a time, in boiling salted water. Drain the leaves and place them a little apart from one another on your work surface. Cover with a towel.

Meanwhile, prepare a sauce as follows: chop the tomatoes, put them in a skillet, salt them, and cook them over low heat for 10 minutes; then add a small garlic clove, a pinch of sugar, and olive oil. Cook until the sauce thickens - it should be quite dense - stirring from time to time and adding basil at the end. Cook the ground meat separately with a little oil in a small frying-pan; break it up with a fork and let it brown for a few minutes.

Cook the rice (not too soft) in boiling water, drain, and season with some of the grated Parmesan, the diced mozzarella, the browned meat, and some grated nutmeg.

Spoon this mixture onto the cabbage leaves and roll them up. Use tooth picks to hold each leaf closed.

Line up the stuffed leaves in a lightly oiled baking-pan, cover them with the tomato sauce, and sprinkle them with the remaining grated Parmesan.

Bake them crusty in a 400° oven for 15 or 20 minutes, and serve them hot.

Lasagna (Lasagna)
(serves 10)

For the pasta: 2 cups white flour - 2 cups semolina flour - 5 eggs
For the meat balls: ½ lb ground pork - ½ lb ground beef - 2 eggs - salt - pepper - 2 tbsp grated Parmesan - 1 tbsp bread soaked in water - olive oil for frying.
For the filling: ragout - grated Parmesan - 1 lb mozzarella - 4 eggs

According to Neapolitan tradition, lasagna is a typical Carnival dish. We begin with the preparation of the pasta, which requires approximately 1 egg for every 100 grams (1 cup) of flour.

As for any pasta dough, mound the sifted flour onto a hard, flat surface, make a well in the center, and break the eggs into it. With the aid of a fork, slowly blend eggs and flour, then work the dough manually until it becomes soft and springy. Let it rest.

After about an hour, divide the dough into the number of leaves or layers that you want. Using a rolling pin, roll out each piece until you obtain very thin sheets, circular if possible. At this point, gently fold each sheet back upon itself, forming a hollow cylinder, and cut each cylinder crosswise into strips about 1/2 inch in width. Unroll the strips and carefully place them on a towel. Let them dry for about 2 hours.

To cook the pasta, use a large pot with plenty of water, properly salted; when it boils, pour the lasagne a few at a time. Cook them briefly; the pasta should still be al dente, as it has to cook further in the oven. Remove the lasagne from the water with a skimmer or slotted spoon, and plunge them at once into a bowl with cold water. Remove, brush off all excess water with your fingers, and place your lasagne on a towel.

Earlier, while the pasta dough was resting, you will have prepared a ragout as described on p.89. In addition, you must prepare the little meatballs that will so worthily accompany the lasagna. Blend ground pork and ground beef, eggs, salt and pepper, the cheese and the bread soaked in warm milk. Mix well, shape into tiny meatballs, and fry them in hot oil. Put a few tbsp. of ragout in a baking-pan, arrange a layer of lasagna on top, add plenty of grated Parmesan, diced mozzarella, and the meatballs.

Beat eggs with more grated Parmesan in a separate bowl, and drizzle some of this onto the contents of the baking-pan. Then continue layering as before: ragout, lasagne, filling, and so forth.

This should bake in the oven at a moderate temperature for about an hour, until you see that the lasagna begins to simmer in the center of the pan. Before serving lasagna, let it rest for 10 minutes.

Linguine con scampi
(Linguine with prawns)
(serves 6)

1 lb linguine - 18 scampi or langoustines (Dublin prawns) - 5 tbsps olive oil - 2 cloves garlic - 1 hot pepper - salt - parsley - 1 lb whole tomatoes - ½ lb tomatoes passed through a food mill - 1 oz butter

The intense red of ripe tomatoes, the shocking pink of prawns, the pale pink of the linguine, and the clear green of the fresh parsley make this dish unique in fragrance, taste, and color: beauty, in short, that transforms itself into delight.

Pour plenty of oil into a skillet. Immediately add a small chili pepper cut into rings and two crushed cloves of garlic. Remove garlic when it just begins to turn golden. Meanwhile cut the prawns lengthwise, wash well in cold water, and de-vein. Lightly sauté the prawns so that their flesh becomes white and their shells pink (no more than 2 minutes). Put them underside up into a baking-pan. Cut the whole tomatoes into quarters and cook them, together with the tomato pulp, in the oil flavored by the garlic and hot pepper. You'll get a lovely, dense red sauce. Add salt. Spread a tsp. of sauce and the butter on each prawn and bake for 4 minutes at 400°.

Boil the linguine, remove while still "al dente", and pour them, not completely drained, into the sauce.

Stir over high heat and turn out onto a warmed platter. Sprinkle plenty of minced parsley on the linguine. Finally, adorn the dish with the scampi. Serve at once.

Linguine ai capperi (Linguine with capers)
(serves 6)

1 lb linguine - 3 ½ oz capers - 4 ripe tomatoes - 3 tbsp olive oil - 1 onion - 2 tbsp grated pecorino cheese - salt - pepper - basil

Cut the onion into thin slices and sauté them in the oil. When they are soft, limp, and clear, add the well-washed capers and stir for two minutes. Add tomatoes chopped into small pieces and pepper, and cook 10 minutes. Meanwhile, boil pasta in plenty of water with a pinch of salt, drain, and pour into the sauce. Mix and remove from heat; add grated cheese and fresh basil.

Linguine al tonno del marinaio
(Sailors' linguine with tuna)
(serves 6)

1 lb linguine - 2 tbsp olive oil - 1 clove garlic -
½ cup black olives - 3 tbsp capers - 1 lb ripe
tomatoes - 7 oz canned tuna with oil

The art of preparing a delicious dish at any time of year with foods stored in the galley is proper to professional seamen, but we'll gladly appropriate it.
In a skillet, fry garlic in olive oil until golden. Remove, and substitute with pitted olives and capers. Stir for a few minutes over a lively fire; add peeled ripe tomatoes. Cook this sauce about 10 minutes before adding the canned tuna with hi oil.
Pour linguine into boiling salted water. When they're cooked al dente, place them in the skillet with the sauce to absorb the flavor.
Stir quickly and serve hot.

Linguine con cozze e polipetti
(Linguine with mussels and octopus)
(serves 6)

5 tbs olive oil - 4 lbs mussels - 2 cloves garlic - 1
hot pepper - parsley - 1 lb small octopus - 1 lb
linguine

For best results with this dish, begin by making sure there's a full moon; in Naples, they say, "Waxing moon, and all is heavy; waning moon, and all is empty." So shellfish will be plump and juicy when the moon is full, but they'll dwindle gradually as the moon begins to wane.

In a frying-pan, sauté the sliced garlic and hot pepper until the former begins to turn golden. Wash octopus well, cut into small pieces, and add.

The octopus should be a "true" octopus, that is, it should have two rows of suckers on each tentacle. After about 5 minutes the octopus will take on a nice red color.

Meanwhile you will have prepared the mussels for cooking.

Open them with a pointed knife - exerting slight pressure will enable you to cut the tendon that holds the shell together - and collect the juices they contain, as well as the molluscs themselves. If you encounter no resistance when prising them open, beware; they're probably dead and may have a bad odour, or contain sand, which will contaminate the sauce.

Add mussels and their water to the skillet and cook for about 20 minutes. Boil the pasta (strictly al dente) and sauté it in the pan with the sauce for a few seconds. Pour the whole onto a serving platter and sprinkle with minced parsley.

Linguine con i ricci
(Linguine and sea-urchins)
(serves 6)

1 lb linguine - 5 tbsp olive oil - 4 lbs mussels - 1
hot pepper - 1 lb small octopus - 18 sea-urchins -
1 lemon - salt

A prerequisite for this dish is proximity to the sea, because seaurchins, or echinoids, must be really fresh, just caught from the sea. After preparing the sauce as in the preceding recipe (Linguine with mussels and octopus), add the sea-urchin eggs at the last moment, a few drops of lemon juice, and the usual minced parsley. Stir well and serve at once.

Migliaccio rustico sorrentino
(Sorrento-style country porridge)
(serves 6)

*2/3 lb spaghetti - 1 tbsp lard or butter - salt - pepper - 2
cups yellow semolina flour - 3 tbsp grated Parmesan -
½ cup sultana raisins*

Migliaccio is a direct descendant of certain Roman porridges (*farinate*).
These were little meal-cakes made with coarsely ground flour, milk or water,
and salt, mixed well into a dense gruel, and eaten with a spoon. A little bit of
everything was poured into this doughy mixture: peas, chickpeas, chicken,
fish, herbs.
For this dish, bring 2 quarts of water to boil and then add the lard, the
spaghetti broken into pieces, salt, and pepper. When the pasta is half-done,
slowly pour in the semolina, stirring constantly with a wooden spoon.
After 20 minutes, turn off the heat and add the grated cheese and the sultana
raisins. Mix well, pour into a greased bakingpan (use a little lard or butter),
and bake for 20 minutes at 400°.

Orecchiette con cime di rapa
(Little ears and greens)
(serves 6)

*1 lb orecchiette ("little ears": disc-shaped pasta
with a hollow in the center) - 1 lb broccoli - 5 tbsp
olive oil - 1 clove garlic - 2 salted anchovies -
grated cheese*

Apulian tradition almost always requires home-made pasta composed of
semolina flour, white flour, water, and salt. This pasta takes various forms,
including the orecchiette or "little ears". The right kind of greens, a typically
Apulian vegetable (sometimes called broccolirab, broccoli rabe, or rappini in
America), may be difficult to find. You can use broccoli instead; choose

those richer in tops than in leaves and you'll approximate the tenderness of the Apulian greens. Boil greens and pasta together. When the pasta is cooked but not soft, drain pasta and greens. Pour olive oil into a skillet, brown the garlic, remove it, and add the washed, boned anchovy fillets, which will dissolve in a few seconds. Add pasta and greens and toss. At table, sprinkle this dish with grated cheese, preferably cacioricotta (a very tasty Apulian cheese made from goat's milk, sheep's milk, or sometimes both).

Pasta alla Campolattaro
(Campolattaro pasta)
(serves 6)

2 lbs beef (rump or round) - ½ hen - 1 quail drumstick - parsley - 2 celery ribs - 1 onion - 1 carrot - salt - 1 lb penne (short, tubular pasta) without grooves - 2 tbsp butter - 1 cup grated Parmesan

A recipe from the ancient Neapolitan family of Count Paolo Gaetani.
Make a stock with the various meats and vegetables. Cook the pasta so that it's still "al dente", drain, and dress it with the melted butter, a few ladles of stock, the grated cheese, and pieces of the meat cut into small cubes.

Pasta alla caprese
(Capri-style pasta)
(serves 6)

1 lb penne - 1 lb salad tomatoes - 1 clove garlic - oregano - basil - 3 tbsp olive oil - salt - 7 oz mozzarella

Like rice, pasta can be boiled, cooled, and used as a base for salads with excellent results.
The pasta should be cooked on the spot, as in any normal warm pasta dish, then drained and cooled rapidly in cold running water. After rubbing a platter

with garlic, dress the pasta with enough olive oil to keep it from sticking, and turn it onto the platter, accompanied with the cubed tomatoes, a pinch of oregano, salt, plenty of minced fresh basil, and little cubes of mozzarella.

Pasta alla Norma
(Pasta alla Norma)
(serves 6)

1 lb short rigatoni or tortiglioni - 1 lb Italian eggplant - olive oil for frying - 7 oz mozzarella – 5 tbsp grated dried ricotta - basil
For the sauce: 3 tbsp olive oil - 1 clove garlic - hot pepper - 2 lb ripe tomatoes - salt

Harmonious as the music of Bellini, the Sicilian composer of Norma, this pasta offers a marvelous and unforgettable balance of ingredients.
To begin, make a rather light fresh tomato sauce: sauté garlic in oil, remove garlic, and replace it with the chili pepper and the peeled, sieved tomatoes; add salt and cook uncovered for 20 minutes.
Meanwhile slice the eggplant and fry in olive oil. With the eggplant, the sauce, the cubed mozzarella, the grated dried ricotta (a cheese similar to the cacioricotta the Apulians use on Orecchiette, p. 105), and fresh basil, dress the boiled pasta. The result will indeed be like a symphony.

Pasta con i broccoli in tegame
(Pasta and cauliflower in a pan)
(serves 6)

1 lb maccheroncini or bucatini (long, narrow, hollow pasta) - 1 cauliflower (about 1 ½ lb) - 1/3 cup sweet seedless raisins - 1/3 cup pine nuts - 1 onion - 1 tsp saffron - hot pepper - 4 anchovies - 4 tbsp olive oil - salt

This specialty of Sicilian cuisine is particularly popular in Palermo. Note that Sicilians call *broccoli* what we call cauliflower. Wash this, chop it small, and put it in plenty of cold water. Boil and cook for 10 minutes. If you want to accentuate the cauliflower taste, save this water to cook the pasta in.

Grate or slice the onion very thinly, place in a pan, add salt, and let stand 10 minutes (this will make the onions more digestible). Now add a generous amount of olive oil and lightly sauté the onion with the hot pepper; then add the anchovies, well washed, the cooked cauliflower, the saffron, the raisins, and the pine nuts (toast these in the oven first).

Cook the pasta al dente, drain it, and pour into a bowl. Dress with the sauce and let stand for 10 minutes before serving.

Pasta con la purea di zucca
(Pasta with pumpkin purée)
(serves 6)

*2 lbs pumpkin - 5 tbsps olive oil - 3 cloves garlic -
hot pepper - parsley - 1 lb pasta (penne) - salt*

At the end of the summer and in the fall you can find big pumpkins of a lovely orange color, available most of the winter and considered a "winter squash."

Take about 4 lbs. of pumpkin, peel and seed it, cut it into pieces, and sauté it in olive oil with the garlic and hot pepper. Cook until the pumpkin comes apart and is reduced to a very soft pulp or purée. Season with salt and fresh minced parsley.

This is excellent by itself as a side dish, but it's also good on pasta, cooked al dente in lots of salted water. Mix into the pumpkin purée and serve.

Pasta con le costolette
(Pasta and cutlets)
(serves 6)

*1 lb spaghetti - 1 lb pork cutlets or loin chops - ½
cup grated Parmesan - 1/3 cup grated pecorino
cheese - salt – pepper*

This is decidedly a rustic, unsophisticated dish, but most delightful if you're careful to warm the plates before carrying them to the table. Chop the pork cutlets into small cubes and cook them in a skillet without any fat; this type of meat provides enough of its own. Meanwhile cook the pasta very al dente in lots of salted water, drain the pasta, and pour it into the skillet with the meat. Sautè. Powder with generous amounts of grated cheese and freshly-ground pepper.

Pasta con le melanzane
(Pasta with eggplant)
(serves 6)

*1 lb penne - 2 tbsp olive oil and vegetable oils for
frying - 1 onion - 2 lbs peeled tomatoes - basil -
salt - 1 lb Italian eggplant - 7 oz mozzarella - 1
cup grated Parmesan*

The calendar rigorously schedules our gastronomical cycles and habits, and so summer brings us the delicious aroma of basil, the fragrance of ripe, sun-filled tomatoes, and the cheeky eggplant; and all these, mixed with the classic flavors of mozzarella and Parmesan, blend into a charming symphony.
In a saucepan, prepare a tomato sauce by first cooking the sliced onions in olive oil until they become golden, then adding the tomatoes.
Season with salt and plenty of basil and cook over low heat for about 30 minutes, until the oil separates from the tomato. Rub through a sieve or food

mill. Meanwhile cut the eggplant into small pieces and fry them in plenty of hot vegetable oil.

Drain on paper towels and season with salt and a little grated Parmesan. Cut the mozzarella into small cubes.

Cook the pasta al dente; sprinkle it with the rest of the Parmesan, then add the tomato sauce, followed by the mozzarella, the eggplant chunks, and the basil. Toss everything and serve immediately.

The determining factor here is the flavorful Parmesan cheese, which is so compatible with the intense taste of eggplant!

Pasta con le sarde
(Pasta and sardines)
(serves 6)

1 lb bucatini or large perciatini (slender, hollow pasta) - 1 lb fresh sardines - 2 oz sweet seedless raisins - 2 oz pine nuts - 1 little bunch wild fennel - 3 salted anchovies - 1 tsp saffron - 1 onion - 5 tbsps olive oil - salt

A characteristic common to every "poor" cuisine is the universal dish, a dish based on an element widely consumed in the region (pasta, in this case, naturally) and enriched with meat or fish or legumes or vegetables or eggs or cheese. In Sicily the universal dish is baked pasta in its various versions, or, in and around Palermo, pasta and sardines.

In the coastal regions, the important food fish are sardines, anchovies, and tuna; especially at certain times of the year, the sardine catch is enormous, and thus a large part of it can be salted and preserved. The juxtaposition of contrasting tastes typical over all of western Sicily is due to the Arabs; notable examples are the agrodolce, or sweet and sour sauce, and the use of raisins and pine nuts in pasta dishes. We can recognize this practice in the present recipe, a dish typical of Palermitan cuisine, complex, fragrant, original, and intense.

Wash the fennel well and boil it in a lot of salted water for 10 minutes. Drain it and save the water, which is now full of flavor, to cook the pasta in later.

Squeeze the fennel well and mince it very thin. Put the raisins in lukewarm water for 5 minutes to plump them. Meanwhile, in a saucepan, slice the onion very fine, season with a pinch of salt, and let stand for some minutes; this procedure will make the onions more digestible. Then add a generous amount of olive oil and cook it until it becomes golden. Warm the saffron on the lid of the hot water pot before adding it to the onion. Wash the sardines, opening them halfway, and remove their heads, tails, bones, and skin. Put four or five aside. Add the others to the onion; mash the fish to a pulp in the pan. Now add the minced fennel, then the raisins and the pine nuts. Wash and clean the anchovies, and, using a separate pan, dissolve them by cooking in a little oil. Add them to the other ingredients.

Finally, cook the remaining sardines. Don't break them up, as they are to garnish the pasta. Boil the latter in the fennel water; when the pasta is nearly cooked, drain it, and finish cooking it in the sauce. Let the pasta rest for 5 minutes in a serving-dish before bringing it to the table.

Pasta di mezz'estate
(Midsummer pasta)
(serves 6)

*1 lb small penne - 1 yellow pepper - 2 Italian
eggplants - 2 zucchini - salt - 5 tbsp olive oil - 1
clove garlic - ½ lb peeled tomato - ½ cup grated
Parmesan - 7 oz mozzarella - basil*

A stunning palette of colors, worthy of Caravaggio.
Chop all the vegetables into cubes of equal size and fry them in oil in separate pans so that they become soft and juicy.
In another pan, sauté a garlic clove in a little of the oil you used for the pepper. Remove the garlic when it begins to turn golden, and replace it with the peeled, seeded tomatoes and a pinch of salt. Let this cook about 20 minutes. Cook pasta al dente and pour it into the tomato pan, add the vegetables, the grated Parmesan, the mozzarella (cut into tiny cubes), and stir. Complete with basil leaves.

Executing this dish will promote you past master of using what Cicero called the *captatio benevolentiae*, "the seizure of good will," since this provocative, tempting dish captures attention through its appeal to both nose and eye.

Pasta e patate del contadino
(Country pasta and potatoes)
(serves 6)

5 potatoes - 1 slice of pancetta (unsmoked, salted bacon) about 3 ½ oz - 1 lb of mixed pasta - 3 tbsp olive oil - 1 cup of various cheeses - basil - salt - pepper

A very quick but tasty recipe.
First put the peeled, very coarsely chopped potatoes into plenty of boiling water, then add the pasta and let everything cook. At the same time, using a skillet, sauté the diced pancetta in oil or butter. After this has cooked for a while, it will be ready for the pasta and potatoes, which you should take out of the boiling water with a slotted spoon. Stir and mingle the tastes; season with pepper. Add the grated cheeses and some aromatic basil leaves.
Serve this pasta very hot.

Pasta fresca al limone
(Fresh pasta with lemon)
(serves 4)

2 cups flour - 1 egg + 1 egg white - 1 tsp olive oil - 1 tsp salt - water - 2 lemons - 7 tbsp dry white wine - 1 cup cream - ½ cup grated Gruyère cheese

A surprisingly delightful dish of fragrance and freshness. To prepare the pasta, sift the flour, add the egg, egg white, olive oil, salt, and enough water to obtain a firm, elastic dough. Let this rest for about an hour. Lightly flour your work surface and roll out the dough upon it with a rolling pin. Make thin sheets, cut them into strips, and put them to dry on white towels. Wash the lemons well, dry them, and grate their peels. Cook the *tagliatelle* (your pasta) in abundant, boiling salted water. Meanwhile put the grated lemon peel and wine in a saucepan. Cook this briefly, reducing the wine by half. Then slide the pasta into the pan and add the cream. If the pasta absorbs all the cream, add more cream or some milk to obtain the right consistency. Check the degree of creaminess, then add a few drops of lemon juice and the grated Gruyère. When sauce and pasta have completely mingled, serve at once.

Pasta gratinata con la besciamél
(Baked pasta with béchamel sauce)
(serves 6)

1 lb pasta (pennette) - 4 oz butter – ½ cup flour -
1 quart milk - salt - pepper – nutmeg - 1 cup grated
Parmesan – 7 oz mozzarella

The Marquis de Béchameil's invention was certainly a happy one. The sauce named after him takes an important part in our cuisine; it lost the last of its exotic aura when Pellegrino Artusi (author of a well-known Italian cookbook) rebaptized it in Italian balsamella.
After the butter has liquefied, remove the pot from the heat and add the flour, mixing it with a wooden spoon. Add warm milk, at first a few drops at a time, then gradually the rest of the required amount. Make sure that the milk is absorbed slowly into the mixture, stirring constantly to avoid unattractive lumps. Season with salt to taste, then nutmeg, and return the pan to a very low fire, stirring until the sauce comes to boil.
Now cook the pasta in plenty of boiling, salted water.
Don't overcook; as it has to continue cooking in the oven. In cooking pasta, it's a good rule to use a large pot. When the pasta enters the water, its temperature drops. This fall in temperature is briefer in a larger pot.
Dress the pasta with a little more than half of the béchamel sauce, some freshly ground pepper, and the grated Parmesan. Coat a bakingpan with some béchamel and pour in half of the pasta. Place a layer of diced mozzarella on

top of the pasta. Add the rest of the pasta and, finally, a layer consisting of the rest of the béchamel sauce.

Put into the stove to form a crust, about 30 minutes, or until the golden color of the pasta tells you it's done.

Pasta "sfincionata"
(Pasta with anchovy and tomato sauce)
(serves 6)

1 lb pennette (short, tubular pasta) - 2 onions – 4 tbsp olive oil - 1 lb tomatoes – 1 tsp oregano - 3 salted anchovies - hot pepper – 3 tbsp stale breadcrumbs - salt - 1 clove garlic

Like all *sfincione* dishes, this one comes from western Sicily.

Slice the onions very thinly, salt them, and let them stand for 10 minutes in order to become more digestible. Then pour a little olive oil on them, cook them slowly until they're limp, and add the peeled, seeded, and minced tomatoes. Cook for 10 minutes before adding plenty of oregano and the anchovies, which you have already washed, boned, chopped, and blended in another pan with a little olive oil and crushed garlic.

After the anchovies, add the hot pepper and leave this sauce on very low heat. Meanwhile toast the breadcrumbs in a skillet with a little oil and a pinch of salt; stir until they become brown.

Cook the pasta al dente and dress it with the prepared sauce. At table, offer fresh olive oil and the toasted breadcrumbs for your companions to add as they please.

Pennette al tonno alla siciliana
(Sicilian-style penne with tuna)
(serves 6)

6 salted anchovies – 4 tbsp olive oil - 1 clove garlic - parsley - 7 oz oil-packed, canned tuna – 3 tbsp grated breadcrumbs, toasted – grated pecorino cheese (optional) - 1 lb penne (short, tubular pasta)

Sauté the garlic in pure olive oil . Remove garlic and turn off the heat. Wash the anchovies very carefully under running water Add them in the pan. We recommend salted anchovies rather than the canned, oil-packed kind, which have less personality. Meanwhile drop the penne into boiling water, reheat the anchovy pan, and add the canned tuna. Drain the pasta and dress it with this sauce, with freshly-minced parsley, and with the grated and toasted breadcrumbs.
Grated pecorino is optional.

Ravioli donn'Amelia
(Donna Amelia's ravioli)
(serves 10)

For the pasta: 4 cups all purpose flour - sufficient boiling water (about 2 cups) – salt - 1 tbsp butter
For the filling: 8 eggs - 1 ½ cups grated Parmesan - 1 cup ricotta - 1 lb mozzarella - salt & pepper

Felix qui potuit rerum cognoscere causas. "The man who has been able to understand the causes of things, is lucky." This is a line from Vergil's Georgics, praising the good fortune of those whose insight into nature's secrets raises them above the superstitions of the crowd. We may paraphrase this line saying that he is lucky who knows the secret of obtaining the softest, most impalpable pasta for ravioli. Mound the flour on a flat surface, make a well in it, and put the water on the fire. When it boils, pour it slowly into the well, mixing flour and water with a fork. You should do this so that about half of the flour absorbs the water and becomes very soft. At this point, add the salt, the lard (or butter, if you prefer), and continue to work the pasta until it becomes velvety and smooth. Let it stand while you make the filling.
Beat the eggs in a bowl with the grated Parmesan, salt, pepper, ricotta and mozzarella (cut into tiny pieces).

Roll out part of the pasta into a thin sheet with a rolling pin and, on one half of the sheet, outline the ravioli in the shape and size you desire. Spoon the filling onto the pasta, keeping within your outlines. Cover with the other half of the sheet, press the edges together lightly with your fingertips, and cut out the ravioli with a ravioli cutter. Gently place the ravioli, one at a time, on a towel. When they're all ready, drop them with the towel into plenty of boiling, correctly salted water. Then dress the ravioli with a good tomato sauce, a sprinkle of grated Parmesan, and, if the season permits, some fresh basil.

The great ballerina, Carla Fracci, a frugal eater, once broke her regimen for these lovingly-prepared ravioli. It's well known that love is the ingredient that the good cook has to add to his operations. It must make its presence known and tasted, and capture the interest of whoever's going to eat; it's an indispensable factor in the success of a dish.

Risotto alla pescatora
(Fisherman's risotto)
(serves 6)

1 lb Carnaroli rice - 1 lb fish (small fry) - 1 cuttlefish or 1 squid - 1 small octopus (1 lb) – ½ lb. shelled shrimps – ½ lb shucked mussels – 1 tbsp shucked clams - 4 peeled tomatoes - 4 white peppercorns - carrot, celery, onion, garlic, 1 tbsp vinegar, 3tbsp olive oil, salt

Risotto, an intensely northern, winter dish, puts on a summery, Mediterranean look in this recipe because of the absence of butter and the presence of some delicate sea creatures.

The result is cheerful and quite lovely.

In a pot with 2 1/2 qts. of water put a peeled carrot, an entire onion gashed crosswise, 4 peeled tomatoes, one garlic clove, 2 celery ribs, a bunch of parsley, and the peppercorns. When the water boils, salt it and add the small fry and 1/2 cup of vinegar. Cook over moderate heat for 20 minutes. Strain the broth and return to boil. Add the cuttlefish or squid and the octopus, and, after 10 minutes, the shelled shrimp, the mussels, and the clams, and continue to cook for 5 minutes.

Cut the octopus into pieces and the cuttlefish or squid into little rings. Sauté a garlic clove in 3 tbsp. of oil; remove garlic and replace with chopped octopus, cuttlefish or squid, shrimp, mussels, or clams, and sauté everything briefly. Keep it warm.

In a pot pour 2 tbsp. of oil and fry a finely-chopped onion. Add rice and toast it well before beginning to pour in the boiling stock, which you will add slowly.

Salt if necessary, and continue to cook for about 20 minutes. At the very last moment add the other warm ingredients, turn the risotto into a serving-dish and sprinkle with minced parsley. Send it steaming to the table.

Risotto con carciofi
(Risotto with artichokes)
(serves 6)

2 ½ cups rice - 4 Italian (or small) artichokes - 1 lemon - 6 tbsps olive oil - 1 onion – 1 ½ qts vegetable broth – ½ cup grated Parmesan - 1 clove garlic - parsley

The artichoke, *Cynara scolymus*, a distinguished vegetable whose floral receptacles are consumed when incompletely mature, is rich in cynarin, a substance that promotes the influx of bile into the intestine. Eating artichokes often is conducive to a healthy liver.

To clean Italian artichokes, remove the layered outer leaves, keeping only the tender central portion of the receptacle; cut off the tip of this as well. Place cleaned artichokes in a mixture of lemon juice and cold water for at least 15 minutes to avoid their turning black.

When you're ready to cook them, cut the artichokes into small pieces and arrange in a saucepan with oil that has been flavored with garlic and minced parsley. Pour in a cup of water, cover the pan, and cook for about 15 minutes. While you're waiting for the artichokes to cook, put some oil and thinly-sliced-onions - spring onions, if available - into another pan. When these have browned, add the cooked artichokes, then the rice.

Flavor the rice by stirring it in, then add stock a little at a time (the stock should, of course, be at a constant, boiling temperature).

You can also use bouillon cubes for this stock - 2 for every qt. of water is enough.

Stir the rice constantly with a wooden spoon until done.

To complete the dish, enrich its taste with plenty of grated Parmesan.

Risotto con favette e finocchio selvatico
(Risotto with fava beans and wild fennel)
(serves 4)

1 ½ cups rice - 1 lb fava or broad beans - 1 tuft of wild fennel - 2 spring onions – 1 tbsp butter - 3 tbsps olive oil – 2 tbsp grated Parmesan – 1 qt vegetable stock - salt - pepper

This simple preparation is related to certain traditional Sicilian pasta and fava dishes, although here, in deference to the lighter tastes and different requirements of today, the favas are exempted from undergoing their traditionally aggressive treatment with lard or animal fats.

Shell the beans, removing their thin pods and tips. In a pan, cover them with water and a thread of olive oil and cook them slowly; salt them at the end of the cooking period.

Boil the wild fennel and mince it. In another pan, cook the thinly-sliced onions in a little butter. When they're soft, add the rice, toast it briefly, and then add ladles of boiling vegetable broth gradually, allowing the rice to absorb it. When the rice is cooked halfway, add the beans and the fennel. At the end, remove from the heat and flavor the rice with plenty of grated Parmesan.

Rich in flavor and strong in fragrance, wild fennel, native to the Mediterranean coast, is preferably eaten cooked. When raw, it has a bitter taste.

Risotto con fegatini di pollo (Risotto with chicken livers)
(serves 6)

2 ½ cups rice - 6 very fresh chicken livers - 2 oz butter - 1 oz beef bone marrow - 1 young onion - 2 tbps olive oil – 2 tbsp grated Parmesan - 1 ½ qts beef & chicken stock - pinch of saffron - salt

Lightly brown the thinly-sliced onion in the butter, together with the minced beef marrow. When the onion is soft, add the rice, toasting it so that it will cook better. Dissolve the saffron in a tablespoon of stock and add it. Continue to cook over brisk heat (as in any risotto dish) pouring in boiling stock from time to time and stirring constantly. When the rice is almost done, cook the chopped livers in a little olive oil; be careful not to overcook them or they will become tough. Season with salt. Mix grated Parmesan into the rice, turn out onto a large serving-dish, arrange the livers in the center, and serve at once.

Risotto con gamberetti (Risotto with shrimp)
(serves 6)

2 ½ cups rice – 10 oz shrimps - 2 oz butter - 1 onion - 1 carrot - parsley - 1 bay leaf – 5 tbsp olive oil - 1 cup white wine (distinctive-tasting; Vernaccia, for example) - salt - pepper – 1 ½ qts fish broth

Put a saucepan on the fire; dribble in a thread of olive oil, then add half sliced onion. When this has softened, add chopped carrot, 1 bay leaf, and a bunch of parsley. Let this sauté lightly for a bit, then add the shrimp; as they change color, stir well for 5 minutes.
Pour in the wine and let it evaporate. Turn off heat, peel the shrimp, and put them aside. Grind their shells together with the cooked vegetables in a mortar, making a creamy mixture. Pass this through a food mill, adding 1 oz. soft butter. Save.

Using the rest of the butter and a thin line of oil, brown the other half of the onion finely chopped in another pan. When the onion has withered, add the rice, toast it in the pan, then continue cooking it by pouring in boiling fish broth or water as for a normal risotto.

Season it with salt and pepper, and add the peeled shrimps and the creamy ground shell mixture, which will give the whole a handsome rosy colour. Complete with the ubiquitous minced parsley.

Risotto con "langoustines"
(Risotto with Dublin Bay prawn)
(serves 6)

2 ½ cups rice - 9 "langoustines" or scampi (Dublin prawn) – 4 tbsp olive oil - 2 cloves garlic - hot pepper - parsley - 1 celery rib - carrot – onion - 4 cloves – ½ cup white wine - 2 oz butter - salt - pepper – cognac

Begin by preparing a shellfish fumet (broth or coulis): toast scampi or prawns in a saucepan with a little olive oil, crushed garlic, and chili pepper. When the carapaces begin to open, remove the fleshy parts of these crustaceans and set aside. Add the aromatic vegetables to the shells in the pan and "sweat" everything together. Then pour in the white wine, let it evaporate, add water, and let this mixture simmer lazily over a very weak flame for about twenty minutes. Salt as desired, and remove the foam that will rise to the surface. Filter the *fumet* through a fine strainer. Return a little of this to the fire, add the rice, and cook it slowly, occasionally pouring in more stock as the rice continues to absorb it (you will need about 1 and a half qts. to cook your rice).

When the rice is done, add butter, salt, pepper, and a splash or two of cognac. Stir again. Finish with the langoustines and some parsley. Serve it hot.

Risotto Primavera
(Springtime risotto)
(serves 6)

*2 ½ cups rice - 2 lbs fresh green vegetables of
the season - 2 oz butter - 1 onion – 4 tbsp olive
oil – 1 ½ qts beef or chicken stock – 1 cup
grated Parmesan – salt*

Rice arrived in Italy from Spain, which had imported it from Arabia. Italy produces about 100,000 tons of rice annually, of which the most highly regarded comes from Piedmont.

The indispensable secret one must know about risotto dishes is that the heat must be quite high at the moment when you pour the stock into the rice, which will have been impregnated already by the cooked-in flavors of the other ingredients you've chosen. For this dish, select spring vegetables for freshness and tenderness: peas, zucchini, artichoke hearts, asparagus tips, parsley, basil. Chop them into small pieces and cook them separately in a little butter and olive oil. Should they become too dry before they're done, pour in some boiling water. Season with salt. In another pan brown a thinly-sliced onion in a little butter and olive oil, then soften it further with some white wine. Let this evaporate and then add the rice, toasting it so that it won't get overcooked. Continue cooking the rice, pouring into it, a little at a time, the boiling, well-skimmed stock. When the rice is almost done, add all the cooked vegetables and plenty of grated Parmesan.

Serve at once.

There are many kinds of Italian rice.

The most common, roundgrained variety is rich in starch and does well in soups and stuffing; a more refined type, the excellent Vialone, is right for sartù and timbales; the best of the superfine rices is Carnaroli, magnificent for risotto dishes.

Sartù
(Neapolitan rice timbale)
(serves 6)

2 cups rice – ½ lb Italian pork sausage - 2 chicken livers - meatballs (½ lb ground meat, 1 egg, 1 slice of bread softened in milk or water) – ½ lb shelled small peas – 1 young or green onion - 2 oz prosciutto - 7 oz mozzarella - 2 eggs - olive oil - ragout sauce – ½ cup grated Parmesan - grated breadcrumbs - butter - salt
For the béchamel: 1 oz butter - 1 tbsp flour - 1 cup milk - salt - pepper - nutmeg

Rice, considered in Campania almost as a last resort for a weak stomach, is accepted here only in the guise of a sumptuous sartù - indeed, it gains the place of honor in the center of the table, perhaps on the magnificent sort of worked-silver tray that the French call *surtout*.

The French style of dinner-service - not much food, but many dishes - scored its first success in Italy at the court of Cosimo III de' Medici (1642-1723), consort of Marguerite-Louise d'Orléans; The surtout was placed in the center of the table. Soon this custom was introduced by the *monsù* (as the Italians called the French, the *monsieurs*) at Naples.

These were French cooks who proudly, if somewhat obstinately, promulgated their transalpine laws among us.

Making sartù is a long and complex job, a complicated architectural feat based on a proper balance of ingredients, whose desired effect is a delicate harmony of many diverse elements which preserve their own identity and submit to no sort of tyranny.

Be patient, therefore, and prepare the various elements of this dish: ragù according to its recipe (p. 89), béchamel sauce, and tiny meatballs fried in hot vegetable oil. Then cook in a skillet, with a little olive oil, the minced onion and prosciutto, add the peas and, if necessary, a few spoons of water. In separate skillets, cook the sausage and brown the chicken livers in a little olive oil. Dice the mozzarella very small.

At this point cook the rice al dente in boiling water; let it cool. Then dress it with grated Parmesan to begin with, then the béchamel, and then a little ragout sauce and the beaten eggs.

The result should be a pretty, uniform pink.

Oil a baking-pan and powder it with grated breadcrumbs. Make a first layer of rice, lining the pan as though it were a box, then a layer of mozzarella, meatballs, peas, another of rice, another of sausage and livers (both chopped small), then rice again.

Sprinkle with breadcrumbs and add a few dollops of butter. Bake in a hot oven (350°) for about 50 minutes. Before serving the sartù, let it cool for 10 minutes; it will be easier to remove it from the pan.

Sformatini di riso
(Little rice molds)
(serves 6)

2 cups rice - salt – pepper – ½ cup grated Parmesan
- 7 oz mozzarella - 2 eggs - grated breadcrumbs
For the béchamel: 2 oz butter - 2 tbsp flour – 2 cups
milk - salt - pepper – nutmeg

Rice, like wine, is alive. Regular rice can last up to 12 months in your pantry; whole or brown rice, less durable, will last only 3 months. Neapolitan cuisine uses rice in the traditional ways: for timbales, sartù, croquettes. molds. Rice dishes loaded with cream or flavored with strawberries or rosepetals or caviar or champagne do not belong to our cuisine. Too much imagination, too little substance! It's difficult - almost impossible - to invent a new dish. Anthelme Brillat-Savarin's aphorism is well known:
"The discovery of a new dish is more beneficial to mankind than the discovery of a star." To make these rice molds, cook the rice in as much water as necessary, leaving it very al dente. Season it with salt and pepper. Shower with plenty of grated Parmesan. Add béchamel sauce - which should be velvety smooth, the eggs yolks, the diced mozzarella and at the end the firmly beaten egg whites. Grease small molds with butter and sprinkle them with grated breadcrumbs.
Fill the molds and bake them until the rice turns a lovely golden color (about 40 minutes at a medium high temperature). After 2 or 3 minutes of cooling, remove the molded rice and despatch it to the table at once.

Spaghetti con bottarga
(Spaghetti with mullet roe)
(serves 6)

6 tbsps olive oil - 3 tbsp minced bottarga (dried, compressed mullet roe) - 1 clove garlic - 1 onion - 2 carrots - 2 celery ribs - hot pepper - parsley - 1 lb spaghetti

The name derives from the Arabic batarikh. This is an old Sardinian speciality, particularly esteemed in Alghero, Cabras, and Carloforte, and obtained from the compressed and dessicated eggs of the mullet, a fish typical of the Gulf of Oristano on Sardinia's west coast.

Something similar is found in Sicily. Leonardo Sciascia writes: "If you see it in the delicatessen shop-windows (in Cefalù and a few other Sicilian towns), it looks like a dessicated, petrified beef fillet. It's compressed tuna roe." This is the caviar of the poor. You slice it thin, season it with oil, and enjoy it with dark bread fresh from the oven.

The ancient drying process goes back to the 13th century, when the method was first tried out on stock-fish and herring.

For full success with this dish, it is essential that the oil be light and fragrant, at the peak of its excellence. Traditionally correct oil must be perfectly pure and extracted by millstones that move no faster than 9 revolutions a minute, the number of turns that, in the past, the ox harnessed to the mill would make. In point of fact, if the oil is pressed out too rapidly, the excessive heat will cause it to lose vigor and upset its subtle balance.

Heat the extra-virgin olive oil with a clove of garlic, which you will remove as soon as it becomes golden. Add the onion, the carrot and the celery cut in very small pieces, and the chilli pepper. Sauté few minutes. Cook the pasta al dente, move it in the pan. Take off the heat.

Finish with the minced bottarga and the parsley.

Spaghetti al sugo di pesce
(Spaghetti with fish sauce)
(serves 6)

1 lb spaghetti - 5 tbsp olive oil - 2 cloves garlic
– ½ lb sword-fish - 2 lbs mussels in their shells -
1 lb clams in their shells – ½ cup white wine - 2
ripe tomatoes - 4 mint leaves – parsley - salt

Scrub and wash mussels and clams in plenty of water, then put them in a skillet with three tablespoons of oil. Set the pan on heat, cover it, and shake it so that the heat reaches all the bivalves.
The shells will open in 2 or 3 minutes.
Collect the mussels and the clams out of their shells and filter the liquid. In another pan, heat some more oil, brown the crushed garlic in it, remove the garlic, and add the swordfish, cut into small cubes.
Sauté briefly and pour in wine. When this has evaporated, add sliced tomatoes and a little chopped mint and parsley.
Boil the pasta al dente in plenty of salted water and dress it with this sauce, the mussels, the clams, and their cooking liquid.

Spaghetti con i calamari
(Spaghetti with squids)
(serves 6)

1 lb spaghetti - 4 small squids - 1 clove garlic –
1 lb peeled tomatoes – 1/3 cup pitted black
Italian olives - 1 tbsp pine nuts - 1/3 cup sultana
raisins – 5 tbsp olive oil - salt – pepper – parsley

This simple, traditional preparation of the Mediterranean coastal regions yields a tasty sauce for spaghetti.
Clean, wash, and dry the squids before cutting them into small pieces.

Brown the garlic in oil. Remove the garlic from the pan and replace it with the squid and all the other ingredients. Season with salt and pepper and cook covered over low heat. Add water if the sauce becomes too dry.
Boil the spaghetti al dente and finish cooking them in the sauce.
Complete the dish with a handful of chopped parsley.

Spaghetti con le zucchine
(Spaghetti with zucchini)
(serves 6)

1 lb spaghetti - 2 lbs zucchini - 1 cup olive oil - 2 oz butter - 1 cup grated Parmesan – 1 slice caciocavallo cheese or provolone - salt – basil

Maybe it's that special sun, maybe it's the sea or the smell of rocks and seaweed, but there's no doubt that you eat the world's best spaghetti with zucchini at Nerano. One can try and try to penetrate the secret or reproduce the magic ingredient, with delicious results, but perhaps that ineffable element will be missing.
Nevertheless, here is an excellent recipe. Cut the zucchini into little cubes and fry them in the oil a few at a time, removing them as soon as they begin to brown. After they've fried, put them in layers in an earthenware bowl and season them with salt, grated Parmesan, and very fresh basil. Finally add 2 tbsp. of the oil they cooked in and let these flavors mingle for an hour.
Then boil the spaghetti al dente, drain, and return to heat with about 1/2 cup of their cooking water, the butter, the zucchini, and the caciocavallo cut into thin strips. Add the remaining parmisan. Flavor everything with a lot of basil.
The caciocavallo (one of the so-called "spun" cheeses) will melt and coat the strands of spaghetti, to their great advantage.
It's a curious fact that the name of this ancient cheese, among the most popular in Campania, probably comes from the custom of tying two fresh cheeses (caci) together and hanging them on a reed to dry, as though astride a horse (a cavallo).
Caciocavallo is round and oblong in shape, similar to a pear, with a very short neck that becomes quite narrow just below the rounded top or head.

One of my usual trips, during my summer in Capri, is the short nautical dash to Sorrento. I am bound to this dream land by a far and unforgatable memory: the Sorrento – Sant'Agata car race, one of the most glorious uphill races of my youth, valid for the Italian championship of this speciality, in which I triumphed over any previous record in 1929.

What a marvellous and superhuman time in my life: I was twenty-one and I considered myself – and maybe I was – the master of the world. In my moral integrity I was thanking God in every moment, for being so generous to me.

Today, after more than half century, my attraction in Sorrento is Rita and Mariano's villa, open to the sun and their friends. Their ospitality has become a way of saying: one says "hospitable as the Panes", and this exquisite and humane quality makes them beloved and popoular to all of us.

One day during the summer when I was a guest at the Panes for lunch, Rita told me: in today's menu there is a surprise for you. I'll offer you "Tagliatelle alla Sirignano".

Suddendly I racalled how the recipe was born. A couple of years before in Netrano, a little town on the sea, less than four sea miles from Capri, in Positano-Amalfi direction, there was just one small restaurant named like its owner, Maria Grazia, my favourite destination out of Capri. I used to go with Fred Chandon, one of the most famous champagne producers, and his divine wife Francesca, of Italian descendent. I was often a guest of the Chandon's in their fabulous castel in Fiertè, 300 km. from Paris.

Once we arrived there, Fred with the sarcasm, sometimes frienfudly, typical of the French towards the Italians talking about gastronomy, told me "Enough spaghetti with tomatoes, your Southern Italians' national dish! I want to see if you are able to offer me something newer or more original".

The stimulating question lightened up in me all my culinary idealisations and I begged M.G. to prepare me a sauce made with zucchini fried in half oil, one quarter butter and one quarter lard. Our cordon bleu, appreciating my suggestion, performed the recipe adding to the spaghetti "al dente" two kinds of cheese: parmesan and provolone, to exalt the Neapolitane origin of the recipe.

The invention has become a huge success and M.G. had lived thanks to it, and it's know how to my friend as "Tagliatelle alla Sirignano" and for her clients as "Spaghetti alla M.G.".

Francesco Caravita
Prince of Sirignano

Spaghetti con le acciughe salate
(Spaghetti with salted anchovies)
(serves 6)

*1 lb spaghetti – ½ cup breadcrumbs - 5 tbsp olive
oil - salt - 2 cloves garlic - 6 salted anchovies - hot
pepper*

This is a speciality of Syracuse, where the preferred way of cooking pasta, as in the rest of Sicily, is to flavor it with olive oil and the hearty taste of salted anchovies.

Heat olive oil in a skillet and sauté the garlic cloves. When they turn brown, remove and replace them with the anchovies, after boning and washing these in running water. They dissolve quickly in the hot oil and make a homogeneous sauce, to which you may add, if you wish, some chili pepper. Now turn off the heat. In the meantime, you will have boiled the spaghetti in plenty of salted water and toasted the breadcrumbs to a fine golden color in the oven. Dress the spaghetti with the sauce, and, at table, sprinkle it with the breadcrumbs. It's even better to make your own grated breadcrumbs at home. Bake stale bread for a while and then crush it up fine with a bottle.

Spaghetti con le noci
(Spaghetti with walnuts)
(serves 6)

*1 lb spaghetti - 5 tbsps olive oil - 1 clove garlic -
1 cup shelled walnuts - 4 anchovies - parsley*

The walnuts of Sorrento, the best in the world, have been famous forever. So how could the Sorrentines not invent a dish with walnuts?

Like the dried fruit that cheers the table on cold days, this recipe is proper to winter. ince it's very "simple," it requires the greatest care! The only risk you run is that of either burning or undercooking the walnut kernels.

In hot oil, sauté the crushed garlic, remove when golden, and replace with the nuts. Cook for 3-4 minutes over moderate heat. Be careful, since the heat of the oil contained in the kennels will continue to toast them even after the heat is off. After they are cooked, add the anchovies without the bones and already washed. They will break up in the hot oil. Cook the spaghetti al dente and drain them, leaving them lightly moist, and put them in the pan with the sauce. Sauté the pasta a bit, stirring well and add some finely minced parsley. Send them to the table on warmed plates.

Spaghetti o linguettine aglio e olio
(Spaghetti or linguettine with garlic and oil)
(serves 6)

1 lb spaghetti or linguettine – ½ cup extra-virgin olive oil - 6 cloves garlic - hot pepper - parsley – salt

The magic formula of the "Mediterranean diet," which is based upon vegetable oils, green vegetables, and farinaceous foods, which limits consumption of meat to a minimum, and which prefers seafood in its stead, is expressed in this synthesis: spaghetti, garlic, oil, and green pepper. This is a simple diet, the descendant of a way of nutrition built upon basic products of the land and the sea.

Garlic (*Allium sativum* of the family *Liliaceae*), originally from Asia, takes on the appearance of a bulb formed by a cluster of many smaller bulbs or cloves and possesses antiseptic and bactericidal properties; together with the onion, it has the power to neutralize the cholesterol-producing action of fats.

The olive (*Olea europaea Olivaster or Olea europaea Sativa of the family Oleaceae*), originally from Asia Minor, has been cultivated for millennia in the Mediterranean regions. Its oil is obtained by pressing the washed fruit; after about three months of settling, the oil is filtered.

The sweet or green pepper (*Capsicum annuum acuminatun* or *Capsicum frutescens* of the family *Solanaceae*) comes from the Americas; cultivated principally in warm climates, it is a berry which assumes various shapes and different levels of pungency.

Until the discovery of America, Europeans used black pepper imported from the East Indies by the Phoenicians and the Arabs. When the Turks conquered Constantinople in 1453, commerce in this spice came to a halt. Henry the Navigator, king of Portugal, organized an exploration of the western coast of Africa, but the black pepper discovered there was inferior to the Asian variety. Meanwhile, Christopher Columbus, thinking to circumvent the Turkish obstacle, planned to reach the East Indies by sailing west.

And so the sweet pepper arrived from America and was well received. Unlike black pepper - which, after long use, may damage the liver and intestines - the sweet pepper has healthful properties. It contains much vitamin C, vitamin K (which promotes blood clotting), and vitamin E; it assists in resisting infectious diseases; and it contains a particular oligomeric protein that is ingested when smoking. Thus sweet pepper can help ease the withdrawal symptoms of those who are trying to quit smoking. It is, moreover, a vasodilator and therefore a powerful remedy for hypertension. Ground pepper of this type is called cayenne or paprika. "Holy oil" is oil in which an infusion of pepper has been left for at least fifteen days.

For all of the reasons stated above, this spaghetti recipe is the healthiest that the "Mediterranean diet" can offer.

The Neapolitan imagination has conceived many sauces that can accompany delicious pasta dishes, but this is the most classic, as well as the simplest, of all.

Lightly sauté a garlic clove in plenty of olive oil.

When the garlic clove begins to brown, remove it and replace it with the rest of the garlic, thinly sliced, the hot pepper, a little minced parsley, and a pinch of salt.

Cook the spaghetti al dente in abundant salted water. Pour it into the garlic skillet while still very moist, and cook pasta and sauce together over a high heat for a few seconds.

Serve spaghetti on a warmed platter.

At the last moment, mince a lot of parsley and sprinkle it over the spaghetti.

Spaghettini alla ricotta
(Spaghettini with ricotta cheese)
(serves 6-8)

1 lb spaghetti - 1 ½ lbs ricotta cheese - salt - 2 oz butter - ½ cup Parmesan - 2/3 cup sultana raisins - 5 eggs - 1 tsp sugar

A simple little pasta pie, to be baked crusty in the oven. It's best if prepared in a large pan, so that it can brown properly and achieve the desired level of crunchiness.

Break up the spaghettini and cook them in boiling water. Remove them while they are still al dente, and season with butter and Parmesan.

Beat the eggs in a bowl with a pinch of salt, blend in the ricotta and a teaspoon of sugar, and mix all this into the cooked pasta. After plumping the raisins in warm water, add them to the mixture, and pour everything into a buttered bakingpan.

Cook in a hot oven until shiny and golden.

Spaghetti in frittata
(Spaghetti omelette)
(serves 6)

*1 lb spaghetti - 6 tbsps tomato sauce - 3 eggs -
parsley - butter - olive oil - 4 oz prosciutto - 6 oz
mozzarella – 3 tbsp grated Parmesan - basil - salt*

This dish recalls happy days at the sea and the delight of eating a slice of an
omelette like this after a long swim. Why? Because a few decades ago, kids
took along such food to eat out at sea when they went boating.
Cook the spaghetti al dente in plenty of salted water, and dress it with some
fresh tomato sauce. Beat the eggs in a bowl with a pinch of minced parsley
and add them to the spaghetti. Heat as much olive oil and butter as you think
you'll need in a large skillet, and spoon in a layer of the spaghetti and egg
mixture. Cover this with the diced prosciutto and mozzarella, a handful of
grated Parmesan, and some chopped basil leaves. Cover this in turn with the
rest of the spaghetti and brown on both sides.

Spaghettini in involtini di melanzane
(Spaghetti-stuffed eggplant)
(serves 6)

*3 Italian eggplants - vegetable oil for frying - 1 lb
spaghettini - 2 lbs ripe tomatoes - 1 onion - olive
oil - 2/3 cup grated Parmesan - basil - salt*

For this dish, which comes from Catania in Sicily, it's essential to find long
and not to thin eggplants. Peel them, slice them lengthwise, and place them in
salted water to purge them of their dark liquid. Let them stand for about an
hour, press them dry, and fry them.

Place the fried eggplant slices on absorbent paper. Now take the spaghettini, boil them in salted water, and remove them while they are still al dente. Dress them with a fresh tomato sauce and grated Parmesan. For the sauce, just brown the thinly-sliced onion in a little olive oil and then add the sieved, ripe tomatoes. Cook this, seasoned with salt and perfumed with basil, for about 20 minutes.

With the help of a fork, spread the spaghettini and sauce on the slices of fried eggplant, then roll up each slice lengthwise to hold the filling.

Cover the bottom of a baking-pan with tomato sauce and arrange the eggplant rolls in the pan. Pour more sauce over the rolls and sprinkle grated cheese on them. Turn these tidbits golden in an oven, under low heat, and serve them hot.

Tìmballo alla genovese
(Pasta timbale with meat gravy)
(serves 12)

For the "Genoa-style" sauce: 2 lbs beef rump - 2 oz bacon - 1 lb onions - 2/3 lb carrots - parsley - 4 celery ribs - salt - 1 cup dry white wine - 3 tomatoes - 1 cup olive oil

For the little meatballs: ½ lb ground meat - 1 egg - 1 slice bread soaked in water - 2 tbsp grated Parmesan - parsley

For the béchamel sauce: 2 oz butter - 3 ½ tbsps flour - 2 cups milk - salt - pepper - nutmeg

For the short pastry: 2 cups flour - 4 oz butter - 1 egg - salt - 1 tsp sugar.

1 lb tagliolini (a kind of thin tagliatelle) - 1 lb shelled peas - 1 oz butter - 2/3 cup grated Parmesan – 7 oz mozzarella

In order to make a good Genoa-style timbale, you need tagliolini of excellent quality - such as those made by hand with only two ingredients, flour and eggs. If you don't have these or, frankly, the time to make them, an acceptable variety, similar to the one just described, is commercially available. Cooked properly and decidedly al dente, tagliolini produce an excellent dish.

To begin preparing our timbale, we put together a "Genoa-style" sauce, *salsa alla genovese*, which is typical of Neapolitan cuisine and totally unknown to the citizens of Genoa. This sauce originated with certain Genoan restaurant owners who set up shop in Naples in the 1600's and who knew how to prepare admirable meat dishes.

The best cut of beef for this sauce is the rump. To tenderize the meat, you should lard it by making small incisions in it and stuffing them with little cubes of lard or pancetta. Having done this, give the meat an attractive shape by tying it together with some string. The classic vessel for cooking this sort of pot roast is a large, oval-shaped, tin-plated copper pot, of the kind that used to be essential equipment in big old kitchens and then suddenly fell into obscurity. There was a time, in fact, when shining copper pots, hung up on the brick walls, were on display in many kitchens.

Such a pot has the advantage of distributing heat and flavor evenly, but, if you haven't got one, a good stainless steel pot will do fine. Place the meat into it, pour in some oil - base the amount on the number of diners and the quantity of meat – the onion cut in slices, the carrots, three or four aromatic celery ribs, some flavorful tomatoes, and a little bunch of the freshest parsley possible.

Brown the meat very slowly in the pot with the vegetables. Pour in the wine and cook until it vaporizes. Now add one or two cups of salted water, cover the pot, and lower the fire. In this way you'll produce a lovely brown sauce and well-cooked meat after about 2 hours.

Make the sauce smooth by removing the meat and passing the vegetables and liquid through a food mill.

While you're waiting for the sauce to cook, make some tiny, pretty meatballs. Blend together some high-grade ground meat, as much egg as necessary, grated Parmesan, and a sprinkle of finely minced parsley. Prepare the little peas too by cooking them in butter (use just enough, because too much butter will make the dish oily) with a small amount of water, just enough to cover them. The water should have evaporated by the time the peas are done.

Prepare the béchamel sauce (sauce à la Béchamel), named after Louis de Béchameil, Marquis of Nointel and maître d'hôtel to Louis XIV, according to the accepted rules.

A kind of short or flaky pastry also plays a part in this timbale. Sift and mound the flour, make a well in the center, and place therein pieces of butter, then an egg, a pinch of salt, and a little sugar. Carefully blend everything to make a dough of the proper consistency. Let it rest from all this agitation for about an hour - a good rule to follow, by the way, anytime you make a dough.

Now that all our characters are ready to recite their roles, the author himself enters the scene. Cook the tagliolini, very al dente, if you please. Unite this pasta with the French white sauce and then with our so-called Genoan sauce. You should obtain a soft, sensuous sauce. New characters now join the scene: lots of grated Parmesan, along with some mozzarella cubes.

Roll out the pastry dough very thin and line a baking-pan or mold with a sheet of it. Gently add part of the tagliolini, then the meatballs, the peas, more tagliolini, and thereupon another thin sheet of pastry. Brush some beaten egg on top to make the surface bright and tempting. Bake in a moderate oven until golden; this should require about 40 minutes.

Where can one eat better in Rome? Mac Donalds in Piazza di Spagna.
Where can one eat worst? At Mariano and Rita's Pane home.
This from the point of view of one that is on a forced diet.
In a fast food you can eat in five minutes and you are far away from temptations.
At Rita Pane's home you are lost as soon as you step inside, even Pannella and Sant'Antonio would have some problems to resist.
Also if you have firm and detached intentions (I'll go, I'll only grab something, let's say a salad and a steak), she comes up with a steaming dish, one of those to which you can't say "no", and you collapse at the first scent coming from the kitchen.
Last time I was at Rita's, she cooked genovese sauce, an open attack on my diet.
Who doesn't know it, genovese is a meat and onion based sauce, which is highly appreciated in Naples and surroundings. God only knows why, being a Neapolitan dish, it's called "genovese ": maybe it was imported from Genova or maybe the cook who invented it was called Genovese...
what's sure is that it is exquisite, too good to get along with triglicerids and cholesterol.
Usually you prepare genovese sauce with thick pasta, like rigatoni, maltagliati, mezzani and so on.
In Naples there are different schools, or ways of thought on genovese, the Santa Lucia one and the corso Garibaldi one.
At my home, when I was a child, there was a continuous dispute between the two representatives: one claiming that the piece of meat should be rump and the other arm clod, some were claiming that the onion shouldn't be cut ("the onion -dad said- should never get to know metal...") and some were pointing out on the meat onion amalgam, on the reciprocal taste osmosis ("That's a wedding between two essences!" uncle Alberto was usually screaming).

Another discussion issue was the final colour: "dark amber" according to the corso Garibaldi school, "monk's cloak" according to the Santa Lucia one.

Uncle Alberto had a jacket just that colour which he used to compare the sauce with.

And Rita Pane? Well, to be sincere, I don't have a master in genovese to be able to make a suitable review of "hers" : if dad and uncle Alberto were alive, l could set up a jury, unfortunately both of them are in the afterlife, and I hope for them that they are now in Paradise eating an angel prepared genovese.

What I know for sure is that Rita uses the rump (Santa Lucia school), cuts the onions (corso Garibaldi school), adds the carrots by colour, then celery, bacon, a tomato and some wine.

What else can I say?

My diet dies in front of Rita Pane's genovese.

The sauce is as thick as San Gennaro's blood in it's first minutes before melting, the scent is even thicker than the sauce and the taste is such that you have the feeling you have committed a mortal sin, a sin which won't easily be forgiven on Judgement Day.

In my life I never experimented heroin, but I am sure that if injected the Pane's Genovese sauce in my veins, the effects would be more or less the same.

Luciano De Crescenzo

Timballo alla sorrentina
(Sorrento-style timbale)
(serves 6/8)

For the ragout: 1 lb prime cut of beef (rump or round) - 4 tbsp olive oil - 1 onion - parsley - 1 tbsp. sultana raisins - 1 carrot - 1 celery rib - 2 lbs peeled, seeded tomatoes - salt - basil
For the little meatballs: ½ lb ground pork loin - 1 egg - 1 bread slice soaked in water - parsley - salt - olive oil for frying
For the short pastry: 1 ½ cups flour - 1 egg - 7 tbsp butter - salt - 1 tsp sugar - 1 lb maccheroncelli (small macaroni) - 7 oz mozzarella – 2/3 cup grated Parmesan.

First prepare the ragout: brown the meat in olive oil, add thinlysliced onions and the carrot and celery chopped into small pieces. After the vegetables become limp, add a small bunch of parsley, the sultana raisins, the tomatoes, a few pinches of salt, and the basil.
Let all this cook for about 1 hour over very low heat, until the oil separates from the sauce. Then remove the meat and rub the sauce through a sieve.
Make the little meatballs with the ground pork and the other listed ingredients, fry them in hot olive oil, and put them on paper towels to drain. You should have the short pastry dough ready - just blend all the ingredients rapidly. Finally, cook the pasta al dente in plenty of salted water. (Remember that the best way to cook pasta is to figure on using 1 quart of water and 2 tsp of salt for every ¼ lb of pasta.) Dress the pasta with the ragout sauce, the grated Parmesan, and the little cubes of mozzarella.
Roll out a thin sheet of the flaky pastry dough, line a baking-pan with it, and fill the pan with the pasta intermixed with the meatballs.
Cover with another sheet of pastry dough and bake this delight at 400° F for about half an hour.

Timballo del Gattopardo
(Leopard timbale)
(serves 10)

1 ½ lbs maccheroncelli (small macaroni) – ½ cup grated Parmesan
For the short pastry: 2 ½ cups flour - 7 oz butter - 2 tbsp sugar - 2 eggs - salt
For the filling: 3 ½ oz prosciutto – 3 ½ oz mushrooms - 1 onion - 1 carrot - 1 celery rib - 6 oz chicken livers - 7 oz boneless chicken - 1 cluster of unborn chicken eggs - 1 shot glass of Marsala - pinch of cinnamon –1 tbsp shelled pistachios - salt & pepper
For the béchamel: 3 oz butter – 6 tbsp flour - 1 qt milk - salt – pepper

Blend a short pastry dough with the ingredients listed above and let it rest. Fry lightly in a saucepan a mixture of chopped onion, celery, and carrot. Add the chicken, the very thinly sliced mushrooms, salt, pepper, cinnamon, and pistachios. Pour in Marsala. Cook everything over a slow fire.

Pour a thin stream of oil into a frying pan and cook the chicken livers and the eggs, separated from one another. Meanwhile prepare the béchamel: melt the butter in a sauce-pan over low heat; away from heat, add the flour and mix in well. Pour in the lukewarm milk a little at a time, stirring constantly. Season with salt and pepper.

Return sauce to heat, stirring until it reaches the proper consistency. Then, turn off the heat.

Cook and drain the pasta (very al dente). Add to the chicken mixture the chicken livers and eggs, the béchamel, the diced prosciutto, and the grated Parmesan. Stir all this into the pasta.

Divide the short pastry dough into two parts, one slightly larger than the other. Roll out the larger part into a thin sheet. Line a bakingpan with it. Pour in the dressed pasta, cover with a sheet made from the remaining part of the pastry dough, and seal the edges.

Brush one egg white on top.

Bake the timbale in a hot oven (400°) for about one hour, take it out, and let it stand for a few minutes before removing it from the pan.

Timballo rapido di tagliolini
(Quick tagliolini timbale)
(serves 4)

3/4 lb tagliolini - 1 egg - 5 oz mozzarella - 3 ½ oz butter - 1/3 cup grated Parmesan - grated breadcrumbs - salt

Butter a baking-pan and sprinkle it with grated breadcrumbs so that they adhere all over.

Boil the tagliolini very al dente and drain them somewhat, leaving them rather moist. Dress with the softened butter, the grated Parmesan, and the beaten egg. Put half of the tagliolini into the pan, arrange little cubes of mozzarella on top, and cover with the rest of the tagliolini.

Press down lightly so that there won't be hollow spots.

Powder the surface with more breadcrumbs and add a few dollops of butter.

Put into a hot oven (400°) for 20 minutes and let the timbale set. It should rest for a few minutes more before being removed from its pan and served.

Timballo soffice di tagliolini
(Soft tagliolini timbale)
(serves 4)

*3/4 lb tagliolini - 1/3 cup grated Parmesan - 2
tbsp flour - 7 tbsp butter - 1 pint milk - salt -
pepper - nutmeg - 2 eggs*

Prepare a béchamel sauce in the following way: melt half the butter over low heat, remove pan from heat, and add flour; mix well, add lukewarm milk a little at a time, season with salt, pepper, and nutmeg. Return to heat and cook, stirring constantly, until the sauce has thickened and is about to simmer. Remove from heat and add the rest of the butter, saving only enough to grease the baking-pan.

Add Parmesan, stir again, and, after the mixture has cooled a little, add the yolks of the eggs, one at a time, stirring constantly. Lastly, and very gently, fold in the egg whites, beaten stiff. Boil the pasta al dente, drain, dress with the prepared sauce, pour into the buttered baking-pan, and put at once into a hot oven (400°) for 20 minutes.

Serve the timbale in the dish it baked in.

Tubetti con salsa di cavolfiore
(Tube pasta with cauliflower sauce)
(serves 6)

*1 cauliflower - 5 tbsp olive oil - 1 garlic clove - hot
pepper - parsley - 1 lb mid-sized pasta tubes*

This dish is humble, simple to make, but very tasty. Crush the garlic and sauté it in a saucepan with the oil. Remove the garlic (its flavor will stay behind) and throw in, all at once, as much chili pepper as you want and the cauliflower, well-washed and cut into little groups of flowers.

Cover and cook over very low heat for about 30 minutes. If the cauliflower isn't moist enough by itself, you can pour ½ cup of hot water over it. When the mixture has reduced itself to a blondish mush, its ready to receive the pasta, boiled al dente. Blend the ingredients into a single delicious whole.

Before serving, add minced fresh parsley.

Vermicelli con le vongole
(Vermicelli and clams)
(serves 6)

1 lb vermicelli (thick spaghetti) - 2 lbs clams in
their shell - 2 cloves garlic - hot pepper - 1/2
cup extra-virgin olive oil - parsley

For vermicelli and clams to turn out as well as they do in Naples, certain essential conditions must be observed: the vermicelli must be of the best quality, there must be a very great deal of water, boiling infernally, the olive oil must be extra-virgin, and, naturally, the clams must be fresh, large, and genuine bivalves.

While the pasta is boiling, make sure all the clams are good, by taking four or five at a time and passing them from one hand to the other; if you notice that some of them sound empty, identify and eliminate them.

Brush and clean the clams. Steam them in their water until their shells open. Some sea- water will be expelled in this process; strain it before you use it. Discard the opened clams. Set aside the removed clam flesh and the strained cooking liquid. Brown the garlic cloves in plenty of oil, remove them, and replace them with the hot pepper, the shucked clams, and the filtered seawater.

When the vermicelli are cooked al dente, drain them (but not completely), pour them into the pan with the clams, and stir rapidly for a minute over the heat. Sprinkle the whole with very freshly-minced parsley.

VEGETABLES

Barchette di peperoni
(Little pepper boats)
(serves 6)

3 sweet yellow peppers - 4 Italian eggplants - 2 eggs
- 3 tbsp grated Parmesan - salt - parsley - 1 clove
garlic - vegetable oil for frying

Calabrian peppers, very sweet and fleshy, lend themselves well to various dishes. Some of the best of these require the peppers to be cut in half so that they look like little boats.

They are then seeded and filled with a mixture like that described for Polpette di melanzane, p.170.

Chop the eggplants coarsely and boil them in plenty of salted water. When they're cooked and soft, squeeze them dry and mince them with a *mezzaluna* ("half-moon": a two-handled knife) so that you obtain a kind of mush. Combine this with the eggs, the grated Parmesan, and the parsley, finely minced together with the garlic.

Stuff the peppers with this filling and then fry them in plenty of hot oil, first on the bottom or pepper side, then on the top or filling side.

These are excellent lukewarm.

Caponata alla siciliana
(Sicilian-style eggplants in sweet-sour sauce)
(serves 6-8)

1 lb onions - 1 lb ripe tomatoes - 3 stalks celery - 2/3
cup pitted olives - 1/3 cup capers - 2 lbs Italian
eggplants - 2 tbsp sugar - ½ cup vinegar - basil - 4
tbsp olive oil - vegetable oil for frying

Caponata, in its original Spanish form, was a laborious dish that included fish and molluscs with the various vegetables. Something similar can be found in Apulian tiella dishes. The caponata in this version contains no fish and gives pride of place to the vegetables.

Brown the thinly-sliced onions in olive oil. When they are soft and golden, add the blanched, peeled, seeded, and chopped tomatoes; then the celery, chopped into small pieces, the pitted olives, and the capers. Blend all these flavors well.

Prepare the eggplants in advance by washing them, chopping them very coarsely, and frying them in plenty of hot vegetable oil. Add them to the first mixture. Stir while adding sugar and vinegar. Lower the heat and continue to cook until the vinegar has completely evaporated. At this point add a new flavor with some very fresh basil.

Caponata can be served lukewarm or cold. There's also a variation that includes one or two fried sweet peppers.

Carciofi con la mozzarella
(Artichokes with mozzarella)
(serves 6)

6 Italian (or small) artichokes - salt - parsley - fresh garlic - 2 tbsp lard - 10 oz mozzarella

A variation of artichokes Parmesan, this dish revels in greater simplicity while simultaneously paying all due respect to these peerless vegetables. Here, in fact, the artichokes, after being cleaned and cut into thick slices, need simply to be boiled in plenty of water. Add salt only when they're just about cooked, and then remove them from the water while they're done. After they've cooled, arrange them in a baking-dish and season them with a pesto made from parsley, fresh garlic, and lard. Cover them with slices of mozzarella and put them into the oven for about 20 minutes. Serve them hot.

Carciofi imbottiti
(Stuffed artichokes)
(serves 6)

6 artichokes - 2 lemons - 4 eggs - 4 tbsp grated
Parmesan - 1/3 cup sultana raisins - 2 tbsp pine
nuts - 5 oz mozzarella - parsley - vegetable oil
for frying - salt - olive oil

You need medium-sized American (or large Italian) artichokes for this delicious dish. Clean them correctly and thoroughly, and put them in a mixture of water and lemon juice while you prepare the stuffing.

In a bowl, mix the eggs, the Parmesan, the sultanas (plump them first for a few minutes in a little warm water), some pine nuts, cubes of mozzarella, a sprinkling of finely minced parsley, and salt. Drain the artichokes well, and then stuff them by pressing down between the leaves the flavorful mixture you've prepared. It should be rather thick and creamy, because once the artichokes have been stuffed, you're going to flip them *ex abrupto* into hot oil and fry them carefully, topside down. This operation will require but a few seconds, enough time for the stuffing to set.

Then arrange the artichokes (bottomside down) in a saucepan, dribble some olive oil on them, pour in a cup of water, cover the pan, and let it cook over a very low flame for about forty minutes.

Carciofi in tegamino
(Artichokes in a pan)
(serves 6)

12 small (or Italian) artichokes - 2 lbs potatoes -
2/3 lb small or spring onions - 6 tbsp olive oil -
salt - pepper - 3 cloves garlic - parsley - 2 lemons

Inside that spiky, forbidding armor, the artichoke encloses a tender core, rich in flavors and fit for a connoisseur: "the vegetable for the top ten thousand" (*das Gemüse der oberen zehntausend*), as the Germans say.

Remove the toughest outer leaves from the artichokes. Cut off the pointed tips, spread out the leaves with fingerpressure, and immerse the artichokes in water and lemon juice. Mince the parsley with the garlic, add salt and pepper, and stuff the artichokes with this mixture. Arrange them upright, one next to the other, on a bed of sliced onions in a saucepan. Put small chunks of potato around each artichoke and pour a generous amount of oil over the whole. Add a cup of water and cook, covered, over low heat for about forty minutes.

Carciofi ripieni in tegame
(Stuffed artichokes in a pan)
(serves 6)

6 small (or Italian) artichokes - 1 lemon - 3 slices stale bread - parsley - 3 eggs – 6 tbsp olive oil - 3 tbsp grated Parmesan - 2/3 lb young or spring onions - salt – pepper

Clean the artichokes well, detaching their tough outer leaves and cutting off the points of the artichokes with one clean slice. Put them in a bowl with water and lemon juice so they don't turn black.

Cut off the stems. Pare away their stringy outer layer and use their tender insides, chopping them up into small pieces and putting them into the lemon water too.

Prepare the stuffing mixture in this way: in an earthenware bowl, blend together the beaten eggs, the crumbled slices of stale bread, some minced parsley, salt, pepper, grated Parmesan, and the tiny pieces of the chopped stems. Make all this cohere with 2 tbsp. of oil.

Spread the artichokes' leaves gently and use a teaspoon to stuff them with the filling.

Heat some olive oil in a pan and cook the thinly-sliced onions until they become limp. Place the stuffed artichokes on top of the onion slices, add a cup of water, cover the pan, and cook over very low heat.

Check the salt when the cooking is almost done; artichokes are greedy for salt. If necessary, add a thin stream of olive oil.

Cavolfiori al gratin
(Cauliflower au gratin)
(serves 6)

1 cauliflower - 3 tbsp butter - 1 ½ tbsp flour - 1
½ cup milk - salt - pepper - 1 egg - 2 tbsp grated
parmesan

Partially cook the cauliflower in boiling, properly salted water - it must finish cooking in the oven. Remove the cauliflower from the water. Meanwhile, you will have prepared a rather soft béchamel sauce with butter, flour, and milk.
As usual, blend the flour and the melted butter, add the milk a little at a time, and then season with salt and pepper. Cook this over a low heat, stirring constantly, until it boils. When the béchamel has cooled somewhat, add to it the egg yolk, then fold in the stiffly-beaten egg white. Chop the cauliflower into little clusters of flowers, butter a baking-pan, and put them into it. Cover with the prepared sauce, sprinkle with plenty of grated Parmesan, and bake in a hot oven until a lovely golden crust forms on the top of this dish.

Cianfotta fritta
(Fried vegetable stew)
(serves 6)

2 lbs Italian eggplants - 2 lbs sweet peppers - 1
lb potatoes - 1 onion - 2/3 lb tomatoes – 2
cloves garlic - plenty of basil - salt and pepper
- 6 tbsp olive oil

Seasonal conditions obviously account for the origins of this dish, wherein tradition is wedded to disarming simplicity.
Without peeling the eggplants, wash and chop them into cubes. Wash the peppers, remove their seeds and the fibrous portions around them, and cut the peppers, too, into small cubes. Peel and julienne the potatoes, then put them in water so they don't darken. Mince the onion.
Put a large skillet containing about half a cup of olive oil on the fire. Brown the garlic, removing it as soon as it changes color. Then add to the hot oil, in

order, the eggplants, the peppers, and, lastly, the potatoes. Cook all these ingredients until they become rather soft. Remove them from the oil and place them in a bowl. In the same skillet, lightly and gently sauté the minced onion. Pour in the chopped, fresh tomatoes, and cook over high heat for about 10 minutes. Season with salt and pepper, add the eggplant, the peppers, and the potatoes, and let all these tastes mingle. At the end, strew basil leaves over everything.

Fagiolini all'olio
(Green beans in olive oil)
(serves 4)

1 lb green or snap beans - 1 clove garlic - 2 tbsp
olive oil - 1 lemon - 2 tbsp vinegar - salt

Although the science ot nutrition tells us that vegetables cooked in large quantities of water lose a lot of their nutritive properties, since vitamins and minerals are dispersed into the water and only vegetable fibres, which the body cannot assimilate, are left behind, we must nevertheless acknowledge that this is the best cooking method in certain cases, as here, for example, in a recipe that treats the dignity of the green beans with the greatest respect.
In order to preserve the brilliant green typical of fresh beans, you must cook them in plenty of heavily-boiling water, in an open pot, adding salt and 2 tbsp. of vinegar almost at the end. In this way the chlorophyll won't be attacked by the acids that cause it to change colour - these will be dispersed into the air - and the vinegar, for its part, will keep the vegetables from becoming too soft and enhance the bright green colour that attracts the eye, piques the palate, and stimulates the gastric juices.
Rub a serving-platter with garlic, then pour on some excellent olive oil.
Drain the beans and put them on the platter.
At table, invite everyone to sprinkle a few drops of fresh lemon juice onto the beans.

Fagiolini al pomodoro
(Green beans and tomatoes)
(serves 6)

2 lbs green or snap beans - 1 lb peeled, seeded tomatoes - 6 tbsp olive oil - 1 clove garlic - salt – 1 tsp oregano.

Cut off the tips of the beans and remove any stringy fibers. Cook them al dente in boiling water, adding salt almost at the end. Drain them.
Make a quick sauce in a skillet: sauté crushed garlic in the oil, remove the garlic when it begins to color, and add the tomatoes.
Cook for about 15 minutes with a little salt. Then add the beans and continue cooking for 10 minutes more.
Turn off the heat and finish with a sprinkle of oregano.

Finocchi al gratin
(Fennel au gratin)
(serves 6)

9 fennels - 2 tbsp butter - 3 tbsp grated Parmesan
For the béchamel: 2 oz butter - 2 tbsp flour - 2 cups milk - salt - pepper - nutmeg

Remove the tough outer leaves from the fennels, wash them well, and boil them in plenty of salted water for 20 minutes. Drain them, let them cool a little, and slice them. Sautè them in butter to get rid of their moisture. Meanwhile, prepare the béchamel: melt the butter over low heat, remove from heat, and add the flour, blending well. Then add the lukewarm milk, a little at a time, stirring constantly. Season with salt, pepper, and a little nutmeg, return to heat, and cook (stirring all the time) until the sauce thickens. Butter a baking-pan and arrange the fennel in it. Sprinkle with Parmesan, cover with the béchamel, and bake in a hot oven (400°) until the top is golden (about 20 minutes).

"Gattò" di patate
(Potato cake)
(serves 6)

3 ¼ lbs potatoes - 7 tbsp butter - 1 cup milk - salt - pepper – 1 cup grated Parmesan - 4 eggs - grated bread crumbs (as much as necessary) - 7 oz mozzarella – 3 ½ oz salami or prosciutto cotto

Nowadays the potato (*Solanum tuberosum*), in a thousand guises, occupies a prestigious position on even the most refined tables. Originally grown in the Peruvian Andes, the potato was not immediately appreciated upon its entrance into Europe in the 16th century.

It was only later (in the 18th century), after the French agricultural economist Antoine Augustin Parmentier produced a thorough study of the potato, that its high nutritional value was discovered. Potatoes are rich in starch and vitamin C.

Potatoes with yellowish flesh are used above all for frying and roasting, while the white-fleshed, more floury variety is called for in making gnocchi, purées, and "gattó."

It would be more proper to call this dish gateau (French for "cake'), but it has always been called gattó in Naples, and its French origins were forgotten a long time ago.

To make a good *gattó*, boil the potatoes and rub them through a sieve or food mill while they're still very hot; this is the only way to make them light and tenuous and to avoid unattractive lumps. Then add the butter, milk, salt, and pepper, a goodly amount of grated Parmesan, the egg yolks, and, lastly, the stiffly-beaten egg whites. At this point, butter a baking-pan, sprinkle it with grated breadcrumbs, and put half the potato purée into it.

Top this with diced mozzarella and salami or prosciutto, cover this in turn with the rest of the potatoes, and sprinkle the surface with more breadcrumbs. Add a few dollops of butter. Bake in the oven for a half-hour, or until the surface becomes golden.

Gratinato di finocchi alle uova
(Crusty-baked fennel and eggs)
(serves 6)

6 fennels - 6 eggs - 6 tbsp grated Parmesan -
7 tbsp butter - parsley - salt – pepper

This is a simple dish, homely but flavorful, typical of the cuisine of Capri.
Remove the toughest leaves from the fennels. Cut the fennels into small spikes and boil them in salted water. When they're halfcooked, take them out of the water and set them aside.
Beat the eggs in a bowl with the Parmesan, the salt, the pepper, and the minced parsley. Add the fennels to this pasty mixture and turn the whole into a buttered frying-pan. Add a few dollops of butter and bake in an oven at 350° for 10 minutes.
Serve this dish hot.

Involtini di melanzane
(Stuffed eggplant rolls)
(serves 6)

3 Italian eggplants - 2 cups tomato puree - 1 onion
- 4 tbsp olive oil - basil - 3 ½ oz mozzarella - 1
pinch of sugar – 2/3 cup grated Parmesan -
vegetable oil for frying - salt

This is a lighter version of the traditional Eggplant Parmigiana, presented in the form of tiny, miniaturized tidbits.
Cut the eggplants into long slices, sprinkle with salt, and let them sweat in a colander for about an hour. Then dry and fry them in plenty of boiling vegetable oil. Place them on paper towels. Brown the onion slices in a pan with a little olive oil. As soon as they become golden, pour in the puréed tomatoes, season with salt, and cook until the oil separates from the tomatoes (about twenty minutes). Take the eggplant slices one by one, sprinkle them

with a very little sugar, the grated Parmesan, place a cube of mozzarella and a basil leaf in the center of each slice, and roll up the slices lengthwise. Pour a little of the tomato sauce into a baking pan, arrange the eggplant rolls in it, and cover them with more sauce and grated Parmesan.

Bake in an oven at 350° F for about 15 minutes.

After a concert at Pompei, Isaac Stern, great violin-player and notable fork-wielder, ate practically nothing but stuffed eggplant rolls, exclaiming continually: "Sublime! Sublime! "

Involtini di peperoni
(Stuffed pepper rolls)
(serves 6)

3 sweet or green peppers - 3 tbsp olive oil - 1 small onion - 1 ½ cups tomato purée - 3 Italian eggplants - ½ cup olives - 1 tbsp capers - vegetable oil for frying - salt

These little tidbits will please demanding eaters who want small portions but lots of courses. Wash and dry the peppers. Cook them on a grill, turning them to make sure they're done on all sides. Remove from heat. Peel them, empty them, and cut them into broad slices. Fry the finely-diced eggplants in hot vegetable oil until tender.

Season with a little salt and place them on paper towels.

Prepare a sauce as follows: brown the thinly-sliced onion in some olive oil; add the puréed tomatoes, the pitted, chopped olives, the capers, and a little salt. Cook for 10 minutes before adding the eggplant.

Let these flavors mingle for a few minutes; then, using a tablespoon, put some filling on each pepper slice and roll it up.

Line up these rolls in a baking-pan, dribble some olive oil onto them, and cook for 10 minutes in a hot oven (350°F).

Melanzane alla griglia
(Grilled eggplants)
(serves 6)

2 lbs Italian eggplants - 3 cloves garlic - minced parsley - hot pepper - 2 tbsp vinegar - a splash of balsamic vinegar - salt – 6 tbsp olive oil - mint - pink peppers (from Madagascar)

Peel the eggplants and cut them into slices. Grill them on a griddle with some olive oil, preferably a ridged one that will score them. Remove them.
Now make a sauce with minced garlic, finely-chopped parsley, hot pepper, the vinegar, salt, and plenty of olive oil, mint and pink pepper from Madagascar. On a platter, arrange a layer of eggplant slices, pour sauce over them, then add another eggplant layer and more sauce. Let stand about 1 hour before serving.

Melanzane a barchetta
(Eggplant boats)
(serves 6)

3 long, medium-sized Italian eggplants - peanuts oil for frying - 2 tbsp olive oil - 1 clove garlic - 1 lb ripe tomatoes - basil - oregano - salt - 3 tbsp grated Parmesan - 1 tsp sugar.

Cut the eggplants in half lengthwise. Don't peel them. Score the flesh of each half rather deeply in a crosshatch pattern. Fry the eggplants in plenty of hot oil, cut side down, pressing them frequently with a long-handled spoon so that they release all their moisture, and rendering them very soft.
Place the eggplants on a plate covered with paper towels. Meanwhile, in a copper pot, brown the garlic in olive oil, then remove and replace the garlic with the peeled, seeded tomatoes. Season this sauce with salt, oregano, and fresh basil, and let it cook for 20 minutes. Pour some of the tomato sauce into a baking-pan, arrange the eggplant slices (cut side up) in the pan, and

sprinkle them with a pinch of salt and a pinch of sugar. Pour the rest of the sauce into the pan so that it covers the eggplants equally, then sprinkle with grated Parmesan.

Let this cook in a moderate oven for about a fifteen minutes, or until the eggplants become golden. Decorate with fresh basil before serving.

Melanzane a barchetta del "monzù"
("M'sieur's" eggplant boats)
(serves 6)

3 long, medium - sized Italian eggplants - 3 eggs - 1 cup grated Parmesan - 1/3 lb minced beef - 6 ripe tomatoes - ½ lb mozzarella - basil - 6 tbsp olive oil - salt

Like timbales and *au gratin* recipes, this dish shows the French influence that is present in many of our oven-baked dishes. These go back to the French cooks who arrived in Naples between 1700 and 1800 and entered the service of the court or the patrician families. For the Neapolitans, these French messieurs were the "monzù." Although both aristocrat and bourgeois at Naples are proud of their city's former prestige as the capital of the kingdom, the Neapolitan upper classes have always fused their sumptuous gastronomy with the humble cuisine of the narrow side-streets. In the present recipe, the eggplants, so abundant during the summer months in the countryside around Naples, are combined with cheeses and meat and then baked crusty.

The result is an exquisite dish. Cut the eggplants in half lengthwise, scoop out and set aside their pulp in an earthenware bowl, and fry them in a skillet in plenty of oil. Drain them on paper towels. Now chop the pulp into cubes and fry also these in the same skillet. Brown the minced meat in another pan in a little oil. Blend the eggs with the Parmesan, salt, and eggplant pulp in a bowl, and add the meat to this. Stuff the little eggplant boats with this mixture, then add to each a long slice of mozzarella and another of tomato. Pour some oil into a baking-pan, arrange the eggplants in it, and bake at 400°for 10 minutes to form a crust. At the moment of serving, decorate with fresh basil.

Melanzane in bianco
(Eggplants in white)
(serves 6)

*1 ½ lbs Italian eggplant - sufficient flour - 4 eggs - 1
lb mozzarella – peanuts oil for frying - salt*

The eggplant, a rather ambiguous member of the family *Solanaceae*, Asiatic in origin - perhaps from India - and familiar to the Arabs, spread to the Mediterranean Basin towards the 8th century and, in approximately the 13th century, arrived in Italy, where it was viewed askance and called *mela insana* or "mad apple." These days, throughout the Mediterranean area, the eggplant enjoys a success unparalleled among vegetables, thanks to its intense, irresistibly enticing flavor. Peel the eggplants, cut them lengthwise into rather thin slices, and flour them lightly.

Dip the eggplants into the eggs, which you have beaten with a pinch of salt. Fry the slices two at a time in plenty of moderately hot oil. When they've cooked on one side, turn them over; when this side too becomes golden, place a slice of mozzarella on it, preferably from the previous day and therefore not containing too much milk.

Cover immediately with the other eggplant slice and place the pair on a paper towel. Continue the operation with the other eggplant slices. Serve them attractively arranged on an oval platter and garnished with basil.

Parmigiana di carciofi bianca
(Artichoke parmesan style in white)
(serves 6)

*6 small or Italian artichokes - 2 lemons - sufficient
flour - 6 tbsp olive oil - salt - 10 oz mozzarella - 3
tbsp grated Parmesan*

This vegetable was known to the ancient Egyptians. By the 15th century, Italians were cultivating it in Sicily, Tuscany, and Campania. Whenever preparing an artichoke dish, begin by eliminating the tough parts of the artichoke's many layered leaves, retaining only the fleshy portions and cutting off the blunt point. In this way the most interesting part of the artichoke will remain, the receptacle of its inflorescence, whose center, the artichoke heart or bottom, is plump and tender. Artichokes contain a substance called cynarin, remarkably effective in preventing the formation of bladder and kidney stones, and in promoting the secretion and influx of bile into the intestine. Accordingly, artichokes are used in medicine to help treat liver ailments. Once you've cleaned the artichokes, plunge them immediately into a bowl filled with water and lemon juice so they don't turn black. After about 15 minutes, cut the artichokes into slices, dredge them lightly with flour, shake off the excess flour, and fry them in olive oil. Place them on paper towels. Put some of the artichoke slices into a baking-pan, add a pinch of salt, slices of mozzarella, and cover with another layer of artichoke slices. Sprinkle with grated Parmesan and bake for a few minutes, enough time for the cheese to melt and form an intimate union with the artichoke. Serve this dish hot.

Parmigiana di carciofi rossa
(Artichoke parmesan - style in red)
(serves 6)

6 small or Italian artichokes - 1 lemon - 6 tbsp
olive oil - sufficient flour - 1 clove garlic - 1 tbsp
sultana raisins - 1 onion - 1 carrot - 1 celery rib -
parsley - ½ cup white wine - 2 lbs ripe tomatoes -
10 oz mozzarella - 3 tbsp grated Parmesan - salt -
basil

If the season of the year allows it, let's continue with our artichoke preparations; we'll vary the traditional Parmesan dishes, which call for eggplants, and use artichokes instead. Clean them as usual and set them in lemon water for 15 minutes. Then dry them and cut them into moderately thin slices, dredge them in flour, shake off the excess, and fry them in olive oil. Drain them on paper towels so they won't be too oily.

You will have previously prepared a light tomato sauce: sauté the garlic in olive oil, remove the garlic after it has flavored the oil, replace it with the onion, a carrot, and a celery rib - all chopped very small - and a small bunch of parsley.

When the vegetables are soft and wellcooked, add the sultanas and the white wine. After the latter has evaporated, add the tomatoes, season with salt, and cook for about half an hour over low heat. The result will be a tasty sauce, just right for Parmesan dishes, whether they contain artichokes or eggplant or zucchini - a sort of mock ragout.

Put a few tablespoons of sauce in a baking-pan, then the fried artichoke slices, cubes of mozzarella (from the day before, if possible, so that it's not too moist), plenty of grated Parmesan, basil, a little more sauce, more artichoke slices, more mozzarella, more Parmesan, basil, and sauce.

Top with one final layer of artichokes and bake for about half an hour. Serve it hot.

Parmigiana di melanzane
(Eggplant parmesan - style in red)
(serves 6-8)

For the tomato sauce: 4 tbsp olive oil - 1 clove garlic - 2 tbsp sultana raisins - 1 onion - 1 carrot - 1 celery rib - parsley - ½ cup white wine - 3 lbs ripe tomatoes -
4 lbs eggplants (Italian if available) - 1 lb mozzarella - 1 ½ cups grated Parmesan - basil - salt - sugar - peanuts oil for frying

There are two types of Neapolitan dishes that deceptively claim a paternity not their due: genovese or "Genoan" sauce, foreign to Genoa, and Parmesan preparations, sublime glories of summer unknown in Parma. "Parmesan" implies eggplants, but artichoke or zucchini Parmesan is certainly acceptable. This is by no means a quick dish; it requires thought and forbids distraction, but, in compensation, it promotes better human relations, capable as it is of opening the heart at a moment of inexpressible delight.

Begin by preparing a good tomato sauce or light ragout, of the type described in the artichoke parmesan recipes.

Meanwhile, cut the eggplants into long slices and put them to soak in a large bowl filled with salted water so that they lose their bitter taste. After one hour remove and squeeze them to eliminate the dark liquid they will exude, dry them with a cloth, return them to their original shape, and fry them in plenty of vegetable oil. Set aside to drain on paper towels. Dice the mozzarella and get some good, fragrant basil.

Proceed to the construction of the parmesan, which should take place as follows: spoon some tomato sauce into a baking-pan, then begin to arrange the eggplant slices in layers, season them with a pinch of salt and a pinch of sugar, add plenty of mozzarella, even more Parmesan cheese, and small pieces of basil leaf. Then cover with more spoonfuls of tomato sauce and begin again in the same order, completing the operation with a final layer of eggplant slices topped, of course, with grated Parmesan and a little tomato sauce. Bake this marvel in an oven at 350° F for about half an hour, and serve it hot or lukewarm.

Parmigiana di melanzane bianca
(Eggplant parmesan - style in white)
(serves 6)

3 lbs eggplants (Italian if available) - 7 oz mozzarella - sufficient flour - vegetable oil for frying - salt - basil - 2 beaten eggs - 1 cup grated Parmesan

This is faster than the traditional Parmesan recipe. Peel the eggplants, cut them lengthwise, and let them soak for about an hour in a bowl of cold water seasoned with a few pinches of salt. In this manner the bitter juices of the eggplant will be eliminated and the pulp will maintain a more compact consistency and not become soft during the cooking. Squeeze out the eggplants, a few at a time, bring them back to their initial shape, flour them lightly, and fry them in plenty of very hot vegetable oil. When they turn golden, place them on paper towels and continue the operation until all the eggplants have been fried. Cut the mozzarella into tiny cubes and the basil leaves into little pieces. Begin to construct the Parmesan dish by arranging a layer of eggplants in a baking-dish, then a pinch of salt, mozzarella, a bit of the egg, grated Parmesan, and basil.

Repeat this process several times, ending with a layer of eggplant. Bake in a moderate oven for half an hour.

Parmigiana di zucchine
(Zucchini parmesan - style in white)
(serves 6)

3 lbs zucchini - vegetable oil for frying - sufficient flour - 1 cup grated Parmesan - 7 oz mozzarella - basil - 2 eggs - salt

In the summer, when the garden is overflowing with greens and fresh vegetables, imagination helps us to use all this bounty in various ways and often with encouraging results. An admirable complicity of elements produces the following interesting dish.

Cut the zucchini into round slices, flour them lightly, and fry them in plenty of hot vegetable oil. Let them dry on paper towels. Cut the mozzarella into a very tiny dice and begin to build this Parmesan dish.

In a baking-pan, arrange a bed of zucchini, add a pinch of salt, grated Parmesan, mozzarella, basil, and a little beaten egg. Repeat this process, maintaining the same order, until you run out of ingredients, making certain to end with a layer of zucchini. Bake in a 350° F oven for 20 minutes.

Peperonata lucana
(Sweet peppers Basilicata-style)
(serves 6)

2 ½ lbs sweet peppers (choose various colors if available) - 5 tbsp olive oil - 2 cloves garlic - ½ lb ripe tomatoes - 1/3 cup capers

From the homeland of the poet Horace, the simple, ancient land of Lucania, now called Basilicata, come many pasta and vegetable dishes, dressed with good olive oil, with various types of cheese, and with olives or capers. Because of its sunny colors and its flavor, this simple pepper dish is decidedly summery.

Use a high-sided saucepan. Brown the garlic in the oil, then remove the garlic and replace it with the sweet peppers, which you have washed, dried, and cut into little strips. Stir them, let them at first grow brighter and then fade, and, at this point, add the peeled, seeded ripe tomatoes and the capers and let these tastes mingle for a few minutes.

Peperoncini in padella
(Skillet-fried small green peppers)
(serves 6)

2 lbs small sweet green peppers - vegetable oil
for frying - 6 tbsp grated Parmesan - salt

Use minuscule green peppers, all of the same size, if possible. Remove their stems, but don't slice off their tops and don't take out their seeds. Wash the peppers, dry them, and fry them in plenty of hot vegetable oil. Drain them and place them on absorbent paper. Place them next on a serving-platter, and sprinkle them with salt and grated Parmesan. They are good cold.

Peperoni imbottiti
(Stuffed sweet peppers)
(serves 6)

6 sweet or green peppers - 6 tbsp rice - 5 tbsp
olive oil - 1 clove garlic - ½ lb ripe tomatoes
vegetable oil for frying - 2 eggplants - 2 tbsp
grated Parmesan - basil - 7 oz mozzarella - salt

Roast the peppers whole over an open flame; if over hot coals, better yet. Peel them and empty out their seeds. In a separate saucepan, prepare a light sauce with fresh tomatoes, olive oil, and a clove of garlic to flavor it. Add enough water to the sauce to cook the rice, which should be added at the rate ot one tbsp. per pepper, unless the peppers are very large. Cube the eggplants and fry them in plenty of vegetable oil. Add them to the rice, which should be cooked very al dente, and enliven the whole with the grated Parmesan, basil, salt, and cubes of mozzarella.

Stuff the peppers with this mixture, line them up on a baking-pan moistened with oil, and run them into the oven for 20 minutes.

Peperoni in agrodolce
(Sweet and sour peppers)
(serves 6)

2 ¼ lbs sweet peppers - vegetable oil for frying -
salt - 4 tbsp vinegar - 2 tbsp sugar

Preparing sweet peppers in many different ways is certainly part of the Neapolitan flair for interesting cooking, but this dish reveals an Oriental influence which, although it may at first seem bizarre, produces a most delightful summer side-dish.

Choose very fresh red and yellow peppers, cut off their stems and empty out their seeds, rinse them well and cut them into long bands about as wide as your finger.

Dry them with a cloth and fry them in plenty of vegetable oil. Remove them from the pan, put some salt. Heat the vinegar and sugar in a skillet.

Let it boil for one minute. Pour in the peppers, stir for a few seconds, and then arrange them on a pretty plate.

Piselli con le uova
(Peas with eggs)
(serves 4)

1 lb shelled peas – 3 tbsp olive oil - 4 spring onions -
7 oz ripe tomatoes - 2 eggs - basil - salt

These wonderful legumes can be consumed by themselves, in soups, or as side-dishes capable of garnishing even meat courses with little personality in themselves.

Chop the small onions very fine and soften them with a bit of olive oil in a saucepan. Then add the shelled peas, stir, and add the peeled, seeded, and finely-chopped ripe tomatoes.

Let this cook gently. When necessary - that is, if the peas seem to be getting too dry - add a little boiling water, which you should keep handy. When the peas are cooked, season them with salt, add the two previously-beaten eggs, stir everything together, and, at the moment when you serve this dish, strew it with fragrant basil leaves.

Pizza di scarola
(Escarole pizza)
(serves 6-8)

4 lbs escaroles - 2 cloves garlic - 3 tbsp pinenuts
- ½ cup sultana raisins - 6 tbsp olive oil - ½ cup
pitted green olives - 1/3 cup pitted Italian black
olives - 2 tbsp capers - salt
For the dough: 1 tbsp active dry yeast - 2 ½ cups
flour - salt - ½ cup olive oil - ½ cup water

Escarole is a healthy, refreshing, easily-digestible vegetable. You can serve this dish as an intermediate course. This tasty little pie is best when lukewarm, but it's good cold as well.

Wash the escaroles well and steam them in a wide, covered pot; they will shrink quite a lot. Drain them well and press them with a spoon so that they will loose the excess of water. Put a goodly amount of olive oil in a pan and sauté the crushed garlic in it. Remove the garlic once it's roasted, replace it with the pitted olives, the capers, the pine nuts, and the sultana raisins, having first plumped these briefly in warm water. Let everything crackle a little over the fire, then add the smothered escaroles. Blend all this for a few minutes and you will have the escarole pizza filling ready. To make the pizza dough, mound the flour on your work surface and make a well in the center. Dissolve the yeast in ½ cup lukewarm water and pour this into the well, together with some salt and the olive oil.

Work the dough well so that it becomes smooth and elastic, and let it stand for about half an hour. You can prepare the escaroles during this time so as to have them ready at the moment when you roll out the dough. Line a baking-dish with a layer of dough, pour in the escarole mixture, cover it with another sheet of dough, and cook this little pie in a brisk oven 375°F for about 40 minutes.

It's not sour, it's not sweet. It's easy to cut, but it's not soft. It cracks tenderly, like a biblical bread. It splits up and maybe it multiples itself. It warmly takes care of endive, the fine variant, envied by all the earth's tastes. From Rita's hands, white as soft bread on the outside and dark green inside, this is my best "pizza di scarola".

Giuliano Ferrara

Polpette di melanzane
(Eggplant croquettes)
(serves 6)

2 lbs Italian eggplants - 3 eggs - 5 oz (about 4 slices) stale bread - ½ cup milk - salt - ½ cup grated Parmesan - parsley - 1 clove garlic - bread crumbs - vegetable oil for frying.

This dish requires good, fresh eggplants, the kind that take on a different flavor in the lands of southern Italy, dazzled as they are by the sun. Cut each eggplant coarsely into four pieces and cook them in boiling salted water. When they're soft and thoroughly cooked, squeeze them well and mash them with a fork; the result should be creamy and dense. Add the eggs, the grated Parmesan, and the parsley, which you have minced very finely together with the garlic. Soften the stale bread in the milk and add this with a pinch of salt. Blend all this very well and shape it into little balls or croquettes, pass them in the bread crumbs, then fry in plenty of hot vegetable oil.

Polpette di melanzane e tonno
(Eggplant and tuna croquettes)
(serves 6)

2 lbs Italian eggplants - 4 slices stale bread - ½ cup grated Parmesan - 1 cup packed tuna in olive oil - 2 eggs - basil - grated breadcrumbs - oil for frying – salt

Wash the eggplants and put them in the oven for 30 minutes at 300° F. Let them cool, peel them, mince them with a *mezzaluna* (twohandled knife), and mix them together with the Parmesan. Cut off the crusts from the stale bread slices and soak them in water. Mince the tuna and the basil as well. Now blend all these ingredients in an earthenware bowl and add the egg yolks and the salt. Beat the egg whites. Shape little balls out of the eggplant mixture, dip them into the beaten egg whites, dredge them in the breadcrumbs, and, lastly, fry them in hot vegetable oil. Serve these croquettes hot.

Pomodori ripieni
(Stuffed tomatoes)
(serves 6)

6 big salad tomatoes - 2/3 cup black Italian olives
- 2 tbsp capers - 2 tbsp vinegar - parsley - 1 cup
oil packed tuna - ½ cup breadcrumbs - salt - 6
tbsp olive oil.

Wash the tomatoes, cut off their tops, and remove their softest pulp and their seeds. Pass this pulp through a food mill, and add the pitted, minced olives, the capers plumped in a little vinegar, the minced parsley, the tuna, enough breadcrumbs to make a dense mixture, a pinch of salt, and a thin thread of olive oil. Stuff the tomatoes, cover them with their tops, and line them up in a single layer in a lightlyoiled baking-pan. Bake them in a moderate oven for about half an hour.

Scarole imbottite
(Stuffed escaroles)
(serves 8)

4 escaroles - 2/3 cup black olives - 2 tbsps capers -
2 tbsps pine nuts - 1/3 cup sultana raisins - basil –
½ cup breadcrumbs - 2 cloves garlic – 6 tbsp olive
oil.

Clean the heads of escarole well, removing their most damaged outer leaves but leaving them whole. Wash them and put them in a wide pot with a clove of garlic, 2 tbsp. oil, and a cup of water. Let them cook slowly in their own steam, covered, for about 10 minutes. In another pan, separately, flavor some oil with the other garlic clove, remove it, and replace it with some of the breadcrumbs. Brown these, then add the pitted olives, the washed capers, the sultanas (previously plumped in lukewarm water), and the pine nuts. Let these tastes mingle awhile, then add basil leaves. Take the escaroles and gently open their centers, forming a passage which you will stuff with 2 or 3 tbsp. of the filling.

Arrange them close together in a baking-pan, cover them with the rest of the breadcrumbs, and bake them golden in a 350° F oven for 15 minutes.

Sformatini di patate fumè
(Potato mold with bacon)
(serves 6)

1 ½ lb potatoes - 7 oz bacon - 4 tbsp butter - salt
- pepper

Dice 1oz. of bacon and brown it in the butter. Add the potatoes, cut into round slices like french fries. Cook until two thirds done and season with salt and pepper. Meanwhile butter some little bakingpans or molds and line them with very thin slices of bacon as though lining a gift-box. Place the potato mixture in the center of the molds and cover them by folding over the excess bacon, like flaps. Bake in a moderate oven for about 20 minutes, remove from the molds, and place the molded fillings on a serving-platter.

Spinaci con le uova
(Spinach with eggs)
(serves 6)

2 ½ lbs spinach - 2 tbsps olive oil and 1 tbsp
butter - 1 clove garlic - 3 eggs - 2 tbsp grated
Parmesan - salt - nutmeg

Wash the spinach well, drain it somewhat but not completely, and put it in a large pot. Cover and let it soften over moderate heat for 10 minutes. Now drain it very well, pressing it with a wooden spoon to get rid of most of the water it contains. Heat olive oil and butter in a skillet and brown the crushed garlic clove. Remove it and add the spinach. Let this cook dry for about 10

166

minutes. Season with salt and nutmeg. Beat the eggs with the Parmesan. When the spinach begins to crackle, pour in the eggs mixture. Stir well and remove from heat.

Tortino di patate
(Potato pie au gratin)
(serves 6)

2 ½ lbs potatoes - 7 tbsp butter - 2 cups milk - 4 tbsp grated Parmesan - 2 tbsp grated pecorino - 4 eggs - 7 oz mozzarella - grated breadcrumbs - salt - pepper

The potato is the tuber of a plant, belonging to the family *Solanaceae*, that originated in South America. It was introduced into Europe towards the end of the 16th century, but, because of popular opposition to novelty at that time, it began to be cultivated widely only in the 18th century.
Thanks to Antoine Augustin Parmentier - who during the second half ot the 18th century discussed the various ways of cooking potatoes, should there be a need for a grain substitute, in his *Traité sur la culture et les usages des pommes de terre, de la patate et du topinambour* (1789) - the development of the potato, whose nutritive properties were at last recognized, received a great impetus.
To prepare this pie, boil the potatoes, peel them, and pass them through a food mill while they're still hot. Return the potatoes to the heat, stirring them vigorously with a wooden spoon. When they come away from the sides of the pan, add the butter and the milk, a little at a time. The necessary amount of milk varies, because some potatoes are more moist than others. Now add the salt, pepper, grated cheeses, and - away from the heat - the eggs: first the yolks, then the stifflybeaten whites. Pour half of this mixture into a buttered baking-dish sprinkled with breadcrumbs. Then add cubes of mozzarella, cover the whole with the remaining potato mix, level the surface with a knife blade, strew breadcrumbs over everything and bake in a 400° F oven until golden. Serve this pie hot, puffy and steaming.

Zucchine con scaglie di parmigiano
(Zucchini with parmesan chips)
(serves 6)

*2 ¼ lbs zucchini - oil for frying - salt - Parmesan
cheese as needed - basil.*

The flesh of zucchini is sweeter and more delicate if they're picked before
they grow too big, but this recipe produces a praiseworthy result even if the
above precaution is not taken. Cut the zucchini into rounds, not too thick, fry
them in plenty of hot oil, drain them on paper towels, and lay them on a
serving-dish. Sprinkle them with a pinch of salt and top with thin chips of
Parmesan cheese and basil.

Zucchine in crosta croccante
(Zucchini in crunchy crust)
(serves 6)

*2 ½ lbs zucchini - 4 eggs - 3 ½ oz prosciutto
cotto - 2/3 cup grated cheese (Parmesan) - salt -
pepper - 4 tbsp butter - 1 onion - basil - ½ cup
grated breadcrumbs*

Wash the zucchini and cut them into little rounds. Heat the butter in a pan
and lightly sauté the thinly-sliced onion. When it becomes golden, add the
zucchini. Let these flavors mingle, cooking the zucchini very well. Add salt
and pepper. Cover the saucepan and continue cooking for 10 minutes. Check
to make sure the zucchini is not sticking to the pan, and, if necessary, add a
little hot water. Beat the eggs in a bowl with a pinch of salt, the Parmesan,
the minced prosciutto, and the basil. Blend in the zucchini and pour
everything into a buttered pie-pan.
Cover with breadcrumbs and place in a hot oven for 20 minutes.

MEATS

Agnello con tre agri
(Lamb with three-sour sauces)
(Serves 6)

4 ½ lbs lamb - 1 onion - 2 bitter oranges - 2 lemons - 1 cup vinegar - 3 tbsp sugar – 6 tbsp olive oil - salt - pepper

The biblical description of the ceremonies attached to the feast of the Passover allows a glimpse of an archaic ritual practiced among the ancient Semites. At sunset on a mild spring day, when the season's first full moon, the sign of the new year in the ancient Middle East and the symbol of the gentle Sumerian goddess Inanna, patroness of love, was rising in the sky, the nomads would seize their walkingstaffs and, now that winter was truly over, initiate their seasonal movement towards new pastures. The lamb had been slaughtered and offered entire to the goddess of fecundity, and she would restore it many times over in the new births to come among the flock. On redhot slabs of stone, the women were baking the unleavened bread and preparing the bitter, aromatic herbs that would accompany the roasted meat. The ritual spring festival observed by the Semitic tribes suggests to us the Israelites' Passover, which celebrates their liberation from pharaonic slavery. The name pesach ("Passover"), deriving from the Egyptian word for "blow" or "scourge," signified for the Hebrews God's passing over or sparing the houses that they had consecrated with lamb's blood. The unleavened bread is the bread of misery - that is, of slavery - and the bitter herbs recall the bitterness of the Hebrews' lives in thrall to the Egyptians. In this Sicilian recipe, tart flavors accompany the lamb.

Cut it into pieces, wash it, and cook off its moisture in a saucepan over a lively flame. Add a little oil and the uncut onion. Brown the lamb on all sides, season with salt and pepper, and cook it covered for about 20 minutes, adding a little boiling water from time to time. Remove the lamb pieces and save the liquid in the saucepan. Arrange the lamb in another pan, turn on the heat, and pour in the lemon juice, the orange juice, and the vinegar, all mixed together with the sugar. Continue to cook for a few minutes, then add the liquid from the first saucepan and mingle all these tastes for a few seconds. Serve this dish hot.

Agnello in fricassea
(Lamb fricasèe)
(serves 6)

*4 ½ lbs lamb - 2 cloves garlic - 2 lemons - 2 egg
yolks - olive oil - salt - pepper*

In the Bible, in the Book of Exodus, we read: "*And the Lord spake unto Moses and Aaron in the land of Egypt, saying: This month shall be unto you the beginning of months: it shall be the first month of the year to you. Speak ye unto all the congregation of Israel, saying, In the tenth day of this month they shall take to them every man a lamb, according to the house of their fathers, a lamb for an house. Your lamb shall be without blemish, a male of the first year: ye shall take it out from the sheep, or from the goats.*
And ye shall keep it up until the fourteenth day of the same month: and the whole assembly of the congregation of Israel shall kill it in the evening.
And they shall take of the blood, and strike it on the two side posts and on the upper door post of the houses, wherein they shall eat it. And they shall eat the flesh in that night, roast with fire, and unleavened bread; and with bitter herbs they shall eat it. Eat not of it raw, nor sodden at all with water, but roast with fire; his head with his legs, and with the purtenance thereof. And ye shall let nothing of it remain until the morning: and that which remaineth of it until the morning ye shall burn with fire... it is the Lord's passover.
For I will pass through the land of Egypt this night, and will smite all the firstborn in the land of Egypt, both man and beast: and against all the gods

of Egypt I will execute judgment: I am the Lord. And the blood shall be to you for a token upon the houses where ye are: and when I see the blood, I will pass over you, and the plague shall not be upon you to destroy you, when I smite the land of Egypt. And this day shall be unto you for a memorial; and ye shall keep it a feast to the Lord throughout your generations; ye shall keep it a feast by an ordinance for ever."

The people of Catania in Sicily honor the very ancient tradition of eating lamb in commeration of the feast of Pasqua (in Italian, this word signifies both the Jewish Passover and the Christian Easter).

Cut the lamb into pieces, wash them, dry them, and brown them in a pot with a little olive oil and a crushed garlic clove.

Stir often, occasionally adding some water, until everything is evenly browned. Season with salt and pepper, cover with water, and cook covered over gentle heat for about half an hour. Now, in a small bowl, beat the egg yolks with the lemon juice and a tablespoon of water.

Remove the lamb from the heat, quickly add to it the egg and lemon sauce, stir rapidly so that the egg doesn't set, and serve at once.

Braciole o involtini di maiale alla napoletana
(Naples-style pork cutlets or rolls)
(serves 6)

2 ½ lbs sliced pork loin - 3 ½ oz prosciutto crudo - 1/3 cup sultana raisins - 1/3 cup capers - 2 tbsp pine nuts - 1 tbsp grated breadcrumbs - 1 tbsp lard - 4 tbsp olive oil - 1 cup white wine - pepper - salt

The taste for contrasts characteristic of Campania and of southern Italy in general is manifest in this dish, decidedly dedicated to those who appreciate the pronounced flavor of pork, a most versatile meat. Pliny says, in fact, "No other animal provides more matter for gluttony; pork has almost fifty different tastes, while in the case of the other animals there is only one."

The secret of success with this dish is, to be sure, cooking it over a very low fire, so that it produces a dense, flavorful gravy. Plump the raisins in a bowl with a little lukewarm water. Flatten the pork loin slices with a meat pounder and use sharp knife to remove any gristle or fat. Mince the prosciutto very finely and blend it with the raisins (drain them well), the capers, the pine nuts, the grated breadcrumbs.

Spoon this mixture onto the meat slices and roll them up, holding them together with toothpicks or lengths of cotton thread. Put a pan on the fire, add some olive oil, and melt 1 tbsp. lard in it. As soon as the fat begins to pop, add the pork rolls and brown them on all sides. When they're evenly colored, bathe them with a cup of wine, sprinkle them with pepper, and cover the pan. Let this cook very gently for about 2 hours, stirring often; if the gravy reduces too much, add some boiling water, which you will keep handy for this purpose. When done, remove the toothpicks or thread and place the involtini on a plate. Pour their gravy over them.

Capretto all'Aspromonte
(Aspromonte-style roast small goat)
(serves 10)

1 small goat - 1 cup dry white wine - ½ cup olive oil - 5
Italian red onions - parsley - pepper - rosemary - salt

The indispensable prerequisite for success with this dish is, without doubt, a young mountain goat, a kid whose delicious flesh, tender and milky-flavored, possesses so bold and unmistakable a taste that it can stand up to equally bold aromas and flavors, such as are provided, in this case, by the red onions that complement so felicitously the taste of the small goat. Cut up the kid into medium-sized pieces and wash and dry them well. Put the meat in a large saucepan and pour over it a cup of dry white wine. Let the meat marinate for half an hour. Drain it well, and discard the wine. Pour plenty of olive oil over the meat, add the finely grated onions, a little minced parsley, freshly ground pepper, a bunch of rosemary (well tied or wrapped in cloth so it won't lose any leaves), and salt. Cook the kid over very low heat. The result will certainly be more interesting if you use a clay pot for the cooking. The sauce produced by this cooking process is also excellent on spaghetti boiled al dente and sprinkled with grated pecorino.

Capretto o agnello al vino rosso
(Small goat or lamb in red wine)
(serves 10)

*about 8 lbs lamb - the juice of 2 lemons - 1 cup vinegar
- sage - rosemary - 4 cloves garlic - 3 cups red wine -
peppercorns - ½ cup olive oil - 2 tbsp vegetable oil -
salt*

This recipe is perfect for lamb but also appropriate for preparing small goat. If you want excellent lamb, it's useful to remember that it's most flavorful in the spring, the time of year when the animal's bodily structure and plumpness reach a level one could almost call provocative.

The best lambs are those not yet weaned, whose tender flesh still has the flavor of milk. The distinctive, unmistakable taste of ovine flesh comports well with equally bold, imperious flavors. Garlic and rosemary, for example, complement the taste of lamb most compatibly.

Cut the lamb into pieces suitable for serving. Wash them several times, then let them stand for about 20 minutes in plenty of water, to which you have added the lemon juice and the vinegar. When this period of time has passed, remove the meat from the water, place the meat in a pot or bowl, pour the red wine over it, and add a few leaves of sage, a little rosemary, and some peppercorns.

Let the meat stand like this for about 2 hours. Then drain it and put it in a pan with the olive and vegetable oils, salt, and the crushed garlic cloves, which will enhance the flavor of the meat with their own. Add sage and a little rosemary.

Cook it covered for one hour, than uncover and finish the cooking for other fifteen minutes.

Carne con patate al forno alla pizzaiola
(Baked meat and potatoes with tomatoes and oregano)
(serves 6)

2 lb potatoes - 1 onion - 10 oz tomatoes - 1 tbsp
oregano - salt - 2 ½ lbs veal or baby beef (choose
a tender cut) - 6 tbsp olive oil

Get yourself some potatoes of good quality, cut them into thick slices, and add the meat cut as for stew. Season everything with salt. Slice the onion too and add it, along with the chopped tomatoes and oregano. Let stand for 10 minutes. Choose a saucepan with a tightfitting lid, and pour enough oil into this pan to cover its bottom. Heat the oil, add the potatoes, meat, and other ingredients, omitting the liquid that has collected in the first container. Arrange everything in layers as neatly as possible and cover the pan with its lid (aluminum foil will do as well). Cook in a moderate oven for about 40 minutes.

Carne in umido
(Beef stew)
(serves 6)

2 ½ lbs beef for stew - 1 lb carrots - 2 celery ribs - 1
onion - sage – 5 tbsp olive oil - 1 cup white wine - 1
bouillon cube - salt

Chop the vegetables into tiny pieces and place them in a saucepan with the olive oil and the meat, cut into bite-sized chunks. Brown everything, pour in the wine, and let it evaporate. Now cover the contents of the pan with water and add a bouillon cube and salt to taste. Cook covered over a low heat for about one hour.

Coniglio in agrodolce
(Sweet and sour rabbit)
(serves 6-8)

1 rabbit - 1 lemon - 2 tbsp vinegar - 4 cups sweetish white wine - ½ cup olive oil - 2 cloves garlic - hot pepper - 1 lb small or spring onions - 4 celery ribs - ½ lb carrots - ¼ lb tomatoes - parsley - 1/3 cup sweet seedless raisins - 6 plums - 1 apple - salt

Rabbits (*Lepus cuniculus*), together with hares, pheasants, quail, woodcocks, and partridges, make up what is properly called "game." Rabbits are delicious to eat, but it's up to the cook to bring out their best qualities. Rabbit meat is subjected to a great many tried and true modifications and transformations.

First of all, the rabbit should be cut into small pieces. This method, which we share with the cooks of the Orient, allows the meat to cook faster and gives a result that is pleasing to the eye. A basic rule, however, is not to cut against the "grain" or fiber of the meat. Once this operation is complete, wash the rabbit in plenty of water flavored with lemon juice and vinegar. Cook the rabbit briefly over high heat in all of the white wine; discard the wine and set the meat aside. Prepare an appetizing, gaily-colored sauce with olive oil, garlic (which you'll remove after it has impregnated the oil with its flavor), hot pepper to your taste, plenty of thinly-sliced small onions, celery, the carrots chopped into small pieces, and a small amount of tomato. When the vegetables have become soft and bright, add the raisins (previously plumped in water), the pitted prunes, and the grated apple.

Regarding the rabbit, we can say, as Juvenal does in his Satires, *Gustus elementa per omnia querit* ("It seeks flavor in every element").

When all these ingredients are singing happily in the pot, add a cup of white wine.

Let the sauce cook for about 20 minutes. It should be amber-colored, almost brown, and at this point you can add the rabbit. As it cooks, it will absorb all the flavors at hand.

Cover the pan and add more wine a little at a time.

When the cooking is completed, it's a good idea to strew the meat with minced parsley.

Fagottini mediterranei
(Mediterranean bundles)
(serves 6)

2 ½ lbs veal noisettes or medallions - 2 oz prosciutto crudo - 3 tbsp grated Parmesan – ½ cup grated breadcrumbs - parsley - 1 chicken liver - salt - pepper - nutmeg - sage - flour – ½ cup marsala – 3 cups stock - 1 egg - 2 oz butter

Have the meat cut into twelve small slices. Pound these thin and flat. Cook the chicken liver in a little of the butter. Now prepare the stuffing by amalgamating in a bowl the thinly-sliced prosciutto, the cooked, crumbled chicken liver, the grated breadcrumbs, the Parmesan, and the minced parsley, incorporating the whole with the egg, and seasoning with salt, pepper, and nutmeg. Parcel out this filling onto the meat slices and roll them up. Dredge them in flour, brown them in the rest of the butter, and perfume them with a few leaves of sage. When these little bundles have browned on every side, pour marsala over them, add the stock as needed little at a time, and finish cooking them slowly for about half an hour or more.

Fegatini di maiale
(Pork livers)
(serves 6)

2 lbs pork liver and pig's caul or omentum - salt - pepper - vinegar - fresh bay (laurel) leaves - lard or oil for frying - 1 lemon

According to Sicilian tradition, the tastiest liver comes from the sow, while the best blood-pudding is made from the hog.

Cut the liver into pieces about the size of a walnut. Let the pig's caul (intestinal membrane, also called "omentum") stand for a short while in lukewarm water to which a few drops of vinegar have been added.

It will soften, and you can then spread it out on your work surface.

Season the chopped liver with salt and pepper in a bowl. Roll up the liver slices and wrap each in a fresh bay or laurel leaf. Cut little squares from the pig's caul - be sure they're the right size - and wrap each liver-and-leaf roll tightly in one of these. After making up the rolls, fry them in hot lard over a slow flame, so that the meat is well done on the inside yet remains tender inside and out.

Sprinkle just few drops of lemon at the table.

Fegato d'oca al marsala
(Goose liver with Marsala)
(serves 6)

1 goose liver (about 1 ½ lb) - 6 sclices of bread -
3 oz butter - 1 cup marsala - salt and pepper

Eliminate from the livers any bilious or greenish traces and any gristly or fatty parts. Season with salt and pepper and brown in melted butter in a skillet over gentle heat. High heat takes the liver by surprise, making it tough on the outside and leaving it raw inside. When you're through cooking it, the liver should still be rather pink on the inside. Well-done liver is dry and grainy and has definitively sacrificed its original flavor.

Halfway through the cooking process, pour in the marsala, tilt the saucepan, and flame the wine.

Meanwhile, toast the bread slices in the oven. Place livers on them, along with the juices accumulated in the skillet.

Fesa mosaico
(Smothered veal roll)
(serves 6)

2 ½ lbs veal or baby beef - 1 lb spinach - 5 tbsp olive oil - 1 oz butter - 1 clove garlic - 2 rather thick slices of prosciutto - salt - pepper - 1 cup white wine - rosemary - sage

Use a lean cut of veal or baby beef, such as the sirloin upper leg sections. Such a cut, because it s not rich in connective tissue, can easily tolerate prolonged cooking. Cut the meat so as to obtain a single large, thin slice, and pound it well.
Steam the spinach. In a large skillet, melt the butter and flavor it with the garlic clove. Sauté the drained spinach briefly in the butter. Arrange upon the meat the prosciutto - which should cover the surface of the veal completely - and then the spinach, and season with salt and pepper. Roll the meat up upon itself very tightly and truss it well with some strong cotton twine. Put the meat in a saucepan with some oil and cook. When the cooking has colored the meat on every side, pour the white wine over it, season it with rosemary and sage, cover the pan, and continue cooking over very low heat for an hour. Should the meat become dry, add white wine.

Fianchetto al ragù
(Steak in ragout sauce)
(serves 6)

2 ½ lb beef steak, preferably a round steak - 2 eggs - 3 ½ oz prosciutto crudo - 1 cup shelled peas - ½ cup grated Parmesan - salt – pepper - parsley - ½ garlic clove - 1 onion - olive oil - 2 lbs ripe tomatoes

Get a single whole steak, such as a round steak. Take this broad piece of meat and sew its edges partially together so as to obtain a kind of pouch, which you are going to fill with a very tasty stuffing. Beat the eggs in a bowl with a pinch of salt, add the grated Parmesan, the finely-diced prosciutto, the peas (already boiled and seasoned), the very finely minced parsley, a little pepper, and the tip of a garlic clove, finely minced. Stuff the meat with this mixture, sew the pouch shut, and put it in a saucepan with olive oil and the very thinly-sliced onion. Brown all this. When the onion is completely limp and the meat nicely browned all over, add the peeled, seeded, and sieved ripe tomatoes and some salt. Stir this occasionally while you let it cook for about an hour and a half.

Fianchetto in bianco
(Stuffed veal pouch)
(serves 6)

2 ½ lbs boneless veal loin steak - 1 onion - 3 tbsp butter - 3 slices stale bread - ½ cup grated Parmesan - parsley - basil - 1 carrot - 1 celery rib - 2 cloves - 2 eggs - salt - pepper - nutmeg - olive oil - 2 cups dry white wine

Flatten the piece of meat by beating it well until it forms a nearrectangle. Season it with salt and pepper, fold it in half, and sew it up on two sides so as to obtain a little bag or pouch, which you will stuff with the following delicious mixture. Sauté the onion in a saucepan with half the butter until golden, then place the sautéed onion in a bowl with the bread (which you have soaked in water and then squeezed) the grated Parmesan, and the parsley and basil, minced together. Add the two beaten eggs, salt, pepper, and nutmeg. Stuff the veal pouch with this thick mixture, sew the opening shut, and truss the meat to give it an attractive form.

Place in a high-sided clay bakingdish, add the remaining butter and the olive oil, pour in the white wine, cover with aluminum foil, and cook in a moderate oven for about two hours.

According to a variant of this recipe, it's preferable to cook the meat in approximately 4 qts. of water, which you should first bring to boil (because in this case you want the meat to retain its flavor and not give too much of it to the broth), then add the meat, a modest bouquet of aromatic vegetables and herbs, and a clove. Let the whole simmer very slowly for 3 hours; the pot should merely "smile."

Ficedula
(Songbird)

Some dining experiences are impossible to repeat, because the respect due to nature has banished from today's "civilized" tables the little winged creatures that once were victims of our barbarous aggressiveness. And so we have given up eating the warblers that the Romans call *ficedule* and the Neapolitans *focetole*, extremely delicate little birds that eat figs in autumn and become very plump.

One would take very large onions, cut off their tops, and hollow out their centers. The little birds were seasoned with salt and pepper, then with garlic and parsley minced together, and smeared with lard and placed inside the onions. These were laid among coals that had been burning for some time and had become white. In this way, the cooking process would be very slow, and the fat, after having absorbed all the flavor of the birds, would liquefy and consign all its flavors in turn to the enclosing onions.

Let's content ourselves, like Benedictine monks, with crostini, little toasts.

<*Crostinum, deinde vinum, deinde crostinum usque ad matutinum*>.

You can recreate the gamy flavor of these birds by skewering pieces of onion, bread, and quail, seasoned like the warblers, and then cooking these over hot coals as described above. All the flavor will penetrate the succulent pieces of toasted bread.

Gallina con piselli
(Hen with peas)
(serves 6)

1 hen - 1 lemon - 4 tbsp olive oil - 3 cloves garlic
- 1 cup dry white wine - salt - pepper - 6 small,
spring, or pearl onions - 2 oz bacon - 1 lb shelled
peas - parsley

Nature certainly manages things exceptionally well. In the spring, when hens reach their plumpest, most tempting state, the best time for pea-picking arrives as well. Together, these two ingredients make a marvelous dish.

Cut the hen into pieces and let these marinate in lemon juice and water for an hour. Drain them well. Heat 4 tbsp. olive oil in a saucepan and cook the garlic cloves so that they transfer their flavor to the oil. Brown the chicken pieces well before adding the dry white wine. Let this evaporate, season with salt and pepper, lower the flame, cover the pan, and let the cooking continue.

Meanwhile, in another pan, cook the little onions, sliced as thinly as possible, in 3 tbsps. olive oil. When they're soft and faded, add the bacon and then the shelled peas and about a cup of water, and let this cook for half an hour.

Salt the peas and add them to the hen pieces.

These will have cooked almost completely in the meantime. Let all these flavors mingle until done.

At the moment when you serve this outstanding dish, strew it with fresh, minced parsley.

Involtini alla sarda
(Sardinian-style stuffed veal rolls)
(serves 6-8)

*2 ½ lbs veal (shank or rump or shoulder roast) -
7 oz prosciutto crudo - flour - 7 oz cheese (Dutch
style) - 1 cup Vernaccia wine - sage - 2 tbsp
butter - 5 tbsps olive oil - salt - pepper - 3 ripe
tomatoes - 1 onion - 3 carrots - 1 celery rib*

Have cut equal-sized slices from the piece of meat. Top each slice with lean prosciutto and a thin slice of cheese (provola if available; if not, use a Dutch cheese such as Gouda or Edam). Make sure the surface area of the cheese is a good deal smaller than that of the slice it's on; otherwise, some cheese could escape during the cooking and vanish into the sauce. Add a leaf of sage to each topping.

Close the slices by rolling them up and fastening them with a toothpick. Flour these involtini. Heat the butter and some olive oil in a skillet, add the veal rolls, and season them with salt and pepper. When the involtini have browned, pour in the Vernaccia. After this has evaporated, add the very thinly-sliced onion, then the carrot, celery, and tomatoes, all chopped small. Cover and cook for an hour. Should the sauce reduce excessively, you can add some hot water.

At the end of the cooking period, rub the sauce through a food mill and remove the toothpicks from the rolls.

Lingua salmistrata
(Pickled tongue)
(serves 6-8)

1 veal tongue – 4 tbsp olive oil - 2 tbsp butter - 1 tbsp lard - 2 oz pancetta or bacon - 4 onions - ½ lb carrots - 2 celery ribs - parsley - 1 clove garlic - 3 ripe tomatoes - salt

Take a whole veal tongue and boil it for a few seconds in salted water. At once, while it's still hot, make an incision in the skin and try to remove it in one piece. If this proves difficult, you can simply peel the tongue like a carrot with a sharp knife. Truss the tongue with string to give it a pleasing, round shape. In a separate saucepan, heat the olive oil, butter, and lard, and sauté the chopped pancetta, the thinly-sliced onions, the carrots and celery chopped small, a bunch of fresh parsley, the garlic, and the sliced tomatoes. Let all these ingredients blend with one another. When everything is soft and amalgamated, put the tongue in the pan, season with salt, cover the pan, and continue cooking slowly until you get a pretty brownishamber sauce; this will require about 2 hours. If necessary, pour some white wine over the meat. Cut the tongue into fine slices, pass the sauce through a food mill, and cover the slices of tongue with it.

"Morseddu"
(Morsels)
(serves 6)

2 ½ lbs veal entrails - 1 tbsp tomato paste - ½ tbsp
hot pepper purée - 1 tbsp lard - salt - oregano - hot
pepper

It comes from Catanzaro in Calabria and it is similar to the Neapolitan *soffritto*. It's a frugal meal, and the peasants eat it very hot in *pitta*, a kind of pizza made from bread dough. The most ancient recipe - perhaps Hebrew in origin, perhaps Saracen - calls for veal entrails, purée of tomato and of hot pepper, salt, and oregano.

Wash the entrails in cold water and clean them carefully. Boil them in plenty of salted water, and drain them when they're halfway cooked. Wash them again in cold water and chop them into small pieces. Melt the lard in a saucepan and add the puréed tomato and puréed hot pepper.

Let this liquefy, then add the chopped entrails. Fry lightly for a few minutes, and cover with lukewarm water.

Cook until done, over a slow fire. Add more water if necessary - keep it hot and handy for this purpose. Season with oregano and, lastly, add some fresh hot pepper.

Oca imbellettata
(Painted goose)
(serves 6)

1 goose, about 4 lbs - 1 small onion - 1 clove garlic -
parsley - salt - 1 tbsp brown sugar - 1 tbsp honey - 1
tart apple

This recipe, reminiscent of the famous Chinese Lacquered Duck, was introduced by a sailor from Sorrento; back from a trip to the East but still deeply fascinated by it, he modified this example of its cuisine to suit Italian palates.

Goose is less digestible than chicken. To reduce its fat content, it must always be baked - never cook it in a sauce. When you buy it, figure about 3/4 lb. per person.

Choose a good-looking goose and singe its skin by passing it rapidly several times over an open flame. Spread salt inside it with your hand, then stuff it with the onion, the crushed garlic clove, and the parsley.

Hold the goose up by its legs over a pot filled with water almost at the boiling point, and use a deep spoon or ladle to bathe it for five or six minutes. It will shine!

Hang it up on a hook overnight in a well-ventilated area. In the morning, when the goose is dry, make a mixture of 1 cup water, 1 tbsp. cane sugar, and 1 tsp. salt. First boil the water, then pour in salt and sugar. When these have dissolved, add 1 tbsp. honey. Paint the goose all over with this mixture, then hang it up to dry again.

Before putting the goose in the oven, place inside it a peeled tart apple.

Place in a 400°oven on a suspended grill, with a pan underneath to collect the drippings.

Let it bake for about an hour.

The Goose

We were young and full of life
We were young and full of life
And I asked you, and I asked you
"Do you want to be my wife?"
But just then a plump and stately
Goose strolled by; I took a look
And amended, and amended:
"Do you want to be my cook?"

Stelio Ricciardi

"Panada" di carne
(Meat pie)
(serves 6/8)

*For the short pastry dough: 3 cups flour - salt - 3
tbsp lard or olive oil - water
For the filling: 8 oz veal or beef - 8 oz pork - 6 oz
beef brain - 3 ½ oz prosciutto crudo - 3 small or
Italian artichokes - 1 lb fava or broad beans - 2
tomatoes - 5 tbsp olive oil - 1 clove garlic - parsley
- 1 egg - salt - pepper - nutmeg*

Sardinia, an island populated more by shepherds than by fishermen, preserves its traditional cuisine; neither peasant nor fisherman cares much for risk-taking or experimentation in eating.

Meat is the protagonist of the table, and it is customarily the man who cooks the meat, from suckling pig to lamb, from boar to kid.

Meat is always cooked over a low fire and according to specific rules: the spit must be made of aromatic wood, likewise the bundles of sticks for the coals, and the meat should be wrapped in myrtle, rosemary, and juniper. In the old days, cooking took place in a primitive oven: a hole dug in the earth and covered with live coals and faggots. On special occasions, different animals were baked, one in the belly of the other - in the calf there was a goat, in the goat a suckling young pig containing a hare that held a partridge, and inside of the partridge a thrush.

Perhaps this practice provided the source for the fad of hidden foods in the so-called *pièces montées*, "mounted" dishes of the kind popular in Renaissance and Baroque cuisine - impossible nowadays - in which the elements of spectacle and ornamentation often dissembled the taste of the food.

The recipe for this panada di carne is more practical and simple; although it combines different kinds of meat, it's easier to put together. Mince the garlic and parsley, brown them in the oil, and then add the meats, chopped into tiny cubes. Brown this duly, and season with salt, pepper, and nutmeg.

In another saucepan, sauté in a little olive oil the chopped onion, add half the minced prosciutto, the beans and the artichoke hearts, sliced very small. If the vegetables become too dry, add a little boiling water.

When they are done, add them to the meats. Clean the brain well, remove the skin, and boil it for a few minutes in lightly salted water. When it is cooled, chop it into pieces. Add these to the meats together with the bean mixture. Remove the pot from the fire, beat the egg, and add it. Season with salt.

Make a short pastry dough with the flour, salt, lard and water. Roll it out with a rolling-pin, making two discs. Line a high-sided baking-dish with the larger of these two discs.

Put the other half of the prosciutto on the bottom, then pour in the filling. Cover with the other disc-shaped dough and bake at 350° F for half an hour.

Petto di tacchino lardellato
(Larded turkey breast)
(serves 6)

Turkey breast (about 2 ½ lbs) - 3 ½ oz pancetta - parsley - 1 clove garlic - 4 tbsp olive oil - 2 tbsp butter - 1 cup white wine - salt – pepper

Although turkey breast meat is tender, delicate, and easy to digest, it can sometimes be too dry and therefore not very pleasing to the taste. You can avoid this problem as follows: mince together parsley, pancetta, and garlic; cover the turkey breast with this mixture. Truss up the breast with string to hold everything in place and put it in a saucepan with the butter and the oil. Season with salt and pepper. Brown the meat on all sides, turning it often; bathe it with the white wine, and cook it until done over low heat.

Pollastrella al pomodoro
(Pullet with tomato)
(serves 4)

1 pullet or young hen (about 3 lbs) - 4 peeled, seeded tomatoes - 1 clove garlic - hot pepper - 3

cloves - 3 tbsp olive oil - 1 cup white wine - salt -
minced parsley

Pluck the pullet, gut it, singe it over an open flame, wash it, and cut it into 4 pieces.
Sauté the garlic clove with the hot pepper in a little olive oil over moderate heat; discard the garlic. Add the pieces of pullet and cook until they are golden brown.
Pour the wine, let evaporate, chop the tomatoes into small pieces and add them, as well as the salt, hot pepper and the clove. Cover and cook for about 1/2 hour over low heat, stirring from time to time so the liquid doesn't stick to the bottom of the pan. Just before serving, sprinkle the dish generously with parsley.

Polpettone
(Meat roll)
(serves 6)

2 lbs ground beef - parsley - 5 eggs - 3 slices of
bread - milk or water - 5 oz mozzarella - 2 cups
meat stock - 2 tbsp grated Parmesan - 4 tbsp
butter - flour as needed - salt

The meat roll has humble origins.
Crumble the bread and soak it in some warm milk or water. Remove and blend with the ground beef, 4 eggs, the grated Parmesan, the parsley finely minced and salt to taste. Use your hands to mix all this. When you've obtained a homogeneous mass, carefully spread it out over a wet dishtowel and shape it into a single smooth, uniform layer. Quickly scramble the remaining egg in a hot skillet, add the cube mozzarella, place this mixture on top of the meat. Now, with the help of the towel, try to roll up the meat around its filling so that this is enclosed inside the meat roll. Adjust the roll with your hands, applying pressure here and there to give it a pleasing oval shape. Then dust it all over with flour.

Next, brown the roll on all sides in a little butter, turning it steadily and gingerly. Transfer it to a baking-dish, cover with stock, and continue cooking your polpettone in a moderate oven for about 40 minutes. Serve it hot, cut into circular slices and dressed with its cooking liquid.

Puntine arrosolate
(Braised pork rib tips)
(serves 4)

3 lbs pork rib tips - 1 lb onions - 3 tbsp olive oil -
salt - 1 cup white wine

The *puntine* ("little points") of pork, called by different names in the various regions of Italy, are cut from around the tips of the ribs and include both meat and bone. This is a cut rich in fat and cartilaginous tissue, ideal as a base for ragout sauces, but it can also assert itself and play a leading role, as in this dish.

First brown the small onions - spring or pearl onions, if the season permits - in the olive oil. Once these are soft, add the rib tips, cut into pieces. Stir them well so that they take on a bright, uniform colour, then pour in the cup of white wine. When this has evaporated, stir again, salt, reduce the heat, and cover the casserole. The dish will be ready in about 20 minutes.

Quaglie al marsala
(Quails with Marsala)
(serves 6)

12 quails - 2 oz pancetta - 1 cup Marsala - 1 tbsp
raisins - ½ cup green olives - 5 tbsp olive oil - salt -
pepper - parsley

This dish is prepared with Marsala, a liqueur-like wine produced from wines made in the Sicilian provinces of Trapani, Palermo, and Agrigento, fortified by the addition of both alcoholized must and "cooked" must, and aged for about three years.

Pluck the quails, gut them, remove their beaks and legs, wash them, and singe them. Chop the pancetta, not too finely. Heat a thin thread of oil in a pan and lightly sauté the quails and the pancetta. Stir over a lively fire until the quails are golden brown, then add the raisins, the pitted, chopped olives, parsley, salt, and pepper. Stir some more and pour in the Marsala. Cover and cook until the wine has evaporated. Serve the quails hot.

Soffritto
(Pig's sauté)
(serves 8)

4 ½ lbs pork heart, lungs and liver - olive oil -1
onion - 1 clove garlic - hot pepper - 2 cups white
wine - 1 ¾ lbs tomato puré - salt –parsley

In winter, richer, more succulent dishes (under the pretext of fortifying us against the cold) appear on the table.

So gourmets and gourmands, connoisseurs and gluttons, await this season with their salivary glands in uproar and their stomachs ready to receive the most appropriately-prepared meats.

The pig, king of the table as far back as human memory goes-pigs were domesticated in prehistoric times-found in the most ancient Chinese recipes, served to the Romans with herbs, sweet wine, and pepper, defined by Juvenal as "animal propter convivia natum" (an animal born for banquets), the most generous of animals, offers literally all of himself during the butchering days, and so provides festive occasions for others.

The present recipe produces a sort of Neapolitan-style soup, very similar to the *Calabrian morseddu (p.202)*, a mixture of pork lights or innards with oil, garlic, tomato, and a plenty of pepper. Humble and rustic, this thick soup is used to stuff hollowed-out loaves of country-style bread.

Before using innards, wash them several times in plenty of water and lemon juice. Then place them in plenty of fresh water, bring this to a boil, and cook for 10 minutes. Remove, cool, and cut into pieces no larger than a walnut. Boil this again for 5 minutes in the white wine.

Meanwhile, heat some olive oil and brown a sliced onion, two garlic cloves, and some minced pepper. Now add all the pork piece, brown them, then fry them over a brisk fire until they start to "sing" in the pot by crackling and popping. Don't forget to stir often. Next, add the puréed tomatoes and continue to cook for about ½ hour over moderate heat. Season with salt. At the end of cooking period, the sauce should be neither too liquid nor too thick. Complete this dish with a shower of finely-minced parsley.

FISH AND OTHER SEAFOOD

Alici in tortiera
(Anchovies in a pie-pan)
(serves 8)

*2 ½ lbs very fresh anchovies - 1 generous cup
grated bread crumbs – parsley - 2 cloves garlic- 1
tbsp grated Parmesan - salt- pepper - 6 tbsp olive
oil - 1 lemon*

Anchovies and sardines are humble fish, but absolutely delicious if eaten very fresh; they're rich in proteins and in certain fatty acids that lower cholesterol and improve blood circulation. Wash the anchovies and discard the bones and head. Keep the fillets joined together at the back. In a bowl, blend the breadcrumbs, the garlic and parsley minced together, and the Parmesan; season with salt, pepper, and a little oil. Oil a rather broad heat-resistant pie-dish, arrange the anchovies in it, strew them with the breadcrumb mixture, and moisten the whole with a bit more olive oil and a few drops of lemon juice.

Put the pan in a pre-heated (350° F) oven for 15 minutes. This "pie" can be served lukewarm as well.

Aragosta all'insalata o alla catalana
(Spanish - style spiny lobster salad)
(serves 4)

1 live spiny lobster (also called rock lobster or langouste) about 3 lbs - 1 onion - 1 tbsp vinegar - salt - 2 lbs salad tomatoes – 3 tbsp olive oil

Catalonia-Style Spiny Lobsters are eaten neither in Barcelona, nor in Valencia, nor on the Balearic Islands, nor anywhere else where the Catalan language is spoken; it is in fact a Sardinian dish, born of a happy intuition in the town of Alghero, on Sardinia's west coast. It is, nevertheless, true that Alghero can boast of Catalonian origins; Pedro IV of Aragon, called the Ceremonious, after expelling all the Genoans and Sardinians from this village, repopulated it in 1354 with Catalonians. Unlike inland Sardinians, whose gastronomic banners display sheeps' milk cheeses, meats, and wines, the Algherese find in the sea the umbilical cord that links them to their motherland.

In this recipe, we're talking about *Palinurus elephas Fabricius*, the Mediterranean spiny lobster or langouste, not to be confused with the Northern lobster (*homard* in French), which is black when alive and turns bright red only when it's cooked. The prized crustacean, which we are talking about, confirms the rules for cooking it, wrote down by Ippolito Cavalcanti, Duke of Buonvicino:

"Boil the lobsters, and peel their tails and claws, for these contain much meat. You can leave the body whole, and make thereof a hot, salty sauce. You can serve them cold as well."

For any connoisseur, the princely condiment to use with lobsters is, without a doubt, a thin trickle of olive oil, in all its fragrant, chartreuse simplicity. Truss the lobster and immerse it alive, head first, in boiling salted water. Cook it for 15 minutes, and let it cool in its own broth.

Meanwhile, slice the onion - a spring onion is best - and let it marinate in a tablespoon of vinegar.

When the lobster has cooled, discard the shell, the antenna, the little legs, and the tailfin, and cut the meat into large chunks. Put these on a plate and add the onion, the sliced, ripe salad tomatoes, salt, and olive oil.

Arrosto di anguilla
(Roasted eels)
(serves 6)

3 lbs eels - salt - 4 tbsp olive oil - 1 pinch oregano -
parsley - 2 cloves garlic - breadcrumbs - lemon

Clean the eels, remove their heads and tails, and cut them into pieces. Season these with salt, oil, oregano, and parsley and garlic minced together.
Oil a baking-pan, powder it with breadcrumbs, and arrange the seasoned eel slices in it. Sprinkle with more breadcrumbs and some olive oil. Roast them in a moderate oven for about an hour.
When you serve the eels, dress them with lemon juice.

Calamari farciti in bianco
(Boiled stuffed squids)
(serves 4)

2 lbs squids - salt - pepper - parsley - 1 cup grated
bread crumbs - 2 tbsp pine nuts - 1/3 cup seedless
raisins - 2 eggs - olive oil - 1 onion

Cut the tentacles off of the swollen bodies of the squid. Cook these long appendages in salted water with some parsley.
After they're cooked, mince them and blend them together with the grated breadcrumbs, the pine nuts, the raisins, and some finely minced parsley. Season this mixture with salt and pepper, bind it with the eggs, and use it to stuff the squid, whose openings you will then sew shut.
Mince the onion and fry it lightly in olive oil. When the onion becomes limp and faded, add the stuffed calamari and cook them, pouring small quantities of hot water over them from time to time. You should obtain a thick, tasty

broth. After about an hour of cooking over low heat, serve the squid in this broth.

Calamari ripieni alla caprese
(Capri-style stuffed squids)
(serves 6)

12 squids, about 6 oz each - 6 tbsp olive oil - garlic - salt - parsley - 10 small ripe tomatoes - 1 lb fresh caciottine or fresh cheeses (see p. 42) - 4 tbsp grated Parmesan - 3 egg yolks - marjoram

Close your eyes and you'll breathe in the aromas and flavors of Capri, because this flavorful dish comes from that blessed isle.

The island of Capri - upon whose shores that "hero of endurance," Odysseus, landed - adorns its hard granite body with the most variegated and fragrant flora that the Mediterranean has to offer, and it presents itself to the senses for their delight.

With the small ripe tomatoes, repositories of fragrance and dispensers of flavor, and with the baby squid, you can prepare an outstanding dish.

Clean the squid, putting the tentacles aside. Combine in a bowl the fresh cheese, the grated Parmesan, the egg yolks, and the marjoram. Stuff the squid with this mixture.

Note that they will swell while cooking, so be sure to close their openings carefully with toothpicks.

Heat some olive oil in a saucepan and lightly fry a garlic clove. When this is roasted, remove it and replace it with the whole stuffed squid and with the tentacles.

Let all this turn golden brown and mingle its flavors for a few minutes, then add the small tomatoes. Salt correctly, cover the pan, and cook over low heat for 40 minutes.

Before serving this dish, sprinkle it with just-minced, very fresh parsley.

Calamari ripieni in forno
(Oven-baked stuffed squids)
(serves 4)

*8 small squids - 1 large onion - 2 cloves garlic -
parsley - grated breadcrumbs - 2 eggs - 8 peeled
tomatoes - salt - pepper - 3 tbsp olive oil - 1 bay
leaf - 1 cup white wine*

The squid (*Loligo volgaris Lamarck*) is a relatively recent gastronomical discovery; the Greeks and Romans, in fact, did not think very much of it. Its very delicate taste was not discovered until the 16th century.

For this recipe, you need 8 small squid. Clean them, discarding the mouth or "beak," the eyes, the transparent bone or cartilage, and the ink sac. Wash the squid and cut off their tentacles. Wash and dry these, mince them finely, and add them to the pan, in which you will have already browned the onion, garlic, and parsley in olive oil. Next, add the tomatoes, 1/2 cup of hot water, and 2-3 tbsp. grated breadcrumbs, so that you obtain a homogeneous paste.

At this point, beat and add the eggs, along with salt and pepper, and let all this reduce over heat to produce a thick stuffing.

Fill the squid with this, then close their openings with a toothpick or a simple stitch or two. Arrange the squid in good order in a heat-resistant baking-dish, moisten them with olive oil and the white wine, season with salt, pepper, and a bay leaf, and put them into a moderate oven for about half hour.

Cernia alla marinara
(Sailor-style grouper)
(serves 4)

*4 fillets (7 oz each) grouper or sea bass - 12 white
olives - 2 tbsp capers - 4 peeled tomatoes - 2 cloves
garlic - 1 tbsp sultana raisins - salt - pepper – ½
cup white wine –3 tbsp olive oil.*

This Sicilian recipe is a more elaborate version of an old dish that was prepared with dessicated fish (ray or skate) and potatoes.

Heat some olive oil in a saucepan and cook the crushed garlic cloves until they begin to change color, then remove them and add the fish slices. After searing them, bathe them with the white wine. As soon as this evaporates, add the pitted olives, the capers (wash these first to remove the salt), the seeded tomatoes, and the sultana raisins. Cover with water, adjust the seasoning with salt and pepper, and cook for 20 minutes. Serve with pieces of toasted bread.

"Cicenielli"
(Newborn anchovies or sardines)
(serves 6-8)

1 lb baby anchovies or sardines - parsley - salt -
pepper - 1 tbsp active dry yeast - 2 cup flour -
vegetable oil for frying

What the Neapolitans call cicenielli and the people of the Ligurian coast *bianchetti* (newborn, transparent anchovies or sardines) are an ineffable delicacy for the connoisseur. They belong to the category of macroplanktons, which can only be fished in the Mediterranean fram January 15th to March 15th . They can be cooked simply by being placed in boiling, lightly salted water until they rise to the surface. The tiny fish are then drained well and dressed with the juice of two lemons and plenty of finely minced parsley.

Otherwise (as here), they are presented in the form of goldenfried pancakes or fritters and should be enjoyed with religious concentration. Wash the *cicenielli* carefully, drain them, dry them, and season them with finely-minced parsley, salt, and pepper.

Prepare a batter by dissolving the yeast with a little salt in a cup of lukewarm water and then amalgamating this mixture with the flour. If necessary, add more water, until you obtain a creamy liquid batter. Let this rise until barely puffy. Mix the baby fish into the batter, and transfer this by tablespoons to hot oil. As soon as these little fritters puff up and turn a lovely golden color, remove them and place them on absorbent paper. Serve immediately.

Capone gallinella o scorfano all'acqua pazza
(Red gurnard or Scorpion fish in tomato and wine sauce)
(serves 4)

3 lbs capone gallinella (red gurnard) or scorpion fish - 5 tbsp olive oil - 1 clove garlic - ½ lb small fresh tomatoes (or cherry tomatoes) - ½ cup of white wine - hot pepper - salt - parsley .

Use a broad, low-sided pan big enough to hold the fish.
Heat the olive oil, color the crushed garlic in it, then remove the garlic and replace it with the tomato.
Let it cook for 5 minutes, add the chili pepper, than the fish, the wine. Let evaporate. Add a bit of minced parsley, a pinch of salt, 2 tbsp of hot water.
Cover the pan and cook slowly for 10 minutes. Then remove the lid and let the sauce evaporate a while longer, until it appears to have the right consistency. At the moment of serving, complete the dish with a little minced parsley.

Dentice in zuppa
(Dentex in soup or stew)
(serves 4)

1 dentex or sea bass (about 3 lbs) - 2 cups dry white wine - ½ cup vinegar - 2 cloves garlic - parsley - celery - salt - few white peppercorns

The dentex, a large white fish already appreciated in Roman times, deserves a special place in Mediterranean cooking. "The best dentex can be caught from the beginning of winter until springtime": this advice comes to us from Corrado, who in the second half of the 18th century wrote a treatise on various kinds of food.
In order to avoid a cottony texture, you must use a fish no heavier than a kilogram. Mince all the seasonings (garlic, parsley, celery) very small and

place them in a suitable saucepan with a quart of water, the wine, the vinegar, the white peppercorns, and the salt. Bring all this to boil. Meanwhile, clean the fish well. Add it whole to the boiling stock and cook until done, usually about 20 minutes. When the fish is cooked, remove the backbone and the head. Cut the flesh into 4 or 5 large pieces, and place these in an earthenware bowl. Continue to reduce the broth, bearing in mind that you should have enough liquid to cover the fillets copiously.

When this stock has reached the proper level of reduction, strain it, and pour it over the fish.

The soup should be served with pieces of toasted bread and boiled potatoes sprinkled with parsley.

Fritto di baccalà
(Fried salt cod)
(serves 6)

2 lbs dried and salted codfish - parsley - 1 carrot - 1 onion - 1 celery rib - 2 cloves garlic - 1 ½ cups flour - 1 tsp active dry yeast - 4 tbsp olive oil - hot pepper or a pinch of ground pepper - 3 lemons - vegetable oil for frying - salt

Chop the *baccalà* (salt cod) into pieces and soak them in plenty of cold water. Change the water often, so that the cod completely loses the salt in which it has been preserved.

Next day, prepare a "bouillon": put plenty of water in a large pot and add a bunch of aromatic vegetables - carrot, celery, onion, parsley - along with a bit of salt. Bring this to boil, lower the heat, and simmer for 15 minutes. Let the "bouillon" cool, add the *baccalà* pieces, and cook for about 5 minutes.

Drain the fish, remove and discard the skin and bones, and chop the cod into small pieces. Wash the garlic and parsley and mince them finely together. Add the flour, the yeast, and the olive oil, diluting the whole with lukewarm water until you obtain a thick, consistent batter.

Season with chopped hot pepper or with ground pepper. Add the cod.

Heat the vegetable oil. Spoon a little of the batter at a time into hot oil, and fry these little spoonfuls until they puff up and turn golden.

Drain the fried cakes, put them on a platter, and serve them hot.

Accompany them with lemon wedges.

Gamberoni in cartoccio
(King prawns in foil)
(serves 6)

18 large prawns - aluminum foil – 6 tbsp olive oil - 3 cloves garlic - parsley - hot pepper - salt & pepper - lemon

You need very few ingredients for this dish, but they must be of the highest quality, the result of a careful process of selection that goes well beyond mere hurried provisioning. The olive oil should be transparent, pure, extra virgin, the product of the first pressing of sound, freshly-picked olives, because otherwise the sourish taste will jeopardize the final result. The parsley, too, should be freshly harvested and fragrant, perhaps from a pot on your window-sill. Ideally, the crustaceans should come from the Bay of Naples and incorporate its familiar scents, evoking images, sensations.

Get some waxed paper or foil and cut it into large squares. In the center of each, place the prawns, two or three to each package, depending on their size. Add the crushed tip of a garlic clove, some minced parsley, a few drops of lemon juice, salt, and pepper (hot or chili pepper is best).

Now close the paper or foil by squeezing the edges together. Leave some space inside for the mingling fragrances. When you open these packages, in fact, after baking them in a 400°F oven for 10 minutes, the aromas thus released will be an olfactory delight, and the prawns will have taken on a handsome red hue.

The effect, in short, will be quite picturesque.

Involtini di pesce spada
(Swordfish rolls in sauce)
(serves 4)

*2 lbs swordfish - 1 generous cup grated breadcrumbs
- 2 tbsp grated pecorino cheese - 1/3 cup sultana
raisins - 2 tbsp pine nuts - salt - pepper - 1 clove
garlic - parsley - olive oil - flour as needed - white
wine*

Fishing for swordfish is a Sicilian tradition and occupies the months from April to September, when schools of these fish, coming from the Sargasso Sea and attracted by the Mediterranean, pass through the Straits of Messina.
The people of Catania prepare swordfish rolls in a tasty, original way.
Cut the fish into thin slices, and pound these so that they will roll up easily.
At the same time, prepare the stuffing. Mix the grated breadcrumbs and the grated pecorino cheese, then add the sultana raisins, the pine nuts, the salt, the minced parsley, the finely-chopped garlic, and the pepper. Moisten all this with some excellent olive oil, to form a good cohesive mixture.
Place some stuffing in the center of each swordfish slice and roll these up upon themselves to form *involtini* or rolls; use toothpicks to hold them together. Dust them lightly with flour and fry them carefully and gently (so as not to break them) in olive oil. Add the white wine and cook everything together over a slow heat for another few minutes.

Nasello alla siciliana
(Sicilian-style hake)
(serves 4)

1 hake or cod, about 3 lbs - parsley - 3 tbsp olive oil - lemon - salt - pepper - 3 salted anchovies - grated breadcrumbs

The hake or Merlucius mediterraneus, although it belongs to the cod family, *Gadidae*, and is often mistaken for cod, is in fact a different fish.

The French call it *colin*, and it is connected to the charming legend of *Cola Pesce*. This is a very ancient story, told for the first time by a 12th-century Provencal poet, and taken up again by Italo Calvino in his *Fiabe italiane* (Italian Fairytales).

The legend, originally concerning the lighthouse of the town of Messina in Sicily, lived on there in multiple versions and passed from there to Naples. Countless writers have retold this story or alluded to it, among them Cervantes in Don Quixote. Benedetto Croce recounts it too, in his *Storie e leggende napoletane* (Naples: History and Legends) and attributes its formidable popularity to the tendency to imagine extraordinary and unnatural aspects of men and animals that have particular connections to the sea; such is the strange attraction and curiosity about the unknown generated by the sea, with all the hidden riches it contains. The legend tells the story of Cola, a boy who remained in the water night and day and was transformed into a fish (pesce). One day the king of Messina sent for him and asked him what things he saw in the depths of the sea. Cola Pesce told him that he saw marvels, but that around the lighthouse everything was obscured by a column of smoke which concealed an enormous fish that would surely devour anyone who disturbed him. The curious, imperious king demanded that Cola explore those waters too. Snatching off his crown, the king flung it into the waters near the lighthouse and ordered the good Cola to go and retrieve it. Cola obeyed, but first he asked for a handful of lentils; should he be unable to return to the surface, he said, he would let the lentils go, and their appearance on the waves would be the proof of his fate. And so it came to pass; the legend tells us that Cola Pesce remained submerged in the depths of the sea. It is not certain, however, whether Cola was indeed a prisoner in the watery abysses, or whether he had taken the prudent decision to swim far away from such an arrogant and capricious sovereign. Or perhaps Cola, with the same artless simplicity that led to Pinocchio's decision to remain a puppet, finding himself at the threshold of normal adult life, at the outer limit of adolescence, and not caring to renounce his desire for freedom, hides himself in the twisting passages of caverns that lie under the sea.

In any event, this recipe is Sicilian in origin. Get yourself a hake (or cod), scale it, open it, and remove its backbone, which you will replace with a sprig of parsley moistened with oil and lemon juice and sprinkled with salt and pepper.

Lightly oil a baking-dish and place the fish in it. Wash, bone, and chop the anchovies then, using a separate pan, dissolve them in a tablespoon of hot olive oil. Pour some of this simple sauce into the fish and the rest onto its back.

Sprinkle with grated breadcrumbs, salt, pepper, and minced parsley. Place the baking-dish in a pre-heated oven and bake for about twenty minutes.

Orata in "court-bouillon"
(Gilthead bream in court bouillon)
(serves 4)

3 lbs gilthead bream - 3 tbsp olive oil - lemon - parsley - garlic - 1 onion - 1 carrot - 1 celery rib - pepper - vinegar - salt

The dorado or gilthead bream (related to the porgies), whom Linnaeus baptized *Sparus auratus* because of the distinguishing golden band on its snout, is a delicate fish, sensitive to cold, that nourishes itself on mussels, oysters, and other delicacies which surely leave their flavors underneath its soft flesh. In deference to the wise principle according to which what counts in the kitchen is refinement, not originality, we maintain that the court *bouillon* is the ideal method for cooking not only the orata, but also any other very fresh fish, whose flesh seems compatible with the process of boiling and the fragrance of delicate perfumes, such as those ingredients that make up the "bouillon."

This method, which limits itself to a subtle transfer of aromas that improves the flavor of the fish, enhances its self-expression.

Light fragrances characterize Neapolitan cooking, which uses only very fresh, simple herbs. Depriving this cuisine of the poetry of its fragrances would be equivalent to reducing it to a primitive way of cooking ingredients, and the result could be only insipid boiled food without any character.

The "scents" (*odori*), as the Neapolitans call parsley, celery, garlic, small peppers, onion, carrot, basil, tarragon, anise, mint, sage, rosemary, and bay leaves, are for the cook what colors are for the painter - instruments for expressing and realizing creative fantasy.

Dumas père, in his *Grand dictionnaire de cuisine*, enjoined the cook to have at hand the 28 essential fragrant vegetables and herbs, in plant, powdered, condimental, and pickled form. The "scents" amalgamate with the dishes and assimilate themselves to our very humors, although the most pervasive of all is a fragrance not found in any garden: it's the smell of home, that familiar aroma of love, of childhood, of fairytales. Pour into a pot enough water to cover the fish, but don't add the fish yet. Instead, put in one onion, one celery rib, a bunch of fresh parsley, a carrot, some peppercorns, one or two tablespoons of vinegar and a few pinches of salt. Simmer all the ingredients, then turn off the heat. Let the pot cool, put the fish into the water, turn the heat back on, and boil it again. This amount of time will be sufficient to cook the fish. Gently place it on a tray and dress it with a little sauce made of finely-minced parsley, a small garlic clove, a few tablespoons of olive oil, and a few drops of lemon juice.

When Alberto Moravia tasted this fish, he was touched at rediscovering the flavors that reminded him of the days of his convalescence at the Hotel Cocumella, towards the end of the 1930's.

Rana pescatrice o coda di rospo in zuppa
(Anglerfish or Monkfish soup)
(serves 6)

1 anglerfish or monkfish, about 5 lbs - 1 clove garlic - 1 onion - 1 carrot - 1 celery rib - salt- 6 tbsp olive oil - 1 lb peeled ripe tomatoes - pepper or hot pepper - parsley

The flesh of the angler-fish or Lophius piscatorius, also called in Italian *coda di rospo* ("toad's tail") or *diavolo di mare* ("sea devil") makes it one of the most delicate and delicious of fishes. One eats the tail of this fish, duly skinned, cut into slices, and cooked in a soup or stew.
For this recipe, clean the fish and place it in a fish poacher with about 1 ½ qts water, the onion, the carrot, the celery rib, and a large pinch of salt.
Boil the water until the bones of the fishtail seem about to detach themselves. At this point, remove the fish, bone it, and chop the flesh into small pieces once it has cooled. Pour plenty of oil into a pan, add garlic, and brown it. Then add the tomatoes, salt, pepper, and a small piece of hot pepper. Stir in the fish pieces. Cover the pan and cook over low heat for about 10 minutes, pouring in enough of the fish broth to obtain a soup of the proper consistency.

Serve it sprinkled with fresh minced parsley and accompanied by toasted bread.

Pesce spada alla marinara
(Sailor-style swordfish)
(serves 6)

6 swordfish slices - flour as needed - vegetable oil
- 1 clove garlic - mint or parsley - vinegar or
lemon juice - olive oil - salt

Lightly flour the swordfish slices, fry them in plenty of hot vegetable oil, and drain them on paper towels. Line them up on a serving-platter and season them with salt. Mince the garlic very finely together with two mint leaves; if you can't obtain any of this wonderfully aromatic herb, use parsley. Sprinkle this on the fish slices and moisten them with a trickle of olive oil and a few drops of white vinegar or lemon juice.
This dish may be served cold.

Polipetti alla Luciana
(Stewed octopus)
(serves 6)

3 lbs small octopuses - 3 fresh or peeled tomatoes -
1 small glass of olive oil - parsley - 1 clove garlic -
salt - hot pepper - ½ cup white wine

"The octopus cooks in his own juice". You can cook octopus without adding water because it gives off its water content as it cooks. This old Neapolitan proverb contains a lesson: the man who does evil ends up punishing himself.
The octopus, or *Octopus vulgaris*, protagonist of various tales of marine horror, considered by A. Duman *"le régal des Napolitains"*, sometimes requires rough treatment to overcome the inconvenient toughness of its flesh.

The fishermen of Bari are experts in this procedure: first they remove the sac of black ink; then they begin pounding it with a block of wood. This results in complete tenderizing.

Small octopuses, more tender by nature, do not require such treatment.

Pour plenty of olive oil into a clay pot. Add the crushed garlic, the small, "genuine" octopuses - they should have a double row of suckers on their tentacles - the tomatoes (chopped small), the salt, the hot pepper, ½ cup of white wine, and a handful of finely minced parsley.

Cover the pot with tinfoil and tie this with string to ensure a tight closure. Cook the octopuses in their own steam over gentle heat for about one hour. Shake the pot from time to time to move them around, but don't remove the foil.

After the cooking time has passed, let the dish rest for 10 minutes before serving it, sprinkled with fresh parsley.

"Salamurigghio"
(Salmoriglio or sicilian sauce)

2 lemons - 1 cup olive oil - 1 clove garlic - oregano
- salt - 1 tbsp vinegar - parsley

This typical, widely-used condiment accompanies boiled meat or grilled fish, and is dabbed on foods at all possible times - before, during, and after the cooking process. This sauce is similar to the Apulian *cimciurro*, whose variations may include thyme or some other herb.

Pour the oil into a bowl and emulsify it with a wire whisk while adding gradually, ½ cup of hot water, the juice of 2 lemons, a pinch of oregano, salt, 1 tbsp. minced parsley, 1 tbsp vinegar, and a crushed garlic clove. Blend completely. At this point, the salmoriglio is ready, but it is generally heated in a double boiler before being served.

Saporiglia di merluzzo
(Codfish in liver sauce)
(serves 4)

1 whole cod ungutted about 3 lbs - olive oil - salt -
parsley - flour - 1 clove garlic - 1 tsp sugar

Remove the liver from the cod, cook it in oil and a teaspoon of water, and put it aside.

Chop the fish into thin slices about the length of a finger, season these with oil, salt, and minced parsley, flour them, and fry them in oil.

In a separate pan, brown the garlic in oil, together with some parsley and a teaspoon of sugar. When everything has changed color, pour in 1/2 cup of water. Pound the cooked liver and mix it into this sauce. When everything is well blended, add the pieces of fried cod and serve them hot.

Sarago (o pagello o fragolino) al forno
(Baked porgy or red snapper or sea bream)
(serves 6)
2 porgies, about 2 lbs each - flour - 2 cloves
garlic - parsley - salt - pepper - olive oil - 1
lemon

Porgies, members of the suborder Percoidea and the family Sparidae, are spiky-toothed fish that prey on crustaceans and molluscs and live in the rocky crevices of the continental shelf down to a depth of 80 meters (about 260 feet). This refined diet no doubt makes their flesh particularly tasty, like that of other members of the family Sparidae that share their feeding habits.

Already in the 4th century B.C. the Greek poet Archestratus, author of the long poem *Delights* (a journey in search of gastronomical curiosities that found favor with Lucilius, among others), appreciated the pleasing taste of the porgy; his only reservation is that the fish is by nature dry and tough-fibered, and therefore he advises his readers to moisten it with vinegar and bake it. We, too, shall follow his suggestion. Gut, scale, and wash the fish. Cover them with a very thin layer of flour, season them with salt, and place them in a rectangular bakingdish. Inside each fish, where its stomach used to be, put a crushed garlic clove, a pretty bunch of parsley (coarsely chopped), salt, pepper, and a few drops of lemon juice. Moisten the fish with a trickle of oil and ½ cup of water, and bake them in a moderate oven for about ½ hour.

Sarde a "beccaficu" (Warbler-style sardines)
(serves 6)
24 fresh sardines - 1 cup grated breadcrumbs
- 2 tbsp   grated pecorino cheese - 2 cloves
garlic - salt - parsley - 1 tbsp olive oil - 2 tbsp
vinegar - flour - oil for frying

The beccaficu ("warbler"), because it feeds on figs, is a particularly fleshy and flavorful bird. It is taken between July and September and prepared with a good stuffing. Likewise the sardines in this dish, designated "Warbler-Style" in Messina, because the fish thus served, like their namesakes the birds, are also plump and delicious. If you can't find sardines for this dish, you may also use anchovies. Clean the sardines carefully: split their bellies and remove their backbones, making sure that all the tiny outer bones are also removed. This operation is more difficult with sardines than with anchovies, because the sardine's flesh is more compact and adheres more tightly to its spine. Wash the boned fish repeatedly in running water and let them drain. Now, prepare the stuffing: grated breadcrumbs, grated pecorino, garlic, parsley, olive oil, and a little vinegar. The mixture should be rather moist and well blended with the finely-minced garlic and parsley.

Distribute this stuffing over half of the open sardines, cover each with another sardine, dredge each sardine couple in flour, and fry them in a lot of very hot oil, first on one side and then on the other. When they're golden, drain them on paper towels.

Like all fried dishes, this one is very good when hot, but it's possible to enjoy these sardines cold, too, if you remember to add a little vinegar to them.

Seppioline o calameretti ripieni alla sorrentina
(Sorrento-style stuffed baby cuttlefish or baby squid)
(serves 4)

2 ½ lbs baby cuttlefish or baby squid - 2 eggs - 1 cup grated Parmesan - 3 ½ oz mozzarella - 1/3 cup sultana raisins - salt - pepper - olive oil - 1 clove garlic - hot pepper - parsley - 1 lb small tomatoes

An unusual marriage between flavors of the sea and of the land (the cheeses are an example of the latter), this pleasing, appetizing dish produces little tidbits fit for a cardinal.

Clean the cuttlefish well, removing all the impurities they contain inside their "sack" or body, remove the internal cartilage, and cut off the tentacles. If you're using squid instead of cuttlefish, remove the eyes and the little sac containing the black ink, wash the squid carefully, and cut off the tentacles.

Prepare the filling in a bowl, amalgamating the eggs and enough Parmesan to make a dense, creamy mixture. Add a pinch of salt and pepper, the finely diced mozzarella, and the sultana raisins.

Fill the body-sacks of the cuttlefish or squid with this mixture, being sure not to overfill them; they swell when cooking, and you run the risk of breaking them.

Sew up the openings with white thread or simpler tight them with toothsticks. From a saucepan where the crushed garlic clove has transferred its fragrance to the hot olive oil and a piece of chili pepper has made the oil more assertive, remove both garlic and pepper and replace them with the tentacles. Fry these well, then add the stuffed cuttlefish or squid and cook for several minutes over a lively fire. Add the crushed ripe tomatoes, adjust the salt, lower the flame, cover the pan, and cook for about 25 minutes. Before serving these, remove the thread you used to sew them up, and place them on a platter. Cover them with their sauce and strew the whole with very finely minced parsley.

Spiedini con involtini di pesce spada
(Skewered swordfish rolls)
(serves 4/6)

2 lbs swordfish, sliced thin - 2 onions - 2 cups grated breadcrumbs - ½ cup grated pecorino - olive oil - 1 tbsp pine nuts - 1/3 cup raisins - laurel or bay leaves

In Southern Italy numerous swordfish arrive with the heat of the summer. From Sicily to Campania, recipes for the preparation of this extraordinary blue fish are numberless. Grilled method is among the best and most common.
Use thin slices of swordfish for this dish, and pound them with a meat pounder until they're supple enough to roll up around the stuffing you're going to prepare as follows. Fry a thinly-sliced onion in a little olive oil, then add the breadcrumbs (reserve enough of these to dredge the rolls in before you cook them), the grated pecorino cheese, the pine nuts, and the raisins. Mingle all these flavors and stuff the fish slices with the resulting mixture.
Roll up each slice around the stuffing, forming little rolled bundles, and fasten each with two toothpicks. Dredge each roll in the remaining breadcrumbs, and then skewer the rolls, separating each roll with a laurel or bay leaf and a slice of onion. Roast these over a grill and serve them very hot.

Spigola all'arancia
(Sea bass with orange)
(serves 6)

4 lbs sea bass or grouper - 1 bitter (or Seville) orange - parsley - ½ cup white wine - salt - pepper - 4 tbsp olive oil - 2 cloves garlic

The delicate flavor of sea bass combines well with the refined fragrance of orange. Scale and clean the fish. Insert into its stomach cavity 2 crushed garlic cloves, a sprig or two of parsley, and a piece of orange peel. Season with salt and pepper. Place the fish in a bakingpan and bake it at 400° F for 5 minutes. Bathe it with the white wine and the orange juice and let it bake for another 5 minutes so that the liquid evaporates. At this point, add a few tablespoons of salted water or fish stock and continue cooking for another 15 minutes. Transfer the fish to a warm serving platter and keep it warm while you strain its cooking liquid into a pan where you have placed the rest of the orange peel, cut into tiny strips. Cook and reduce this sauce. Fillet the fish and pour the sauce over it. Sprinkle the whole with fresh minced parsley.

Spigola in salsa verde
(Sea bass in green sauce)
(serves 4)

1 sea bass or grouper fillets, about 3 lbs
For the sauce: parsley - 1 clove garlic - olive oil - 1
lemon
For the bouillon: 1 small onion - 1 celery rib - 1
carrot - a few parsley sprigs - 1 tbsp. vinegar - 3
whole black peppercorns - 3 cloves

The *spigola*, a kind of sea bass (Dicentrarchus labrax) akin to the groupers, is a fish of the Mediterranean and Atlantic waters, known as far away as England. Like every fresh fish, it requires that its taste not be overwhelmed by heavy sauces or strong flavors.
Clean the inside of the fish, but leave the scales and fins intact. Prepare a bouillon in a large saucepan. Pour in about 2 qts. water, and add a small onion, the washed celery rib, the grated carrot, a few parsley sprigs, and a pinch of salt, together with the peppercorns and the cloves. Bring to the boil for 5 minutes then turn off the heat. When the bouillon has cooled, strain it, add the fish, turn the heat back on, add the vinegar, and cook until the water is to the boiling point. Let the fire agitate the water enough to make it

tremble, but don't let it boil outright before the fish is cooked; this should require about 10 minutes from the moment the water begins to tremble.

Now gently remove the fish, place it on a serving platter, and serve it with the green sauce that you will have produced as follows: mince garlic and parsley together very finely; place this mixture in a sauceboat, and cover it completely with olive oil and the juice of a lemon.

Stoccafisso alla napoletana con pomodoro
(Neapolitanstyle stockfish with tomato)
(serves 6)

4 lbs stockfish (cod, hake, or haddock, dried in the open air) - olive oil - 1 clove garlic - 2 onions - small pepper - 1 lb San Marzano tomatoes - 1 lb potatoes - parsley - salt

Soak the stockfish in water for 2 or 3 days, taking care to change the water every day.

Then boil it in plenty of salted water for 5 minutes, and plunge it at once into a bowl filled with water and ice. Remove the bones and the skin.

Put the oil into a saucepan, together with the garlic clove and plenty of minced onion. Brown everything, then add the small pepper and the peeled tomatoes. After about 15 minutes, when the sauce is cooked but not too cooked, add the potatoes, cut into chunks. Let this cook quite slowly. When the potatoes are almost done, very delicately add the cold fish pieces, arranging them as if they were to be shielded and protected by the potatoes in the pan. Continue cooking over very low heat for 10 minutes. Be careful not to stir at all.

At the moment when you bring this dish to the table, strew it with finely-minced parsley.

Stoccafisso alla pizzaiola
(Stockfish in tomato sauce)
(serves 6)

4 lbs stockfish (see previous recipe) – 4 tbsp olive oil - 1 clove garlic - small hot pepper - 6 tomatoes - parsley

Fry the garlic and the pepper in a saucepan with the oil. Add the peeled, seeded, and chopped tomatoes, and let this cook until you obtain a fine, thick sauce (you will have given the stockfish the indispensable preliminary treatment: three days of soaking, then 5 minutes of boiling, followed by cooling in iced water). Now add the stockfish to the sauce. Let this cook over very low heat. Do not stir.
When the fish is cooked, add some fragrant, fresh minced parsley.
Sun-drying is the most ancient method of preserving coarsetextured fish (generally cod and hake), which are known as stockfish.
This very abundant type of fish represents about one half of the fish caught commercially all over the world.

Stoccafisso e patate
(Stockfish and potatoes)
(serves 6)

4 lbs stockfish - 1 ½ lbs potatoes – 5 tbsp olive oil - salt - 1 clove garlic - hot pepper - parsley - 1 lemon

Towards the middle of the 16th century, the Council of Trent enjoined the return to an austerity modeled on that of biblical days. The strict rule of fasting was established at the same time as the ships of the Italian marine republics were being loaded with dried fish in the ports of Northern Europe.
The stockfish is a type of cod found in northern waters. It is first dried in the sun, without salt, and then rolled up for preservation into tight cylindrical bundles, like so many "stocks" or blocks of wood. Before cooking it, it's a

good idea to pound it moderately with a wooden spoon; this facilitates soaking the fish effectively. It should be soaked in plenty of fresh, cold water. Change the water every day for three or four days before cooking the fish. Alternatively, it's possible to buy stockfish that has already been softened.

Once the stockfish is sufficiently soft, boil the fish for 5 minutes in plenty of salted water, then quickly transfer it to a bowl containing water and ice. This procedure will keep the fish in one piece without crumbling. Remove the bones and the skin.

Now, using the water you boiled the stockfish in, boil the diced potatoes. Put everything on a serving-platter, and dress the dish with a simple sauce, prepared as follows: mix olive oil, 1 clove of garlic, hot pepper and some parsley (mince the latter three together very finely) with the juice of one lemon.

Tonno alla menta
(Fresh tuna with mint)
(serves 6)

3 lbs tuna - several mint leaves - 4 sage leaves - 3
cloves garlic - 2 cups of white wine - ½ cup olive
oil - 2 lemons - salt - pepper

Have the tuna cut into fillets or slices. Make small incisions in them, and insert small pieces of garlic and mint into these incisions. Mix together the wine, sage leaves, salt, pepper, and lemon juice, garlic and mint and marinate the tuna in this for at least an hour, turning the slices from time to time. Then put the fish into a saucepan with the olive oil and cook briefly until the fish begins to brown. Finish cooking the fish on a grill (not too close to the coals); let the tuna roast slowly and baste it from time to time with the marinade.

Tonno fresco in tegame con filetto di pomodoro
(Pan-cooked fresh tuna with tomato and red peppers)
(serves 4)

2 lbs fresh tuna, cut into fillets - ½ lb small onions - 1 lb
tomatoes - 1 lb sweet red peppers - parsley - 3 tbsp olive
oil - 1 clove garlic - salt - pepper - ½ cup white wine

A migratory fish, the bluefin tuna arrives in the Mediterranean during the mating season; but the fish find the tuna-boats and their nets waiting for them, and the cyclical ritual of the kill is repeated once more. *Thunnus thynnus*, with its pink flesh and intense flavor, is a food rich in many proteins but also rather fatty, although its fats are polyunsaturated and therefore don't contribute to the buildup of cholesterol.

By far the greatest consumption of tuna is from cans, in which it is packed in oil. But it is also eaten fresh, either grilled or cooked with herbs and vegetables, and it can make a most delicious main course.

Peel the little onions, peel and seed the tomatoes. Crush a garlic clove, fry it in olive oil in a saucepan, and remove it. Brown the tuna fillets on both sides in this oil. Add the onions and tomatoes, and season with salt and pepper. After 10 minutes, pour in the white wine, cover the pan, and continue cooking for 20 minutes over a low flame. Meanwhile roast the peppers - on a grill, if you can; otherwise, under the broiler in the oven. You'll be able to peel them easily this way.

Now slice the peppers into thin strips and dress them with olive oil.

On a serving-platter, place the tuna fillets with the red pepper strips between them. Pour the cooking liquid over the whole and garnish with fresh parsley.

Totani e patate
(Flying squids and potatoes)
(serves 6)

*4 lbs flying squids - 2 lbs potatoes - a little more than
1 lb peeled tomatoes - 1 cup olive oil - 1 cup white
wine - 2 cloves garlic - parsley - hot pepper - salt*

This is one of those dishes that reveal their true flavor and unadulterated fragrance when eaten in a place that's close to the sea.
Heat the olive oil in a saucepan with some cloves of garlic. When the garlic is blonde, remove it. Place the squid in the oil and heat it until it begins to pop. Add the peeled tomatoes and cook for twenty minutes. Add the potatoes cut into chunks. Leave to cook for another twenty minutes. Add salt. Cover with minced parsley before serving. This dish is at its best when it is lukewarm.

Triglie in brodetto
(Red mullets in fish broth)
(serves 4)

*2 ½ lbs red mullets - 1 clove garlic - 2 peeled,
seeded tomatoes - 1 tbsp capers - 1/3 cup green
olives - 2 tbsp olive oil - salt - pepper - minced
parsley*

Clean the fish well and arrange them in a wide skillet, together with the olive oil, the minced garlic clove, the washed capers, the chopped tomatoes, the pitted olives, the salt, the pepper, the minced parsley, and a little olive oil. Cook covered over moderate heat for about 10 minutes.
To avoid breaking up the fish, do not stir, but shake the skillet often so that the ingredients are well mixed and do not stick to the bottom.

Triglie in cartoccio
(Red mullets in foil)
(serves 6)

4 lbs red mullets - aluminum foil - 4 tbsp olive oil -
garlic - parsley - capers - salt - pepper

Geographical location is an important factor in selecting foods: the red mullets that live in the waters off the rocky Mediterranean coasts are without peer. They should be cooked as simply as possible to bring out their natural, fresh flavor.

In the Middle Ages, people favored very strong tastes, produced by the addition of every sort of condiment and spice. These seasonings were necessary to overcome any unpleasantness that may have arisen from imperfectly preserved ingredients. Today, on the other hand, we try to rediscover the true flavor of foods, without masks and subterfuges. As Paul Bocuse has said: *Culinary fashion has undergone the same evolutionary process as women's fashion. Women haven't worn corsets for some time, and many of them don't even wear brassieres anymore. In the past, when you started to undress a woman, you had no idea what discoveries lay in store for you. Today, at the moment you order a dish, you know exactly what's going to appear on your plate.* We make a similar guarantee for the following recipe. Use the freshest mullets possible, wash them well and arrange them on sheets of aluminum foil. Into the cleaned stomach cavity of each fish, insert a little garlic minced together with some parsley, add salt and pepper, moisten with some pure olive oil, drop in two or three capers, and close up the foil to form an attractive little package. Pour a cup of water into a heat-resistant baking-dish, and place the foil packets in this. Put the dish in a hot oven for about 15 minutes (the cooking time will depend on the size of your fish). Serve this dish in its silver foil so that each guest can have the pleasure of opening his little package and enjoying the inviting fragrance thus released even before his first bite.

Zuppa di gamberi
(Shrimp soup)
(serves 6)

2 ½ lbs shrimps - carrot - parsley - 2 onions - 1
celery rib - 1 laurel (bay) leaf - hot pepper - salt -
stale bread - 4 tbsp olive oil

They prepare this soup in and around the tiny harbor of Crapolla, a fantastic spot hidden between Nerano and Positano on the Gulf of Salerno. The harbor faces the little Galli Islands, the rocky home of the Sirens (women above the waist and birds below, as depicted by the 19th century Swiss painter Böcklin). More distant, on the right, looms the Isle of Capri, called Caprae by the Romans because of the great number of goats that once lived there.

The buccaneers in the service of the fierce Khair-eddin Pasha Barbarossa, Suleiman the Magnificent's admiral and corsair who sowed panic along these happy coasts in the 16th century, no longer sail these waters.

Early in the morning, only a few fishing boats are still lying in wait for unwary fish, and some of these boats dock at Crapolla, carrying baskets of crustaceans. Boil the shrimps in 2 qts of salted water, along with some aromatic herbs: carrots, parsley, a bay leaf, a celery rib, an onion.

When the shellfish are cooked, peel the tails and put them aside. Pound the shells into a paste. Then sautè a thinly-sliced onion in oil; when the onion is well cooked, add the pounded shells, season with salt, hot pepper, and finely-minced parsley, and then add the water you boiled the crawfish in. Let this stock cook over low heat for about half an hour, then pass it through a fine cloth or a food mill. Toast the bread slices, place them in bowls, and pour the broth over them. Sauté the shrimp's tails in butter or oil, season them with plenty of minced parsley, and add them to the soup.

Zuppa di pesce
(Fish soup or stew)
(serves 8)

*1 scorpion fish, about 1 lb - 1 mullet, about 1 lb - 1
stargazer - 1 jack - 1 moray eel or turbot - the head
of 1 grouper - 1 cuttlefish or squid - 1 lb very small
octopuses - 1 crab - 1 lb chopped tomato - 6 tbsp
olive oil - 3 cloves garlic - ½ cup white wine - hot
pepper - parsley - salt*

There is a common thread in the Mediterranean way of eating, even if the variations differ, requiring saffron and wild fennel in the French *bouillabaisse*, or rice and a yogurt-flour paste, as in the Greek *psarasoupa*, or smoked ham, no less, as in the Spanish *sopa del duelo*, or the clams known as sea truffles, mussels, and coriander seed, as in the Portuguese *caldeirada*; this is a grand dish of Mediterranean popular tradition, frankly coastal in nature, which for centuries has constituted the basic nourishment of sea folk and fishermen.

Zuppa di pesce has its origin, in fact, in the necessity of using fish that are less attractive or less marketable because they're small or excessively bony. If, therefore, none of them deserve the honor of playing a leading role, why not cook them in a soup and enjoy them with crunchy slices of fried bread? The Roman Apicius, as witnesses a recipe of his in *De re coquinaria*, had already taken an interest in cooking the "small fry of the sea," notwithstanding the justified attack on him by the famous gastronome Carême in his books, according to which Apicius promoted a "destructive cuisine" because he drowned every food in *garum* (a sauce obtained by the fermentation of the internal organs of fish with the addition of honey, spices, and wine), thus depriving foods of their original taste.

The most interesting fish soup, which buds our taste, comes from Sorrento. Mussels, because of their too distinctive taste, are excluded; the most tolerable crustacean is the crab; blue fish are not well received because they're too fatty. The basic ingredient is the scorpion fish, ably accompanied by the mullet that the Neapolitans call cuoccio, and by the jack. The moray eel or the turbot may also be called upon, but in discreet quantities, because their flesh is a bit fatty. The grouper is appreciated under the same conditions, in small quantities (using the head produces great results), and the torpedo fish (electric ray) and the stargazer can contribute to good effect.

It's not always possible to find all of the kinds of fish called for; you have to content yourself with whatever the market has that's fresh, and draw upon your own culinary good sense to make sure that no fish with too pronounced a taste exercises tyranny over the whole.

Clean and wash all the fish. Chop the moray eel into small pieces after you skin it patiently. In a wide pot (the fish will clump together in a utensil that's too small, forming steam that will give them a "cottony" texture and endanger their tenderness), sauté the crushed garlic cloves - which you will then remove - the hot pepper, and the crushed crab in the olive oil. Add the little octopuses and the cuttlefish or squid.

Evaporate the liquid they give off, and let all the ingredients brown (or redden) for a while. If they pop intolerably, cover the pot. Next, pour in the white wine. Let this reduce, then add the tomatoes. When the octopuses and the cuttlefish (or squid) are cooked, remove them from the pot and replace them with the grouper head and whatever "small fry of the sea" you have on hand. Cook for about 20 minutes, pouring in a little boiling water if necessary. Remove the fish head and the small fish from the sauce, pass this through a sieve, and put the sieved liquid back into the pot. If the sauce seems too thick, dilute it again with a little hot water.

At this point, add the moray eel and the other fish. Adjust the salt. Cook over low heat for about 15 minutes. Now return the octopuses and the cuttlefish or squid to the pot, and, after a few minutes, serve this marvelous stew sprinkled with minced parsley, and accompany it with toasted or fried pieces of bread.

FRIED FOODS

Frying

There exists a theory of frying foods that Anthelme Brillat-Savarin has eloquently elucidated in his *Physiology of Taste*:

"Well, M. La Planche!" said the professor with that grave tane that penetrates to the very bottom of one's heart, "every one who dines at my table proclaims you a soup-maker of the first class. This is very well, for soup is the first consolation of a hungry stomach; but I am sorry to see that you are uncertain as a fryer.

"I heard you yesterday groan when that magnificent sole was served up to us, pale, flabby, and discolored. My friend Revenaz threw on you a glance of disapproval; M. Henri Roux turned his gnomonic nose to the west, and President Sibuet deplored this failure as a public calamity".

"This misfortune has befallen you because you neglected a theory of which you do not feel the full importance. You are a little obstinate, and I have had some difficulty in making you understand that all the operations of your laboratory are naught but the execution of the eternal laws of nature".

"The liquids that you expose to the action of fire cannot all be charged with the same quantity of heat; nature has given them all various properties; this is an order of things of which Nature alone has the secret, and which is called capacity for caloric".

"Thus you might with impunity dip your finger in boiling spirits of wine, but you would take it out quickly enough from boiling brandy, and quicker still if it were water, whilst a hasty immersion in boiling oil would hurt you cruelly, as the capacity of oil for heat is at least three times that of water.

"It is in consequence of this disposition that we see that hot liquids act in a different manner on the sapid substances that are plunged in them. Those which we treat by water are softened, dissolve and are reduced to rags; and

soup or extracts are thus made. Those, on the contrary, which are treated with oil become contracted, are coloured in a more or less deep manner, and finally are carbonised".

"In the former case, water dissolves and draws out the interior juices of the alimentary substances placed in it; in the second case, these juices are preserved, because oil cannot dissolve them; and if these substances dry up, it is because a continuous heat vaporises the humid parts".

"The two methods have different names, and boiling in oil or grease substances intended to be eaten, is called frying".

"All the merit of a good fry is derived from the 'surprise'; thus they term the invasion of the boiling liquid which at the very instant of the immersion carbonises or browns the external surface of the body placed in it".

"By means of the 'surprise' a sort of vault is formed which encloses the substance, prevents the fat from reaching it, and concentrates the juices, which thus undergo a kind of interior boiling that gives to the food all the taste of which it is susceptible".

"In order that the surprise may take place, the boiling liquid should have acquired heat enough for its action to be sharp and instantaneous; but it only reaches that point when it has been a considerable time on a brisk and blazing fire."

After Brillat-Savarin's words, I don't believe there can be anything to add; it will be sufficient to follow his counsels in order to produce fried foods worthy of their name.

Arancini con salsa di pomodoro
(Rice croquettes with tomato sauce)
(serves 6)

1 ½ cups rice - 2 eggs – ½ cup grated Parmesan – 3 ½ lb cream cheese or mozzarella - 3 oz prosciutto cotto - flour as needed - grated breadcrumbs - salt - pepper - oil for frying
For the sauce: 1 lb peeled tomatoes - garlic - salt - basil - 2 tbsp olive oil

These are little golden balls, crunchy on the outside, but revealing on the inside a pure, white soul, swimming in a flood of tomato sauce powdered with good grated Parmesan cheese.

Boil the rice in a sufficient amount of water in order that the rice will absorb all the water. Season to taste with salt and pepper. Add an egg and let the mixture cool in the fridge.

Now dampen your hands a little in water. Take a small amount of the cooled rice mixture between your palms and form it into a hemisphere. In the center of each half-sphere, put a bit of the ingredients listed above: mozzarella and prosciutto, chopped very small, and some of the grated Parmesan.

Cover this with an equal amount of rice so that you're now holding a small sphere, like a "little orange" (arancino). Dredge these very lightly in flour. Beat the remaining egg. Dip the spheres ("croquettes") into the egg, pass them through the grated breadcrumbs, and fry them in plenty of oil. The oil should at first be very hot, so that, thanks to the element of "surprise," a crunchy crust is formed around each croquette. Then reduce the heat slightly so that the croquettes cook on the inside, too, and the cheese melts; when you cut the croquettes, a thread of cheese should wind itself around your fork and follow its movement.

Put the croquettes on some paper towels and serve them at once, very hot, accompanied by some tomato sauce and some more grated Parmesan. Every guest will add some of each to his croquette after slicing it in half.

To make the simple sauce, proceed as follows: in a broad skillet, brown a clove of garlic in oil. Once the garlic has browned, remove it and add nearly a pound of peeled, seeded tomatoes. Season with salt and basil, and let this cook for 20 minutes.

Arancini di riso
(Rice croquettes)
(serves 8)

2 ½ cups rice - 1 ½ qts broth - 3 tbsp butter - 1 small onion - salt - pepper - ½ cup grated Parmesan - 1/3 lb mozzarella - 3 eggs - flour - grated breadcrumbs - vegetable frying oil

First of all, prepare a risotto in the classic style: sauté a small, finely chopped onion in some butter. When the onion has faded, add the rice and toast it for a bit.

Continue cooking it, pouring in a little at a time the stock that you will keep at boiling point and ready to hand. Stop cooking the rice while it's still rather al dente (about 17 minutes). Then add salt, pepper, 1 beaten egg, plenty of grated Parmesan, and the mozzarella in very tiny dice. Stir this in well so that the mozzarella melts. Let the mixture cool.

Beat the remaining eggs, then shape the cooled rice into balls the size of small oranges (arancini), dredge these in flour, dip them into the eggs, then into the grated breadcrumbs, and fry them in plenty of hot vegetable oil.

Calzone alla napoletana
(Neapolitan-style prosciutto and cheese fry)
(serves 6)

4 cups flour - 1 cup milk - 1 tbsp active dry yeast - pepper - 7 oz ricotta - 2 eggs - 7 oz mozzarella - ¼ lb prosciutto or salami - 1 generous cup grated Parmesan - oil for frying

Another typical Neapolitan dish is the calzone, a parcel made of leavened dough rolled out into a sheet (not too thin), filled with mozzarella, ricotta and salami or prosciutto, closed up, and fried or oven-baked.

The leavened dough is the same as for pizze fritte (p. 265); that is, for every 4 1/2 cups of sifted flour you need about 1 cup of milk. Dissolve the yeast in the warmed milk with a little salt.

After the dough rises, cut it and roll it into several little discs. Place in the center of each disc the following: mix together the mozzarella, ricotta, eggs, grated Parmesan, salt, pepper, and the salami or prosciutto cut into tiny dice. Close each *calzone* in the shape of a half-moon. Seal its edges well with a little egg so that the filling won't escape during the cooking. Fry the calzone in plenty of hot oil until it becomes puffy and golden.

Calzone con cipolle
(Onion and cheese pie)
(serves 6)

*4 cups flour - 1 tbsp active dry yeast - 1 cup
lukewarm water - salt - 4 tbsps olive oil - 2 lbs
onions - 4 ripe tomatoes - basil - parsley - 2 eggs –
ground pepper - 1 generous cup grated pecorino -
3 ½ oz mozzarella*

In Apulia, this dish is traditionally prepared on the first day of Lent. A square sheet of dough is rolled out, and half its surface is covered with filling. The two halves are then folded together, thus obtaining the shape of a calzone or "trouser leg."

Mix together the yeast with some water, then add the flour, salt, olive oil, and enough lukewarm water to form a rather soft bread dough. Let it rise for about thirty minutes, so that it will puff up well when baked.

Meanwhile, prepare the stuffing. Slice the onions and keep them in water up to an hour to take some of the "edge" off their taste. Drain them and put them in a skillet with plenty of oil and a few pinches of salt. Stir often. The onion should lose all its liquid and become transparent. Now add 3 or 4 chopped, peeled, ripe tomatoes, some basil, and some parsley. When the tomato is cooked, add 2 eggs (beat them with some salt first), some pepper, and a big handful of grated pecorino. When the egg is well blended with the rest, remove the pan from the fire and let it cool.

While you're waiting, roll out the dough and line a greased bakingpan with a sheet of it. Pour over this the onion-tomato mixture and some diced mozzarella. Cover this with another sheet of dough. Prick the dough with a fork. Then, bake the *calzone* in the oven until it turns golden brown. A variation of the stuffing substitutes for the eggs and the mozzarella 2 salted anchovies, washed and boned, and some pitted black olives, the whole blended completely with the onions.

Cotolettine nuvola
(Soft-as-a-cloud cutlets)
(serves 4)

Rather more than 1 lb chicken breast - 2 cups grated breadcrumbs - 2 eggs - 2 tbsp flour - ½ cup milk - oil for frying

No matter what aspect of these little cutlets you consider - their minuscule size, their tenderness, their appearance - they make a truly sensual combination whose excellence is assured.
First remove gristle and fat from the meat, pound it, and soak it in a bowl with 2 beaten eggs. Then dredge it in the grated breadcrumbs, pressing firmly with the meat pounder to make sure that the crumbs adhere perfectly.
Now prepare the batter. In a rather large container, place 2 egg yolks and the flour. Mix thoroughly, adding as much milk as needed to produce a batter that's not too thick. Beat the egg whites until stiff and fold them gently into the batter, making sure that they don't collapse. Dip the little cutlets, a few at a time, into the batter until they're completely impregnated with it. Then fry them in hot oil in a large skillet and let them drain on absorbent paper.

"Crocchè" di patate
(Potato croquettes)
(serves 6)

2 lbs potatoes - ¼ cup butter - salt - pepper - nutmeg - 2 eggs + 2 egg yolks - ½ cup grated Parmesan - ½ cup grated pecorino - 3 ½ oz mozzarella - flour - grated breadcrumbs - vegetable oil for frying

Peel the potatoes, chop them into pieces, cover them with cold water, and boil them. Pass them through a food mill. Cook the puréed potatoes until they give up their moisture and come away from the sides of the saucepan.

Season the purée with salt, pepper, nutmeg, butter, and the grated cheeses. Add 2 egg yolks. Shape small portions of this mixture into little balls or croquettes. Make a hole in the center of each and fill it with a bit of finely-chopped mozzarella. Close up each croquette. Dredge them with flour. Beat 2 eggs and dip the croquettes into them, then roll the croquettes in the grated breadcrumbs. Finally, fry these tidbits in plenty of hot vegetable oil.

Crochette di riso
(Rice cakes with meat)
(serves 6/8)

2 ½ cups rice - 4 tbsp grated Parmesan - ½ lb ground or minced meat - 3 eggs - 2 cups grated breadcrumbs - oil for frying - salt

Cook the rice as though to make an ordinary risotto, but don't let it get soft. Season with grated Parmesan. Brown the meat in a skillet with a little oil and mix it into the rice.

Spread this mixture out to an even thickness on a plate. When the mixture is cool, use a glass or cookie cutter to cut out many little discs.

Dip these in the beaten eggs, then roll in the grated breadcrumbs. Fry the little cakes in boiling oil, drain them well, place them on absorbent paper, and serve them hot.

Fiori di glicine
(Wisteria flowers)

Wisteria flowers - flour - salt - oil for frying

Wisteria or wistaria belongs to the genus of the same name and to the family *Papilionaceae*; "Wisteria" generally designates *Wistaria sinensis*, sometimes known also as "floribunda." Originally from China, this vine has droopy, pinnately-compound leaves and purple-blue flowers gathered in long, pendent clusters. In the beginning of spring, these flowers open before the leaves appear. Wisteria is one of the most beloved of plants, both for its soft clusters of flowers and for the sweet, spicy perfume they breathe into the air night and day.

For the pleasure of astonishing our guests, we've taken our inspiration from the end of the 18th century and the beginning of the 19th, a gastronomical period that saw the development of a rather ethereal taste for dishes whose principal ingredients were flowers.

Dust the flowers lightly with flour. Just before frying them, dip them in a very light batter composed of flour, water, and a pinch of salt. Fry them in plenty of moderately hot vegetable oil, and remove them while they're still a pale golden color.

Fiori di zucchini
(Zucchini blossoms)
(serves 6)

12 zucchini flowers - 1 cup flour - ½ cup milk – ½ tbsp active dry yeast- salt - 1 egg - 1 tbsp grated Parmesan - oil for frying

Mix the yeast in the milk. To prepare the batter, place the flour in a bowl, then add the milk with the yeast, mixing well with a fork to eliminate any lumps.

The mixture should be smooth and creamy. Now add an egg, a generous pinch of salt, and 1 tbsp. grated Parmesan. Stir. Using a fork and a spoon, dip the flowers in the batter so that it covers them completely, like a second skin. Drop them, enclosed in their batter, into the moderately hot cooking oil. Vapors and perfumes will be released into the air as the flowers puff up in the cooking oil.

Naturally, the zucchini flowers must be absolutely fresh; if you've just picked them in your garden, so much the better (*ça va sans dire*).

Serve them immediately, golden, puffy, and very hot.

Frittelle alle alghe
(Seaweed fritters)
(serves 6)

1 pinch stiff, dried ulva or sea lettuce (a kind of edible seaweed) - 1 cup water - 1 ½ cups flour - 2 eggs - 2 tbsp grated Parmesan - 7 oz shelled shrimps - 1/2 cup milk - 1 tbsp active dry yeast - salt

Seaweed is a daily food in many oriental countries; the idea of using it in the kitchen seems to have reached Naples in the l9th century. Most commonly, sea lettuce (*Ulva lactuga*) is used as a basic ingredient for fritters with *cicenielli* (see p. 219) - plankton-like organisms which are actually tiny white marine fish, about one centimeter long - or, if these are unavailable, with shrimps. The uses of seaweed are many and variable, as are the forms it takes. Agar-agar, a natural gelatinous extractive prepared from *Gelidium corneum*, a red alga with a high content of alginate, is used as a gelling and stabilizing agent in ice cream, gelatine, and bouillon cubes.

Life had its origins in the sea. Algae, including seaweed, contain minerals in large quantities: calcium, iron, potassium, iodine (almost impossible to find in nature, except in the sea), and magnesium. Algae also contain vitamins and proteins, and their fat content is quite low. These days, we're witnessing a return to the use of natural foods, and that includes marine algae. The delicacy of sea lettuce, combined with other ingredients in a proper balance and carefully cooked, produces a dish that's both very tasty and quite nutritious.

Our marine vegetables are used after being dried or freeze-dried by a process of sublimation and then reduced into very light flakes.

Only a very small quantity of dried seaweed is necessary, therefore, for the preparation of our fritters. When water is added, seaweed regains its soft, moist appearance.

Now add the flour to the sea lettuce and water. Continue to blend everything together as you add the eggs, the grated Parmesan, the shelled shrimp, and, lastly, the yeast, which you have dissolved in the milk. Let this mixture stand for about half an hour, then start frying this creamy paste, a tablespoon at a time, in plenty of very hot vegetable oil. When the fritters are golden, place them on absorbent paper and eat them while they're hot.

There are all sorts of batters used to wrap all sorts of foods in an inviting, golden mantle. Vegetables and fish are prepared in various batters, more or less thick, even transparent as Japanese do for their tempura.

Frittelle di cavolfiore
(Cauliflower Fritters)
(serves 6)

1 cauliflower - flour as needed - egg as needed -
salt - vegetable oil for frying

A native of the eastern Mediterranean regions, the cauliflower, with its dense clusters and heavy leaves, can serve as an ornament as well as a food. Break up the cauliflower into single flowers with very short stems. Discard the tougher stem parts and the leaves. Boil the flowers for 7- 8 minutes. Cool them, then cut them into small slices, flour them, dip them into egg beaten with salt, and fry them.

Serve them very hot.

Frittelle di cervella
(Brain fritters)
(serves 6)

1 lb veal brain - 2 tbsp vinegar - parsley - 2 eggs - 1
heaped tbsp flour - 2 tbsp milk - vegetable oil for
frying - salt & pepper

First of all, carefully clean the brains of any blood residue by washing them under cold running water. Then plunge them for a few minutes into boiling water seasoned with vinegar, parsley, and a pinch of salt. After they cool, chop them into pieces.

While you're waiting for the brains to cool, prepare the batter as for *Cotolettine nuvola* (p. 256). In a bowl, blend the egg yolks first with the flour and then with the milk to obtain a smooth batter that's not too thick. Add the stifflybeaten egg whites. Pour the chopped brains into the batter. Use a tablespoon to move them, a little at a time, to the hot oil.

Thanks to the surprise that Brillat-Savarin talks about, the batter around the chopped brain pieces will condense and gradually turn golden, but the meat it contains will be safe from the aggression of the hot oil, which can't penetrate to it, and thus the food will retain all possible taste.

Involtini di melanzane in bianco
(Fried eggplant rolls in white)
(serves 4)

1 lb Italian eggplants - oil for frying - basil - ½ lb mozzarella - flour - salt

To prepare these rolls, cut the eggplants into rather thin slices. Soak in salted water for at least 1 hour. Remove, squeeze, and dry. Fry them until barely golden; remove to paper towels. Then wrap each slice around a cube of mozzarella and a basil leaf with a pinch of salt. Flour lightly and refry these rolls so that the mozzarella dissolves and forms a single whole with the eggplant.

You can also warm them in the oven just for few minutes instead of frying the second time.

Melanzane farcite alla sorrentina
(Sorrento-style stuffed eggplant)
(serves 6)

2 lbs Italian eggplants - 3 eggs - 10 oz ricotta - 2 tbsp grated Parmesan - salt - flour - 2 tbsp crumbled pan di Spagna - cinnamon - oil for frying

This is a very old Sorrentine recipe, surely Arab in origin, it retains its combination of contrasting flavors by mixing the sweet pan di Spagna with the piquant taste of the eggplant.

Blend in a bowl the eggs, the ricotta, 2 or 3 tbsp. grated Parmesan, a pinch of salt, a pinch of cinnamon and a little crumbled pan di Spagna, and you'll obtain a creamy mixture.

Peel the eggplants, cut them into slices, and flour these. Dip them into the egg mixture and fry them. When a slice turns golden, spoon some filling onto it while it's still in the skillet, cover it with another fried eggplant slice, and let this cook for a few seconds until the parts merge into a single whole. Serve these hot.

Mozzarella in carrozza
(Fried mozzarella sandwiches)

Sliced bread - flour - milk - eggs - salt - mozzarella - oil for frying

A simple, tasty, everyday dish from the Naples area, *Mozzarella in carrozza* ("Mozzarella in a Carriage") consists of a slice of mozzarella between 2 slices of bread, floured, dipped in egg, and then fried in abundant oil.

Remove the crusts from the square bread slices. Cut them into 2 or 4 well-shaped pieces. Dip their edges in milk, then dredge the slices in flour.

Next, dip each piece entirely into the egg (beaten with a pinch of salt). Place each piece on a plate. Make sandwiches by placing a slice of mozzarella between two pieces of bread that have undergone the treatment described. Now dip these little tidbits into the egg once again before plunging them into plenty of hot vegetable oil. Cook on both sides. Eat them piping hot, after the mozzarella has formed a soft, single entity with the bread.

Palline di mozzarella
(Little mozzarella bites)
(serves 4)

1 ½ lbs mozzarella - 3 egg yolks - a pinch of pepper - salt - 3 tbsp flour - oil for frying

Cut the mozzarella into tiny pieces and place them in a large bowl.

Mix in the egg yolks, the flour, the salt and the pepper, and make little balls the size of a small nut.
Dust these very lightly with flour and fry them in hot oil.
Serve at once.

"Panelle"
(Chick-pea cakes)
(serves 6)

2 ½ cups chick-pea (garbanzo bean) flour - olive oil
- salt - oil for frying

The Arab influence is apparent in this Sicilian dish and you can find analogies to it in Madrid, in the labyrinth of narrow streets that characterize the old Arab quarter around the Plaza Mayor. The history of the Spaniards and that of the Arabs is often interwoven.
Before arriving in Sicily as conquerors, the Spanish, like the Sicilians, had in fact gone through a period of Arab domination.
Panelle, tasty fried flat cakes made from chick-pea flour, are a speciality of the fry-cooks of Palermo, like *cazzilli* (little potato croquettes) or *quaglie* (fried eggplant sticks).
Put the chick-pea flour into a saucepan and add enough water - about 1 ½ quarts - to obtain a thick batter. Turn on the heat, stirring continuously (always in the same direction) until the mixture boils. When you've obtained a thick, creamy paste, oil a marble or other non-porous work surface with olive oil and pour the batter onto it.
Using a spatula, spread the batter to a uniform thickness of about ½ inch or less. Let this cool. Cut the flour mixture into rhombuses or strips or squares, and fry them in boiling oil. Sprinkle with salt and serve very hot.

Panzarotti
(Fried turnovers)
(serves 6/8)

3 cups flour - 1 tbsp active dry yeast - 2 tbsp butter - salt & pepper - 1 cup milk - basil - 1 lb mozzarella - oil for frying

Fried panzarotti, made with a light, barely risen dough, are airy, crunchy, delightful, and gay. Fried foods, like pizzas and pasta, are among the classic attractions of Neapolitan cuisine, those which most contribute to good humor. Sift the flour onto your work surface. Make a mound with a well in the center, and into this pour the softened butter, the yeast dissolved in a cup of milk, and salt and white pepper to taste. Work into a soft dough, adding water if necessary. Break off a piece of dough, roll it out into a sheet, and mark on this sheet (without cutting the dough) the shape you want your panzarotti to take.

In the center of this outline place a fresh basil leaf, then a small slice of mozzarella (best if made the preceding day, because it will have lost a good part of its milk thus reduced the possibility that some might inconveniently escape into the frying oil). Now place another sheet of dough over the first and join them together with light pressure from your fingertips. To stick the dough brush it with some water.

Cut out the panzarotti, using the same cutter you used to mark the bottom sheet, and transfer them to a plate covered with a towel sprinkled with flour, so that you can remove them quickly when the time comes to fry them.

For successful frying, its necessary that the objects in question be completely immersed in oil that has been brought to a lively temperature. After frying, place the panzarotti on absorbent paper to get rid of as much excess oil as possible. Send the turnovers to the table at once.

Pizze fritte
(Fried pizzas)
(serves 6)

For the dough: 3 ½ cups flour - 1 oz Brewer's yeast - ½ cup water - ½ cup milk - 2 tbsps olive oil - 1 tsp salt - oil for frying
For the sauce: 2 tbsp olive oil - 1 clove garlic - 1 lb ripe tomatoes - salt - oregano - basil - grated Parmesan

The French arrived in Naples some time before pizza and macaroni did. The Neapolitans ate lots of vegetables, so remarkably that their transalpine visitors nicknamed them "leaf-eaters." As always, necessity exerts pressure on the imagination and produces distinguished results. A felicitous gastronomical intuition, born out of the imagination of the Neapolitan people, is the pizza, which requires but a few ingredients: originality, simplicity, taste and fragrance.

It's useful to note that pizza is even a prudent way to combat a sudden drop in blood sugar.

In the intricate warren of tiny Neapolitan streets is where you taste the best pizzas, folded in four (*a libretto*, "like a little book"), offering an irresistible combination of flavor, good fellowship, liveliness, and joy. Behind his marble counter, the pizza-maker demonstrates skills worthy of a juggler, slinging the pizza from one hand to the other, tossing it in the air and catching it gracefully with a deft circular movement of his hands, stretching and pulling it into the form of a perfect circle.

The white, red, and green "pizza Margherita" was invented by Raffaele Esposito, owner of the pizzeria "Pietro e basta così" ("Peter and that's enough"), on January 11, 1889. Queen Margherita, much beloved by her people, asked for something special on that day, perhaps to console herself for the lack of affection shown her by her spouse, King Umberto, who was extraordinarily busy in the alcove bedroom of the Duchess Eugenia Litta di Monza. So it was that Esposito, shunning the traditional pizza with garlic, oregano, and anchovies, invented pizza with mozzarella, tomato, and basil - a stunningly patriotic choice of colors, since Margherita was considered the real political force of the House of Savoy. It was she, in fact, aided by the authoritarian Francesco Crispi, who initiated the colonization of Abyssinia. And the white, red, and green pizza, through its appeal to the taste buds, has continued to colonize the world. But the odyssey of the pizza begins in the remote past. It's connected to the war between good and evil that ensued in Greek myth when Hades, whom the Romans called Pluto, the god of the underworld, abducted Persephone, Ceres's most beautiful daughter. The mother, disconsolate and distraught, began a long journey in search of her daughter. Unrecognized, she reached Eleusis and the house of King Celeus and his wife Metaneira, whose youngest son, Triptolemus, for lack of his mother's milk was about to die. Ceres-Demeter, in compensation for the hospitality shown her, made the infant vigorous again and burned up the seed of old age in him, thus rendering him immortal. And Metaneira offered Ceres a goblet of wine sweeter than honey; but the goddess refused it, asking instead for a drink of water mixed with flour and perfumed with basil. *"The worshipful goddess accepted it: this was the beginning of the rite."*

In the course of the centuries, this drink, thanks to opportune changes in its preparation, became a solid food, but its mythical ingredients remained intact. The amount of flour was increased, oil was added to it, and it was exposed to the flame; thus what the Greeks call *plax* ("flat surface," "flat cake," or "pie") was born. Such "cakes" found great popularity in Pompeii. There, among the ruins of the Via dell'Abbondanza, you can see some shops that still have their little stone brackets with bowls for cheese and jugs or pots for oil. The digs have even turned up a little statue whose configuration shows that it represents a pizza-maker. But pizza baked in an oven and handled with the aid of a wooden shovel, though a typical and delicious product of Neapolitan cuisine, is not the only kind of pizza. Today people use a home variation, quicker to prepare, suitable for kitchens that lack a wood stove - city kitchens, for example. All you need is a burner. Use a bit more than 1 lb of flour and sift it into the shape of a mound on your work surface. Make a well in the center. Dissolve the yeast and some salt in about a cup of milk and water and pour this into the well. Add the olive oil. Using a fork, blend everything together, moving from the center outward, slowly making the flour absorb the liquid and vice versa. Let the resulting dough rest for about an hour in a warm place away from air currents. It will double the volume.

During this time, you can make the sauce that's going to dress the pizzas. Put some oil in a saucepan and sauté a garlic clove in it over moderate heat.

When the oil has absorbed the fragrance of the garlic, remove the latter and replace it with the tomatoes (cherry tomatoes are a good choice), a pinch of salt, and some oregano. Let all this cook together for 10 minutes.

Divide the risen dough into as many little balls as the little pizzas you want to make. Roll these out into small circles or discs, fry them in plenty of hot vegetable oil, then transfer them to absorbent paper. Pour the sauce onto them one at a time, starting from the center and being careful not to let it overflow the edges.

A sprinkle of freshlygrated Parmesan and a little basil leaf or two will give the pizzas the finishing tricolor touch. It goes without saying that these, like all fried foods, should be eaten piping hot.

"Ramacchè" al prosciutto
(Béchamel ham croquettes)
(serves 6)

2 oz butter - 1/3 cup flour - 1 cup milk - salt & pepper -
nutmeg - 4 egg yolks - ½ cup grated Parmesan - 3 ½ oz
prosciutto cotto - oil for frying

These unusual, crunchy mouthfuls are reminiscent of the French cuisine that the *monzù* (as the Neapolitans called the French *monsieurs*) imported into our southern regions.

Prepare a rather thick béchamel sauce as follows: melt the butter over low heat, remove it from the heat, and blend the flour in well; then pour in the warm milk, a little at a time, so that you get a creamy mixture. Season with salt, pepper, and nutmeg. Return to the stove and cook over a weak flame, stirring continuously with a wooden spoon until boiling point is reached.

Remove from heat. When the béchamel is cool, add to it the egg yolks, a big handful of grated Parmesan, and the prosciutto, diced tiny. Stir and let the mixture cool completely. Use a small dessert spoon to transfer the mixture to oil that's hot but not boiling. The result will be many little croquettes or ramacchè.

When they're cooked on one side, flip them over so that they become a uniform goldenblond color. Serve them very hot.

"Scagliozzi"
(Cornflour cakes)
(serves 8)

3 ½   cups yellow corn flour - 2 qts water - salt - 2
tbsp butter - 3 tbsp grated Parmesan - oil for frying
- flour as needed

Neapolitan *scagliozzi* are similar to Sicilian *panelle*. They're great as a side-dish for Sweet and Sour Rabbit - the combination is rich and delicious.

This is how Rosaura explains to Harlequin in Carlo Goldoni's play *"Donne di garbo"* (The Gracious Ladies) the procedure to follow in making polenta.

"We fill up a lovely pot with water and put it over the flame. When the water begins to murmur, I take some of that beautiful golden powder called yellow flour, and bit by bit I add it to the pot. Then I toss in, in order, a goodly portion of fresh, yellow, delicate butter, and an equal amount of rich, yellow, well-grated cheese."

Polenta, in this rich version, is delicious even by itself; but when there's some left over, it's terrific cut into slices and fried or grilled as a handy accompaniment for beef stews.

Now, when the water begins to "murmur," pour in the yellow corn flour and let it cook for 20 minutes, stirring constantly. Season with salt, 2 tbsp butter, and some good grated cheese, and turn this polenta-like mixture out onto a lightly oiled non-porous work surface. When the polenta has cooled, cut it into squares (or into whatever shape you'd like), flour these lightly, shake off the excess flour, fry the cakes in hot oil, and serve them immediately. They should appear slightly crunchy on the outside and soft on the inside.

CHEESE-BASED DISHES

Brioche alla napoletana guarnita
(Naples-style fancy brioche)
(serves 6/8)

4 cups flour - ½ cup butter - 3 eggs - 1 tbsp active dry yeast - ½ cup milk - 1 tsp sugar - ½ cup grated Parmesan - ½ cup provolone cheese (diced) - 1 cup shelled peas - 7 oz prosciutto crudo - onion - parsley - salt - pepper - 2 tbsp olive oil

In a bowl dissolve the yeast in the warm milk. Mix in a little of the flour so that you obtain a dough that's neither too soft nor too stiff. Place this in a warm spot to rise.

When the dough has doubled in volume, mound the rest of the flour onto your work surface, make a hole in the center, and break the 3 eggs into it, together with a pinch of salt, a teaspoon of sugar, the softened butter, the grated Parmesan, the provolone in tiny dice, and, finally, half of the prosciutto, cut into small pieces.

Mix briefly, then add the yeast dough. Work all these ingredients well together for about 10 minutes. Grease a round tube pan with butter, dust it with a little flour, and turn the mixture into it.

When the dough has risen again, bake the brioche in a moderate (340° F) oven for 40 minutes.

When the brioche has cooled, turn it onto a serving-platter and fill the central hole with the peas, prepared as follows. Pour some oil into a saucepan, slice an onion (a young or spring onion is best) very thinly, and cook it. When the onion is soft, add the remaining half of the prosciutto, chopped into small pieces, and then, after a minute, the shelled peas and 1/2 cup water.

Let this cook for 20 minutes, then salt it, sprinkle it with minced fresh parsley, add to the brioche as described, and serve.

Brioche rustica
(Peasant brioche)
(serves 8)

4 cups flour - ½ lb. potatoes - 1 tbsp active dry yeast - 2 eggs - 1 cup milk - 7 tbsp butter - salt - 2/3 cup grated pecorino cheese - 5 oz mozzarella - 7 oz soft cheese (cacioprovola or Swiss or fontina) - 7 oz prosciutto cotto or mortadella

To make a Naples-style peasant brioche for 8 people, you take 4 cups flour and amalgamate it with the boiled potatoes after passing them through a sieve or food mill. You should also add the yeast and some salt (both dissolved in the warm milk), the butter, and part of the grated cheese (pecorino, or, if you want a lighter brioche, Parmesan).

Once you've obtained a soft dough, roll it out into a fairly thick sheet, about 1 inch. On this sheet of dough, place the filling, a mixture made of diced mozzarella, the soft cheese (also chopped into small pieces), the prosciutto (or mortadella, if you prefer), and the rest of the grated cheese. Roll up the sheet of dough around the filling and join the edges. Make this into a sort of ring-shaped bun and place it to rise in a round tube pan previously greased with butter and uniformly sprinkled with flour. The dough should be only half as high as the sides of the pan. It will rise in about an hour, depending on the temperature in your kitchen, the air currents, and the time of year.

Normally, the brioche can be considered well risen when the dough springs immediately back from the indentation left in it by finger.

Bake the brioche, at this point, in a hot oven until it becomes a lovely golden color; this should take about 35 minutes or a bit more.

"Coniglio all'argentiere"
("Silversmith's rabbit")
(serves 4)

1 lb fresh caciocavallo cheese or provolone - 2 tbsp
olive oil - 1 tbsp vinegar - 1 clove garlic - 1 tsp
oregano - salt & pepper

The English jokingly call a slice of cheese melted on toast "Welsh rarebit" or "Welsh rabbit." Even though such a combination isn't nearly as substantial as a real rabbit; this snack is certainly an invitation to share a drink, and to accompany a glass of wine. In Sicily, the story goes that once there was a silversmith, perhaps a bit of a miser, but certainly fortunate in his most beautiful wife. She had the ability to elicit the most enticing aromas from the humblest dishes, so successfully that she could permit herself the luxury of calling her productions by names other than their own. Thus a modest cheese dish became for her "Silversmith's Rabbit," and her neighbors would think that only luxury dishes were good enough for the silversmith's household. The required cheese is fresh, white caciocavallo. Cut it into slices about half inch thick. Place these in small pans, as many as the number of diners.Rub a peeled, crushed garlic clove on the cheese, sprinkle it with some oregano, add a few drops of vinegar and lots of salt and pepper. Finally, pour in some good olive oil and 1 tbsp. water for each little pan.
Place over very low heat, and let the cheese melt. This should be served very hot.

Fagottini al formaggio con pasta sfoglia
(Short pastry with cheese)
(serves 6)

*For the short pastry: 2 cups flour - 9 tbsp butter –
salt, water as needed
Filling: 3 ½ oz mozzarella - 3 ½ oz Emmenthal - 3
½ oz caciottina or ricotta - 2 egg whites - 2 oz
prosciutto - basil - salt & pepper - nutmeg*

Extremely light, crunchy pastries enclosing a pure white mixture of various cheeses. Solidly-beaten egg whites make this dish particularly airy.

These little cheese pastries are at their best, of course, when you use good, fresh cheeses; for example, the caciottina and the mozzarella that you can find in such places as Sant'Agata sui Due Golfi (overlooking the two gulfs of Naples and Salerno) or Sorrento.

To prepare the short pastry, make a mound of the flour on your work surface and blend in salted lukewarm water until you obtain a smooth, well-worked dough. Use a rolling pin to roll out the dough into a rather thin layer, brush it liberally with some of the butter, and then roll up the sheet of dough onto itself as though to form a cylinder. Wrap the dough in thin tissue paper and put it in the refrigerator for at least 1/2 hour.

After you remove the tissue paper, roll the cylinder of dough up upon itself again, then roll the dough out with a rolling-pin as before. The dough will begin to show the markings of a concentric spiral. Brush the sheet of dough with some more butter, roll it up again into a cylinder, and then roll the cylinder up upon itself.

Let the dough stand in the refrigerator again for 2 minutes. Then repeat the whole operation one final time; the pastry dough is now ready for use.

Roll it out into a rather thin sheet, from which you will cut out about 20 squares. You will shape these around the filling into an equal number of delicate fagottini (little parcels).

For the filling, chop into tiny pieces and mix together in a bowl the caciottina, the grated Emmenthal, the mozzarella, and the prosciutto, together with the minced basil and the very stiffly-beaten egg whites. Season with salt, pepper, and a couple of grates of nutmeg.

Close the pastry squares around the filling, brushing the edges with some egg yolk, and cook your little parcels in a 350° F oven for about 20 minutes.

Pasticcio rustico
(Peasant's pie)
(serves 6/8)

4 cups flour - 1 cup lukewarm water - 1 tbsp active dry yeast - 2 tbsp butter or lard - salt & pepper - a bit more than 1 lb ricotta - 8 eggs - 5 oz salami – the zest of 1 lemon

Make the dough as usual: mound the flour with a well in the center, add the butter or lard and the yeast dissolved with some salt in the lukewarm water. Work into a dough, then roll out into a rather thin sheet. Butter and lightly flour one or two baking-pans and line it (or them) with the sheet of dough. Prepare the filling with the sieved ricotta, the egg yolks, the diced salami, the grated peel of a fresh, aromatic lemon, salt, pepper, and, lastly, the stiffly-beaten egg whites.

Pour this mixture onto the sheet of dough and cover it with another thin sheet of dough. Brush with a beaten egg and cook in a moderate oven for about 1/2 hour.

Pizza rustica
(Peasant's pizza)
(serves 6)

Dough : 2 cups flour - 7 tbsp butter - 1 egg - salt -
1 tsp sugar - a pinch of self raising powder
Filling: 6 eggs - 1 lb mozzarella - 3 ½ oz prosciutto
cotto (or ½ cup sultana raisins)

Mound the flour on your work surface, make a well in the center, add all the other ingredients. Mix until you get a smooth, soft dough. Use a rolling pin to roll out the pasta into a rather thin sheet, and line a pizza pan or pie pan with it.

In a bowl, blend the beaten eggs with salt as desired, the mozzarella cut into the tiny dice, and the prosciutto chopped into small pieces (if you use sultana raisins instead, plump them first in lukewarm water).

Cover your pie with another sheet of dough, brush it with egg, and bake until golden (about 30 minutes) in a 400°F oven.

Tortano
(Lard bread)
(serves 6/8)

4 cups flour - 1 ½ cup warm water - 1 tbsp yeast - 5 oz lard - ¼ cup greated parmesan cheese - ½ cup provolone cheese - 2 oz salame - 2 oz crackling: scraps of pork fat or bacon - 6 eggs - pepper & salt

The Neapolitan "tortano" is the ancestor of savoury buns, although the latter are certainly a more refined interpretation. The tortano's original recipe called for the use of crackling or pork fat scraps, but these need to have been prepared at home by squeezing out the grease from the scraps left over after preparing lard.

Pour the yeast with a little warm water and a pinch of salt into a mixing bowl and add enough flour to obtain a soft well-worked dough which must be left to leaven, covered by a cloth, in a warm place for about half an hour or until it has increased in volume.

Place the dough on the work surface and add all the rest of the flour, the lard (leaving a little aside to grease the baking pan) and knead the dough energetically, adding warm water if necessary, to form a very firm dough.

On the work surface roll out a rectangular shape, sprinkling it with small cubes of provolone cheese and salame, two hard boiled eggs which have been cut into segments, together with the crackling, the parmesan cheese and lots of pepper. Roll up the dough to from a cylinder and then join the ends to make a ring shaped loaf.

Grease a smooth sided tube baking pan very well and place the tortano into this. Leave aside to rise again.

During the Easter period, this loaf is decorated with eggs and is called *"casatiello"*. Once the loaf has risen, use fingertips to make four small indentations. Four whole uncooked fresh eggs should be washed and placed in the indentations. The eggs are held in place with small crosses made of strips of dough. They will cook in the oven whilst the loaf is baking.

The oven must be hot (350°F) and the loaf will need to cook for about forty minutes.

The tortano or casatiello can be eaten either hot or cold.

Palm Sunday is an important occasion when not only tortano is offered around, but also a "palm", which is a sprig of olive tree which has been blessed, as a symbol of peace.

The tradition of the palm, in Sorrento, has a particularly romantic significance with the preparation of exquisite small trees made of sugared almonds.

There is a legend, in fact, which relates that sudden panic spread along the Sorrentine coasts at the announcement of the impending arrival of a Saracen force.

It was Palm Sunday, and many of the faithful were in church; the priest who was saying the Mass counseled them to be calm and to continue praying. When the Mass was over, the congregation discovered that the Saracens ship had foundered, and that a young girl was the sole survivor. Around her neck she wore a small bag of sugared almonds.

DESSERTS

Description of a Buffet

In the 18th century, the Golden Age of pastry-making in France, Carême, the great connoisseur of the various European culinary traditions and a reformer in the delicate art of enthralling and delighting the taste buds with unforgettable flavors, maintained that *"There exist five fine arts: painting, poetry, music, sculpture, and architecture, of which the principal branch is pastry-making"*.

The sensitive, jaded creatures of that era needed diets that were light, coddling, soft, sensual, gentle. This was the period when pastrymaking reached its height.

The incredible flowering of gastronomical delicacies coincided more and more with manifestations of joie de vivre and delight in the subtle pleasures of word-games and high-toned conversations, held in what Montesquieu, author of an *"Essay upon Taste"* called the *bureaux d'esprit*, the Parisian salons he frequented so assiduously.

This "gallant" style, affected by an upper class increasingly bourgeois and therefore increasingly liberal, validated the growing importance of the parlor - or, better, the dining room - where seductive dishes contributed no little to the encouragement of brilliant conversation. The baroque fantasy had influenced the dinner-tables of the 17th century and then paved the way in the century following, to a new style, which was called for more order, measure, lightness, and moderation, even if sometimes was accompanied by softness and exoticism. The baroque returned in force, with all its excesses and intemperance, in the 19th century, when magnificent processions of dishes - decorated marvels, multiple roasts, voluptuous pastries, glazed pies, and improbable jellies - reappeared on tables set up for buffets that were literally stunning. In Sicily, at the time of the Italian *Risorgimento* in 1860, extravagant balls took place, where "buffet" rooms were stocked with delicacies in whopping quantities.

*Beneath the candelabra, beneath the five tiers bearing toward the distant
ceiling pyramids of homemade cakes that were never touched, spread the
monotonous opulence of buffets at huge balls: coralline lobsters boiled alive,
waxy chaud-froids of veal, steely-tinted fish immersed in sauce, turkeys
gilded by the ovens' heat, rosy foie gras under gelatin armor, boned
woodcock reclining on amber toast decorated with their own chopped
insides, and a dozen other cruel, colored delights. At the end of the table two
monumental silver tureens held clear soup the color of burnt amber.*

*To prepare this supper the cooks must have sweated away in the vast kitchens
from the night before.*

*"Dear me, what an amount! Donna Margherita knows how to do things well.
But it's not for me!" Scorning the table of drinks, glittering with crystal and
silver on the right, he moved left toward that of the sweetmeats. Huge blond
babas, Mont Blancs snowy with whipped cream, cakes speckled with white
almonds and green pistachio nuts, hillocks of chocolate-covered pastry,
brown and rich as the topsoil of the Catanian plain from which, in fact,
through many a twist and turn they had come, pink ices, champagne ices,
coffee ices, all parfaits, which fell apart with a squelch as the knife cleft
them, melody in major of crystallized cherries, acid notes of yellow
pineapple, and those cakes called "triumphs of gluttony" filled with green
pistachio paste, and shameless "virgins' cakes" shaped like breasts.*

*Don Fabrizio asked for some of these and, as he held them in his plate,
looked like a profane caricature of St. Agatha. "Why ever didn't the Holy
Office forbid these cakes when it had the chance? St. Agatha's sliced-off
breasts sold by convents, devoured at dances! Well, well!"*

From *Il Gattopardo* by
Giuseppe Tomasi di Lampedusa
(*The Leopard*, English trans.
by Archibald Colquhon)

Pasta frolla
(Short pastry)

4 scant cups flour - 1 scant cup sugar - 7 oz butter - 1 lemon peel, grated - 2 eggs - 2 tsp self raising powder

Short pastry is surely one of the cornerstones of pastry-making, but its preparation requires a series of expedients. The particular characteristic of short pastry is its friability, its tendency to crumble. Certain rules must be observed in order to achieve the best results. First of all, the butter must be of the best quality; the better the butter, the better the dough. Cast a suspicious eye on butter that melts rapidly and noisily in the skillet, producing a whitish foam on its surface. Butter, when it's genuine, infuses its own unmistakable flavor into the foods it's called upon to complete.

When working short pastry dough, use the method of stirring or cutting in the butter in little pieces, after it's soft and malleable. To this end, you can remove it from the refrigerator an hour before using it, or you can base your calculations on the temperature in your kitchen; in any case, the butter should barely yield when you touch it.

Sift the flour and mound it on your work surface. Make a well in the center and add the sugar, the butter in little pieces, the eggs, the self raising powder and the grated peel of 1 lemon (optional). Blend all these ingredients, at first with a fork, then with your fingertips.

Mix thoroughly and quickly. Excessive kneading develops gluten, a tenacious elastic substance present in wheat flour, and will cause the dough to become elastic and cohesive, thus losing its friability.

As soon as you've blended all the ingredients, let the short pastry stand for about an hour before using it.

Pasta sfoglia alla francese
(French-style puff pastry)

*4 cups unbleached all-purpose flour - 1 pinch salt -
1 cup butter - 1 cup water*

For good puff pastry, you need excellent flour. An ideal choice is hard-wheat American or Canadian flour, which contains more gluten. The flour must be perfectly dry (you can check this by squeezing a handful of it; when you open your hand, the flour should flow out of it rapidly, without forming lumps).
Blend and knead the flour and water with a pinch of salt and 3 tbsp. Of butter. You should obtain a very stiff dough. Let it stand for half hour so that it loses some of its elasticity. Next, roll out the dough on your work surface, first back and forth, then left and right, so that it forms a cross. Now take the rest of the solid butter and pound it with a rolling-pin to force out all of its moisture. The butter will become malleable and will form a square and place it in the center of the cross-shaped dough. Close up the ends of the dough, lightly pulling the ends over one another to form a square that completely covers the square of butter. Place in the refrigerator or other cool spot for 1/2 hour. Then roll out the dough with the rolling-pin so that it forms a rectangle about 1 centimeter (3/8 inch) thick. Fold it in half like a book. Let the dough stand for 20 minutes, then repeat the entire operation 4 times.
At this point, finally, the dough will be ready for use. Roll it out into a thin sheet, about 1/4 inch thick, and remember to prick it with a fork before baking it in a very hot oven. (Puff pastry bakes in only 5 minutes).

Pasta reale o pasta di mandorle
(Royal paste or almond paste)

2 ¼ lbs sweet almonds - 1 tbsp bitter almonds - 4
generous cups sugar - 2 cups water - 1 tsp vanilla

As its name indicates, this paste is the queen of Sicilian pastrymaking. The recipe goes back to the prosperous period of Arab domination, which was really a moment of high civilization for the island of Sicily.

Very sweet, beautiful to look at, as malleable as clay, almond paste is the raw material for many Sicilian pastries.

The preparation of excellent pasta reale requires almonds of the best quality, such as the ones called "Avola," which come from Sicily, or hand-picked ones from the province of Bari.

Blanch the almonds in boiling water, let them cool, and slip off their skins. Dry the nuts in an oven at very low temperature; their color must not darken. After they've dried and cooled, mince them and pound them to a fine powder in a mortar. Pour the granulated sugar and about 2 cups of water into a saucepan and boil until a pinch of this mixture forms a little ball between your thumb and forefinger when you plunge it suddenly into cold water. Remove the sugar from the heat and add it with the vanilla to the almond powder in the mortar. Continue to pound the mixture until you get a compact, dry paste.

Pour this onto a marble slab and work it as though you're kneading a normal dough.

Let the paste rest in a cool spot for at least one hour before using it. Royal paste treated in this way is ready for use as a crust for pies or, with the help of food coloring, pasta reale can be molded into those beautiful fruits that are authentic masterpieces in Sicily.

Crema pasticciera
(Custard cream pastry filling)

*1 qt milk - 1 scant cup of sugar - 7 tbsp flour - 8
egg yolks - 1 lemon peel*

The cream or filling is certainly among the pastry-maker's most versatile
tools. In order to obtain a flawless result, it's important to let the cream
thicken and to stop cooking it at the right moment.
Just as carefully, you must stir it without stopping and in every curve of the
saucepan, and you must do all this over a very low flame.
First, blend the egg yolks with the sugar and flour (you can use either ½ cup
or 2/3 cup of flour depending on the thickness you like to obtain) in a
saucepan until you obtain a homogeneous, frothy mixture. Then pour in the
milk, a little at a time, and, lastly, add the thin peel of a very fresh lemon.
Heat the saucepan on the stove, stirring with a wooden spoon.
When the liquid thickens and coats the spoon with a smooth, compact layer,
remove from heat. Keep stirring for a few minutes as the mixture cools. If
you wish, you can add a tbsp. or so of butter to make the cream look even
brighter and more attractive.

Glassa montata
(Whipped glaze or icing) n.1

*¾ cup confectioners' sugar - 1 egg white - lemon
juice*

This glaze can be used to dress pies, tarts, and other desserts, or to decorate
certain kinds of petits-fours.
In an bowl beat the sugar with the egg white and a few drops of lemon juice
until you get an elastic, firm, gleaming white mixture.
Spread this light glaze on sweet desserts before baking them in very low heat
(210°F) for 10 minutes.

Glassa
(Whipped glaze or icing) n.2

1 ½ cups confectioners' sugar - 1 egg white - ¼
cup water

Melt sugar and water over very low heat for few minutes until is almost caramel. In the meantime firmly whip the egg white. Gently pour the hot sugar onto the egg white. The glaze is now ready to be used.
To obtain a chocolate glaze add the cocoa at the end.

Glassa al cioccolato
(Chocolate glaze)

5 oz squares unsweetened chocolate - ½ cup sugar
- 1 ½ tbsp butter

To melt the chocolate, use a heat-resistant receptacle that will fit perfectly over a small pan filled with boiling water. Turn off the heat and leave the chocolate in the covered container. After about 10 minutes, the heat from the hot water will melt the chocolate. Boil a scant ½ cup of water with the sugar and let it cool. Blend the melted chocolate into this syrup. Cook in a double boiler, stirring, for 5 minutes. Turn off the heat and add the butter. Spread the glaze on the dessert and let it cool.

Glassa bianca per coperture di dolci
(White glaze for sweets)

1 cup sugar - scant ½ cup water -1 lemon

In a small saucepan, boil 1 cup of sugar in a little less than ½ cup water until a pinch of the mixture adheres slightly to your fingers but doesn't form a thread between them. Another sign that you've cooked the syrup enough is that it will stop giving off steam and instead produce large bubbles. At this point, remove it from the heat. When it's beginning to cool, add the juice of 1 lemon and stir briskly so that the glaze becomes snowy white.

Should the glaze get too hard, add a little water so that it will flow like a rather thick cream.

Pan di Spagna
("Spanish bread" or Sponge cake)

5 eggs - 1/3 cup sugar - ¾ cup flour - ½ lemon

Pan di Spagna is the basis and support for many sweet desserts; it has the ability to tame flavors that are too strong or too tart and lends its own lightness and softness to any dessert. It's also quite delicious by itself, and simple to make if you know a few little stratagems that will help you get the best results.

In an earthenware bowl, beat the egg yolks and the sugar. Rub 1/2 lemon all over the inner surface of another bowl - make sure it's perfectly dry before you start - and beat the egg whites in it until they stand in soft peaks.

At this point, fold part of the beaten egg whites into the yolk and sugar mixture.

You should carry out this operation very, very slowly. Then, little by little, add the rest of the whites, followed by the sifted flour, always working extremely gently. Butter a baking-dish perfectly (leave no spot ungreased), and dust it uniformly with flour. Shake off the excess.

Pour in the mixture and bake your Spanish bread -it's a kind of sponge cake-in the oven at a very low temperature for 45 minutes.

Babà
(Baba cake)

2 + ¼ cups flour - ¼ cup sugar - ½ cup butter - 6 eggs - 1 tsp salt - 1 oz Brewer's yeast - ½ cup milk
For the syrup: 1 pt water - ½ cup sugar - 1 cup dark Rum - 1 lemon peel

The babà, an extraordinary balance of softness and airiness, of sensuality and discretion, appears to have been invented by the cooks of Ring Stanislaus Leczinski of Poland in the beginning of the 18th century. Diderot subsequently referred to it in a text that dates from 1765.

Perhaps the name "baba" was taken from the story of "Ali Baba and the Forty Thieves", because the cake evokes the wonders of the Orient, or perhaps because the "Thousand and One Nights" was the favourite reading of the Polish king. In any case, the word babà exists in the Polish language and means "a good woman." Alexandre Dumas, too, mentions the baba in his Gastronomical Dictionary and describes the origins of the cake. The first traces of a cake similar to this one can be detected in the Austrian Kugelhupf, a sort of cross between a brioche and the Milanese sweet bread known as *panettone*. This cake, moistened with rum by a happy inspiration of the Polish king, was the origin of the delightful treat we know today. It was later, in the 19th century, that the Julien brothers, owners of a pastry-shop in Paris, eliminated raisins from the recipe and added butter to it.

To make a baba cake, proceed as follows. Sift the flour into a bowl. Take about a quarter of the flour and incorporate it with the yeast, dissolved in a little lukewarm milk.

Let this dough rise in a spot protected from air currents; if you cover the container with a dishtowel and then with a woollen cloth, so much the better.

When the fermentation produced by the yeast has caused the dough to rise, add the eggs (beaten with the sugar), the butter (melted but not hot), and a pinch of salt. Use a fork to work this mixture slowly into the remaining flour so that all the liquid is absorbed. You will obtain a very soft dough. Knead this at length (you can use a mechanical mixer if you have one) before pouring it into a ring mold flawlessly greased with butter and sprinkled with flour and a little sugar. The dough should fill the mold to 1/3 of its height. Cover with a woollen cloth and set aside to rise again. It should take the dough about 1 hour to rise to a level slightly more than 3/4 the height of the mold. When the dough has risen to this point, put it into the oven. At first, the heat should be very gentle so that it can penetrate the baba completely and allow it to puff up as much as possible, and then rather more intense to bake it perfectly (from 210° F to 400° F). When the baba has cooled somewhat, unmold it gently. While waiting for it to cool, begin to prepare the syrup. Boil a pint of water and add a fresh lemon peel, cut into a thin spiral, and the sugar. When this syrup is almost cold, pour in a generous cup of high-quality rum to make a kind of punch. Spoon this over the cake repeatedly and patiently until the cake absorbs it. In this way, you'll obtain a baba that is extremely soft, spongy, delicate, airy, and fragrant: it's to say sublime.

Il bianco mangiare
(Blancmanger)
(serves 8)

1 qt water - 1 ¼ cup milk - 2 cups fresh sweet almonds, blanched and peeled - 1 tbsp bitter almonds - 1 cup confectioners' sugar - ¾ cup cornstarch - 1 lemon peel, cut into a spiral - 1 stick cinnamon

Lorenzo Magalotti, 18th-century art connoisseur, student of natural curiosities, polyglot, counsellor of Cosimo III, Grand Duke of Tuscany, and anglophile, wrote a poem about a superb English pudding that resembles to this dessert. With its rare flavor (almost completely vanished from our modern tables), its marvellous texture, its whiteness - like that of milk, or a nun's breast - its voluptuous, almost sinful richness, this refined, delicious sweet calls up an image of convivial living in 16th-century monasteries and convents, where prayers were as frequent as the occasions of the sin of gluttony.

In the first place, you should provide yourself with almonds of the best quality, such as the "Avola" of Sicily or the hand-picked variety from the region around Bari known as "hand picked Bari".

Blanch them, peel them, dry them in an oven at a very low temperature (leave the oven door half-open) , and then grind them in a mortar. Place the pounded almonds in a crockery bowl with cold water and let them stay there for an hour.

Strain the liquid through a cloth, twisting and squeezing it to extract as much flavor as possible from the almonds. The water will become as white and thick as milk. When you've squeezed the last drop of liquid out of the ground almonds, discard them. Now mix the sugar, cornstarch, milk, lemon peel, and cinnamon into the almond milk and heat this mixture, stirring with a wooden spoon until you've got a lovely, thick, fragrant cream that's to the boiling point.

Remove the lemon peel and pour the cream into little molds moistened with cold water or almond oil. Refrigerate for several hours. Make a pretty bed of lemon or grape leaves on a platter and unmold the cold *blancmanger* onto them.

You can grate a raw almond and a bit of lemon peel onto the little puddings and place an almond in the center of each.

"Bicchinotti"
(Almond cream tarts)

For the filling: 1 qt custard cream (p. 288) - 2 cups ground almonds - 1+ 1/3 cups sugar - 3 eggs - 1 tsp vanilla - Maraschino cherries as needed
For the short pastry: 3 + ½ cups flour - 1 scant cup sugar - 7 oz butter - 2 eggs - 2 tsp self raising powder

Bicchinotti are an appealing kind of cookies: little sealed cases of short pastry, still made in some old Sorrentine pastry-shops. Inside the flaky walls of short pastry, concentrated and marvellously balanced, the dignified pastry cream mingles with sensual almond milk, crowned by a cherry, the whole in pretty little molds that must be absolutely smooth, not grooved like the ones used for a variation of this dessert, cherry cream tarts. Prepare the short pastry as usual; when you're making the dough, try not to let all the flour be absorbed. In this way, you'll save a part of it for help in rolling out the dough.

For the filling, blanch the almonds briefly so that they give up their peel without a struggle. Put them into the oven for a few minutes so that they dry thoroughly, then mince them finely and pass them through a sieve with the sugar. Add the eggs to this powder, one at a time, followed by the vanilla and then the lukewarm pastry cream. A heartening fragrance will fill the air.

Roll out the short pastry dough and cut out many small squares.
Use half of these to line the little molds. Into these, pour the filling and decorate it with a delicious sour cherry. Cover the filling with another small square of pastry dough, cutting off the excess that overlaps the sides of the molds. Brush the bicchinotti with beaten egg and bake them in a 350° F oven for about ½ hour.
After they bake, wait a few minutes before unmolding them. When they're cold, at the moment of serving them, sprinkle them with powdered sugar.

Biscotti all'anice
(Anise cookies)

*4 cups flour - 4 eggs - 1 tbsp olive oil - 1 tbsp
vegetable oil - 5 tbsp sugar - 1 tsp baking powder
- 1 shot glass Anise liqueur - 1 lemon zest - 1 cup
almond cut in slices*

The recipe for these Anise Cookies comes from the towns around Mt. Vesuvius.
Sift the flour into a mound. Make a well in the center. Pour everything else into the well. Work into a dough, making sure the flour absorbs the eggs and the other ingredients.
First, blend everything with the aid of a fork, then use your hands to knead the dough well, working more and more vigorously. Let the dough rest for ½ hour.
At the end of this time, take the dough and knead it again. Shape it into a rectangular, rather flat loaf, and score its surface with many little cuts.
Bake the dough in a hot oven. When it's halfway done, remove it, and cut through the incisions you made earlier so that you obtain many small cookies.
Brush some egg white on them to make them shine as they continue to bake until they're golden all over.

Cannoli alla sorrentina
(Sorrento-style fried pastries)

3 cups flour - 1 tsp sugar - 1 tbsp butter - 1 pinch
salt - white wine or Marsala as needed - peanut
oil for frying - custard cream (p.288)

Based on the traditional, famous Sicilian cannoli, this recipe offers delightful, tiny cannoli filled classically and simply with custard cream pastry filling or enriched with chocolate.

With this method, the resulting cannoli (whether because of the type of filling or because of their greatly reduced dimensions) make a discreet, light, genteel dessert, a graceful miniaturization of the centuries-old Sicilian pastry. The texture of the dough must be delicate in the extreme, and it is essential that the pastries are filled with the cream only at the very last moment before serving them; otherwise, the moisture from the filling will impregnate the pastry, depriving it of its natural fragrance and of the fragile quality that makes these little sweets so irresistible.

You can likewise fill cannoli with a cream that's more impassioned, more intense, and perhaps more popular: ricotta passed through a sieve with sugar (in general, you should use ricotta and sugar in the proportion of 2 to 1, respectively), perfumed with grated lemon peel, and aromatized with rum.

To prepare the pastry dough, pour out the flour onto your marble slab in the shape of a crown, and in its center put the lard, salt, and sugar.

Amalgamate these ingredients with sufficient white wine or Marsala to produce a very soft, elastic dough.

Roll it out into a very thin sheet and cut out little squares, which you will wrap around small cannoli molds (little tin or aluminum tubes) so that a corner of dough overlaps each end, remaining stuck thank's to a drop of egg white. Lightly press down these corners with your finger-tips to close up the ends and plunge the tubes, covered as they are with a thin layer of dough, into plenty of hot oil.

The cannoli will turn golden in a few seconds. Remove them with a long-handled fork, drain them well on absorbent paper, and, when they've cooled somewhat, carefully slip them off their tubes with the help of a table-napkin. Fill them with the cream of your choice and sprinkle them with powdered sugar.

Casatiello dolce
(Fortified raisin loaves)

8 cups flour - ½ cup sourdough starter - 12 eggs – 1 + ½ cups butter - 1 + ½ cup sugar - 4 tsp vanilla - 1 ¾ cup sultana raisins - 1 lemon peel - 1 shotglass Strega liqueur - 1 shotglass Rum

The preparation of a good *casatiello*, an old Easter dessert, requires a symbolic and significant sacrifice of time. To begin with, you have to get yourself some sourdough starter, a mixture of flour and water worked into a dough and allowed to ferment and form microorganisms (mostly *saccharomyces* associated with *lactobacilli*). Sourdough starter is used in bread-making and can still be found in the genuine old bakeries that are engaged in making real bread, not the prefabricated, pre-baked loaves that have, unfortunately, invaded the market.

Blend the sourdough with an egg and part of the flour (about a scant cup) to obtain a very light, soft mixture. Let this rest in a bowl, covered with a towel and standing in a spot away from air currents, for about 2 hours or until doubled in volume. At this point, knead the dough again, at length, adding to it 10 eggs, the remaining flour, the butter, the sugar, the vanilla, the sultana raisins, the grated peel of a very fresh lemon, a shot-glass of Strega, and a shot-glass of rum.

Pound and work the dough very energetically. Then break off pieces of the dough and place them in ring molds previously greased with butter and dusted with flour. The dough should fill the molds only halfway. Let it rise in a warm spot by covering the molds with a dishtowel and then with a woollen cloth, and let them stand like this overnight (they'll need about 16 hours).

When the loaves are puffy and light, paint their surfaces thinly with a beaten egg. Bake them in a moderate (350° F) oven for about an hour.
Before removing them from the oven, check to be certain that they're dry on the inside and completely browned on the outside.

Cassata siciliana
(Sicilian cheesecake)
(serves 10)

For the "pan di Spagna": 8 eggs - 7/8 cup sugar - 1 + 1/3 cups cornstarch
For the cream filling: 1+3/4 lbs ricotta - 1+3/4 cups sugar - 3 + ½ oz squares bitter chocolate - 1/3 cup green candied fruit - 1/3 cup candied orange peel - liquor (Strega or Rum) as needed
For the decoration: 3 ½ oz candied fruit, whole and in chopped pieces (oranges, mandarins, pears, etc.) - 3 ½ oz green candied fruit, cut into lang, thin strips - ½ lb royal paste or almond paste, colored green
For the glaze: 1 heaped cup confectioners' sugar - lemon juice as needed

Cassata was at one time the Easter dessert par excellence in Sicily, first baked in the year 998 in Palermo, during Arab time.
For the *pan di Spagna*, beat the egg yolks in a bowl and cream it with the sugar until you have a soft mixture. Then add the cornstarch and stir well. Beat the egg whites separately until stiff. Fold them gently into the mixture, stirring lightly, and pour the whole into a buttered pan. Bake in a moderate oven (300° F) for about ½ hour. Before removing from the oven, check to see if the baking is complete by inserting a toothpick into the cake (if the toothpick comes out moist, bake for a few minutes more). Let the pan di Spagna cool, then cut it crosswise into three round slices.

For the ricotta cream filling, rub the ricotta through a sieve with the sugar. Chop the chocolate, the candied orange peel, and the green candied fruit into tiny pieces and add them. Bind the cream with a little liquor (Strega or rum).

For the Royal Paste, use the recipe already given. Color the paste with green food coloring.

Take a round non-stick pan. Cover the bottom with a layer of pan di Spagna. Moisten this with a little liquor. Line the sides first with Royal paste, then with pan di Spagna. Pour in the ricotta cream and level it with a knife blade. Cover with another round slice of pan di Spagna. Refrigerate the cake overnight. The next day, carefully turn the container over onto a tray or platter and let the cake slide out gently.

For the glaze, cook the confectioners' sugar over a low heat with a scant ½ cup of water. When the sugar has cooked to the point where a pinch of it begins to stick to your fingers, remove it from the heat and let it cool, stirring energetically all the while and adding a few drops of lemon juice. Use a spatula to spread the glaze over the top and sides of your cassata and decorate it with various kinds of candied fruit.

Chiacchiere
("Sweet nothings" or fried pastries)

4 cups flour - ½ cup sugar - 3 eggs - 1 shot glass Rum - 3 tbsp oil - 1 pinch salt - 2 cups honey - oil for frying - 1 shot glass Strega liqueur - grated peels of 1 orange and 1 mandarin

Here's an example of how a simple dessert, originating in the idea of fried strips of dough sweetened with honey, can be transformed into a sophisticated tangle of knots and bows, boldly formed into a little honey-drenched hill. The honey will find its way into every nook and cranny, and the result will be the bright, crunchy, baroque *chiacchiere* ("empty chatter" or "sweet nothings") that are at their best in certain Sardinian pastry-shops. Elsewhere, they're also known as *bugie* ("fibs"), *frappe* ("fringes"), *cenci* ("tatters"), *gale* ("frills") , or *nastri* ("ribbons").

Pour out the flour onto a marble slab in the shape of a crown. Put the eggs, the sugar, a pinch of salt, the oil, and the shot-glass of rum into the hollow center of the crown of flour and blend everything together. Work the mixture energetically so that you obtain a consistent, elastic dough. Let this rest for about an hour. Then cut the dough into pieces and roll these out with a rolling-pin into very thin sheets (no more than 1/8 inch thick). Use a pastry cutter (the kind that has a scalloped wheel attached to a handle) to cut these sheets into thin ribbons. Shape these into bows or knots. Fry them, a few at a time, in smoking oil and drain them on absorbent paper.

Liquefy the honey in a skillet over very low heat with the Strega liqueur and the grated orange and mandarin peels. Pour in the sweet nothings, a few at a time, and turn them over gently to coat them thoroughly without breaking them. When they're gleaming brightly, mound them on a pretty plate.

Traditionally, this dessert is made during the Christmas holidays and at carnival time.

Choux o pasta bignè
(Cream puffs)

1 + ¼ cups water - ½ cup butter - 1 + ¾ cups flour
- 1 pinch salt - 6 eggs

Put a saucepan on the fire with the water, 7 tbsp. butter, and a pinch of salt. When the water boils, pour in all the flour at once and stir over heat for 5 minutes. You should get a stiff dough that comes away from the sides of the pan. Pour this onto your work surface and add the eggs after the mixture cools. Blend thoroughly and at length; if necessary, add another egg to make the dough sufficiently soft. (You should obtain a dough with the consistency of an ointment. When the dough starts to "exit," to move languidly out of its container, that's the sign that it's ready).

Use a syringe to form little balls of dough in a pan well greased with the remaining butter. Put this into a hot oven for 20-25 minutes until the dough rises and turns golden.

When the puffs are baked, make incisions in them with a small knife or cut them in half to fill them with pastry cream or whipped cream and then cover them with a mixture of melted chocolate and liquor; or, more simply, sprinkle them with confectioners'sugar.

Cioccolata calda in tazza
(Hot chocolate in cups)

4 oz squares unsweetened chocolate - ¼ cup cocoa powder - 1 qt milk - 4 demitasse cups strong espresso coffee - ½ cup sugar - 1 lemon peel - 1 shot glass Anise liqueur - 1 shot glass Strega liqueur

We're able to enjoy this seductive beverage today thanks to Hernán Cortés. When he landed in Mexico in 1519, the Aztecs believed him to be the white god Quetzalcoatl and therefore lavished him with gifts, among which were cacao or cocoa beans. Legend narrates that the Aztec king Montezuma managed to drink as many as fifty cups of the beverage made from these beans every day, and very soon it conquered dinner-tables not only in Spain, but also in Holland, Italy, and France - throughout Europe, in short.

Giacomo Casanova and Madame du Barry attributed particular aphrodisiac qualities to chocolate. It's certain that cacao is one of the richest and most complete foods in existence, capable of producing a significant increase in energy with its combination of fats, carbohydrates, and proteins. A cup of chocolate can justly be compared to a drink fit for gods: *theobrama* in Greek. And *Theobrama cacao* is in fact the botanical name of the cacao or chocolate tree, an imposing plant 6 to 8 meters (18-26 feet) high, with large, shiny oval-shaped leaves and beautiful red flowers that turn into large, fleshy fruits of a lovely yellow-gold color.

So let's enjoy this unadulterated pleasure and prepare our hot chocolate according to a ritual that the people of the Sorrentine peninsula celebrate at breakfast-time on birthdays and name-days. Here's a recipe that blends the sweetness of chocolate, that restores with coffee, that encourages reflection.

Mix the cocoa powder and the sugar and dissolve them over very low heat in part of the milk, stirring with a small whisk to discourage lumps. Separately, over a very gentle flame, dissolve the chocolate in the rest of the milk, together with the coffee (it's actually best to perform this operation in a double boiler). Mix the two chocolate solutions together over the heat, continuing to stir; add the liquors and bring to the boiling point. Cut a thin lemon peel into a spiral and add to the chocolate, which should be very hot but not boiling. The taste of the lemon will thus be released slowly, mingling with the chocolate in a voluptuous *crescendo* that can excite strong passions and irresistible infatuations.

Cioccolatini con ciliegina
(Cherry chocolates)

7 oz squares unsweetened chocolate - ½ cup confectioners sugar - cherries preserved in alcohol - lemon - 1 egg white

Melt the chocolate in a double boiler and let it cool. Use part of it to brush the insides of small parchment containers suitable for this use. Distribute the chocolate evenly. As soon as you prepare each container, turn it upside down on a tray so that the chocolate won't collect on the bottom. Place the containers in the refrigerator at once. Slice the cherries in half so that there's a cherry half for each little mold.

Use a fork to amalgamate the confectioners' sugar, the stifflybeaten albumin, a few drops of lemon juice, and a bit of the cherry alcohol in a bowl. You should obtain a smooth, rather fluid cream.

Remove the molds from the refrigerator and place half a cherry in each, followed by some of the prepared cream.

Return the little chocolates to the refrigerator until the white glaze condenses and forms a thin film on the surface.

Now, gently heat the rest of the chocolate so that its barely melted and pour it into each mold to cover the filling competely. Put the chocolates back in the refrigerator until the topping solidifies, then arrange them on a pretty dish. Keep them refrigerated until you're ready to serve them.

Cornetti
(Croissants)

2 cups all-purpose flour - 2 cups Canadian flour -
1/3 cup sugar - 9 tbsp butter - 2 eggs - 1 oz
Brewer's yeast - 1 tsp salt - 1 grated lemon peel

The story is told that, in 1683, thanks to the prompt alarm given by the Hapsburgs' bakers, the Austrian troops were able to thwart the Turkish assault once and for all.

As a memorial to this event, the pastry-makers were granted the right to fashion little sweet pastries in the shape of half-moons (the symbol of the Ottoman Empire) in memory of the Christians' victory over the infidels.

The pastries were also called "croissants," though it's uncertain whether this refers to the crescent moon or to the rising of the dough. But the frankness of Marie Antoinette of Hapsburg-Lorraine, daughter of the Austrian Emperor Franz I and wife of Louis XVI of France, who, on the eve of the French Revolution, invited her famished people to make up for the lack of bread by eating brioches ("cakes"), was partially responsible for the popularity of croissants and brioches first in France and then throughout Europe, including the Kingdom of Naples.

Sift the flour and add to it the sugar, the eggs, half of the indicated amount of butter, and the grated peel of a lemon. Mix the yeast and salt in a bowl, and dissolve this mixture with about 1 cup of lukewarm water. Blend and mix these various ingredients conscientiously; if necessary, add more water until you obtain a homogeneous dough. Knead thoroughly for 5 or 10 minutes. Place the dough in a bowl, cover it, and let it rise in a warm place. When the dough has doubled in volume (this will take about an hour) transfer it to your work surface and use a rolling-pin to spread it out into a rather thick rectangle. Brush a goodly amount of room-temperature (that is, softened) butter onto the surface of the dough, fold it gently into three sections, and let it rest in a cool spot for about 1/2 hour.

Roll out the dough as before, butter it the same way as previously, and fold it in three once more. Let it rest again. In all, you will repeat the whole operation three times.

Finally, roll out the dough on a floured board and shape it into a rectangle (about 10 by 8 inches) . Cut out triangles (of equal size, if possible) from the dough. Roll them up and bend them into the shape of a half-moon.

Place them in a greased pan. Paint them with some beaten egg and let them rise for about an hour before baking them in a hot oven (400° F) for about ½ hour.

Crumbly and light, these are sublime when still eaten hot from the oven.

Coviglia al caffè
(Coffee custard)

For the custard cream: 2 brimming cups milk - 3 tbsp flour - ½ cup (scant measure) sugar - 4 egg yolks - 1 lemon peel
For the coffee flavour: 6 demitasse strong espresso coffee - 4 tbsp instant coffee - 1 cup whipping cream - toasted coffee beans as needed - 1 shot dark Rum

In the 18th century, when the tastes of sensitive, ethereal, "gracious ladies" required diets that were light, gentle, sensuous, soft, and sweet, two Italian luxury items, two tasty delicacies, were renowned throughout Europe: *liqueurs d'Italie, glaces à l'italienne* were what the foreigners wanted. Naples is famous for its ice-cream and its sorbets.

This coffee custard is velvety and elegant. Prepare custard cream with the ingredients listed above, then add to this voluptuous concoction, first, thick, strong, fragrant coffee, and, next, the whipped cream and the Rum, stirring very gently. Turn the resulting creamy mixture into little porcelain or crystal cups, decorate them by placing a toasted coffee bean in the center of each, and refrigerate them for several hours until the custards become very cold, frothy, and delicious.

Crostata al cioccolato
(Chocolate tart)

*7 oz squares unsweetened chocolate - 2 tbsp milk - 3 tbsp
sour cherry jam
For the short pastry: 2 cups flour - 7 tbsp butter - 1 egg
- ½ cup sugar - 1 pinch of salt - grated peel of ½
lemon - 1 tsp self raising powder*

Carolus Linnaeus, the Swedish botanist and taxonomist, called cacao *Theobrama cacao*, "food of the gods." It is indeed a wonderful thing, capable of instigating strong cravings and sins of gluttony. Chocolate was introduced into Europe from the New World by Queen Anne of Austria, wife of Louis XIII of France, during the 17th century.

To prepare this flavorful tart, get some good baking chocolate. Once you've lined a pan with the short pastry dough, melt this chocolate in a double boiler, or in a pan over very low heat, with 2 tbsp milk. Remove the chocolate from the heat and immediately add the cherry jam. Pour this mixture into the short pastry-lined pan. Top with strips of more short pastry, laid in such a way as to form a grill. Brush this with egg whites so that it will turn bright and golden while baking. Use the standard procedure for the short pastry. Mound the flour on a marble slab or other work surface, make a well in the center, and add to it the barely softened butter, the egg, the sugar, a pinch of salt, and the grated peel of ½ lemon. Blend all this together quickly with your fingertips, taking just enough time as required to obtain a soft dough. Let stand ½ hour, then roll out the dough deftly with a rollingpin. Use some of this to line a baking-pan, and cut thin strips of the desired length from the remaining dough. It's best not to add more flour; manage the stipulated amount prudently, because excessive flour inevitably causes short pastry to become too stiff and thus lose its desirable, characteristic friability.

Deliziose
(Delights)

For the short pastry: 2 cups flour - 7 tbsp butter –
½ cup sugar - 1 egg - 1 tsp self raising powder
For the filling: 1 lb ricotta - 1 cup sugar - 2 lemon
peels - 7 oz hazelnuts or almonds

Two short pastry discs enclose a soft, elegant filling which, although based on a common ingredient (ricotta), attains nobility thanks to the addition of fragrant lemon peel. If it's true that *nomina sunt consequentia rerum* ("names and natures do oft agree"), these sweets are truly *deliziose*. The results are particularly interesting if you keep their dimensions minimal; the diameter of the little discs of short pastry shouldn't measure much more than an inch.

For the short pastry, proceed as usual, blending the flour with the sugar, the butter at room temperature, and the egg. Roll out the dough into a sheet (not too thick) and use a small round cookie or biscuit cutter to cut out as many little discs of dough as you can. Put them on a buttered cookie sheet and bake them at 400° F for the few minutes necessary to turn them a pale golden color. Keep an eye on them, though, because a couple of seconds is all it takes for them to cross the line between baked and burnt!

For the filling, rub the ricotta and sugar through a sieve. Add to this cream the grated peel of two fresh, fragrant lemons. Use a teaspoon to place some of this filling between every two discs of short pastry. Then, gently, holding each little "sandwich" with your thumb and index finger, roll them edgewise in a plate where you will have waiting for them hazelnuts or almonds previously toasted slightly and then finely ground. Place the *deliziose* on a serving-platter and sprinkle them with powdered sugar.

Diplomatici
(Diplomats)

*French-style puff pastry (see p.287) Pan di
Spagna (see p.291) - Custard cream (see p.288) -
punch (1 pt water, 1 tbsp sugar, lemon, ½ cup
Rum) - confectioner's sugar*

Diplomats or trifles use French-Style Puff Pastry as their basic structure and
avail themselves in addition of soft, yielding Pan di Spagna and classic
Custard Cream Pastry Filling.

Prepare two identical sheets of dough less than 1/2 inch thick and bake them.
Spread a layer of pastry cream on the first sheet, followed by a 1/2 -inch layer
of pan di Spagna.

Prepare a punch or syrup by boiling a pint of water with 1 tbsp. sugar and
lemon peel for 5 minutes. When the liquid is cool, add 1/2 cup rum. Use this
syrup to moisten the pan di Spagna, top it with another layer of pastry cream,
and, finally, cover everything with the remaining sheet of puff pastry.

The resulting trifle, marvellously alternating firm but fragile crunchy layers
with yielding softness, and sprinkled with powdered sugar, can be cut into
little squares. They're best when they're bitesized, because that way their
whole complex of flavors reaches the palate all at once.

Dolcetti con mandorle
(Cookies with almonds)

*1 + ¼ cups flour - 1 tsp baking powder - 3 heaped
tbsp sugar - 3 tbsp butter - 2 eggs - 1 lemon peel -
peeled almonds as needed*

Cream the butter thoroughly with the sugar, add the egg yolks, the flour (a
little at a time), and the grated peel of a lemon fresh from the garden. Blend
these ingredients rapidly until you get a good, smooth dough that you can

shape into little walnut-sized balls. Dip these in the beaten egg whites and place them on a buttered cookie sheet. Place a peeled almond in the center of each little ball of dough.

Bake these in a moderately hot oven for about 20 minutes.

Dolcetti di pasta frolla con fragoline
(Pastries with cream and strawberry filling)

Short pastry (p.286) - Custard cream (p.288) - small strawberries

Short pastry forms the basic framework of this dessert, delightful little containers filled with simple, creamy flavors. A foundation of crunchy pastry bears the velvety, thick pastry cream, magnificently crowned with fresh fruit.

Prepare the short pastry as usual. While it's resting, cook the custard cream filling. Roll out the pastry dough with a rolling-pin into a sheet - not too thick - and cut from it enough little squares to line the little molds you're using. Bake the molds in a 400° F oven for 10 / 15 minutes.

Once these little pastry containers are baked, let them cool a little, then carefully unmold them. Spread a layer of pastry cream over each, and let the fruit of your choice add the finishing touch. In this case, wild strawberries have been chosen, but many other kinds will work as well.

These desserts must be consumed immediately, before the cream softens the short pastry.

Formaggelle sarde
(Sardinian cheese pastries)

For the filling: less than 1 lb ricotta - ½ cup sugar - grated peels of ½ lemon and 1 orange - 2 egg yolks - 1 shot Strega liqueur
For the dough: 3 cups flour - 7 tbsp butter - 1 tsp salt - 1 tbsp honey - 1 tsp self raising powder - cold water

Formaggelle are a typical Easter dessert in southern Sardinia, particularly tasty in Cagliari.

For the pastry dough, blend the flour with the sugar, the salt, the butter, and the honey dissolved in enough water to obtain a dough that's elastic but a little stiff. Let it stand for a while as you prepare the filling for the *formaggelle*.

Mix the ricotta and the sugar in a bowl. Add the grated citrus peels, the yolks and a shot of Strega liqueur. Next, take the pastry dough and roll it out into a thin sheet to cover little moulds with wavy rims. Place the filling in the center of each with a teaspoon. Bake them in a 400° F oven for 15 minutes. When they're ready, remove from the moulds and serve them lukewarm.

Frittelle dolci di riso
(Sweet rice fritters)

1 pt milk - ½ cup rice - 2/3 cup flour - cinnamon - 6 tbsp sweet almonds - 1 lemon - oil for frying - ½ cup sugar

Pour 1 pt. milk and 1 pt. water into a saucepan, add sugar and the fragrant, grated peel of a lemon, and cook the rice with these ingredients. Pour the cooked rice into a bowl, add the white flour and some powdered cinnamon and mix well. Blanch, peel, toast, and mince the almonds, then add them to the mixture.

Heat some oil in a skillet and spoon the mixture by tablespoons into the boiling oil. Fry the fritters until they take on a handsome golden color. Serve them hot, sprinkled with a mixture of cinnamon and sugar.

Gelati di frutta
(Fresh fruit ice cream)

*2 cups fruit pulp (like peaches) - 1 egg - 2 tbsp
flour - ½ cup sugar - ¾ cup milk - zest of half
lemon*

Ice cream is a very old food whose origins lie in Italy. It seems that the first ices were prepared in the 16th century by the Italian cooks whom Catherine de' Medici brought with her to Paris. Of course, it was much more difficult to freeze liquids in those days (using snow and ice) than it is now, thanks to the use of ice cream makers and freezers, which make the job a lot easier and allow us to enjoy this delicious, voluptuous dessert to the fullest.
Whisk egg and sugar until foamy, add the flour and dilute to milk. Add some parfum with a little lemon zest. Warm gently the cream until thick. Remove from fire before boiling, let it cool. In the meanwhile stone the fruit, whisk it, add the fruit to the cream now cold and either put the mixture in the freezer mixing time to time or use an ice-cream machine.

Gelatina di mandarino
(Mandarin orange gelatin)

*1 cup sugar - 4 tbsp gelatin or icinglass ("fish
gelatin") - 4 cups strained mandarin orange juice - 1
shot-glass white Rum - 2 cups whipped cream*

This stunning and very delicate dessert comes from Sicily, where citrus fruits (leading products of Sicilian agriculture) present their freshest, most charming fragrances.
Soak and squeeze the gelatin or icinglass (if you're using the type that comes in sheets) and add it to 1 cup of mandarin juice in a saucepan. Let the gelatin dissolve over extremely low heat.
In another pan, dissolve the sugar in another cup of mandarin juice. Under no circumstances should you allow the liquid to come to a boil. Add together the

two mixtures plus the remaining juice and the small glass of Rum. Filter the liquid well by pouring it through a linen cloth spread over a strainer. Pour the strained juice mixture into a mold greased with almond oil.

Refrigerate the gelatin for several hours before unmolding it onto a plate strewn with mandarin leaves.

Decorate the gelatin with whipped cream.

Gelato al cioccolato
(Chocolate ice)

1 cup milk - 1 cup whipped cream - ½ cup sugar - 1 egg - 4 oz unsweetened chocolate - 1 tsp vanilla

Gold or silver *sorbettiere* ("ice cream makers"), cylindrical containers of snowy, fragrant delights, machines invented to grant relief from the summer heat, were used in Italy as far back as two centuries ago to regale noble palates and to arouse heavenly ecstasies with sweet cacao, the gift of the blessed New World to Old Europe.

The fashion of the *déjeuner sur l'erbe*, the outdoor lunch or picnic, arose in the 17th century and became a feature of gallant life in the 18th; the proper conclusion to any such meal took the form of ices or sorbets.

To prepare this ice, grate the chocolate and heat it together with a little milk, add the vanilla and let it cool. Whisk the egg with the sugar, add the milk, the whipped cream, the chocolate melted and transfer the mixture in the icecream maker.

Gelato alla veneziana
(Venetian-style ice)

1 cup milk - 1 cup whipped cream - ½ cup sugar - 1 egg + 1 egg yolk - 4 oz unsweetened chocolate - 1tsp vanilla - scales or chips of chocolate for garnishing - ½ cup Rum

Prepare chocolate ice as described in the previous recipe, enriching it with the addition of an egg yolk. Add the Rum.

Pour this cream into the ice-cream maker. When the mixture has reached the desired consistency, garnish it with chips or large flakes of unsweetened chocolate.

Gelato al limone
(Lemon ice)

4 lemons - ½ cup sugar - 1 cup milk - ¾ cup
whipped crea - 1 tbsp lemon liquor - the zest of 1
lemon

It was in the 16th century that the Florentine artist Bernardo Buontalenti discovered that adding egg white to the ingredients of a sorbet successfully transformed its granular texture to a soft, velvety cream.

Catherine de' Medici, wife of King Henry II of France, introduced ice cream to the Paris court. Also in Paris, the Sicilian Procopio Coltelli opened the "Caffè Procope" in 1650, serving exclusively ices made according to Italian recipes. When possible, it's best to use lemons fresh from the garden for this recipe. When they've just been picked, and particularly when they're still slightly green, they have a most pleasing taste and a unique fragrance.

Squeeze the lemons, whisk the juice with the sugar, add the liquor, then the milk and the whipped cream. Pour the mixture in the icecream maker.

Gelato al torroncino
(Nougat ice cream)

1 + ¼ cups milk - ½ cup sugar - 2 eggs - 1 tsp
vanilla - 1/3 cup honey - ½ cup sugared almonds
- 2 tbsp candied fruit - 1 tsp cinnamon - 2 tbsp
Rum

Chop up the candied fruit in small pieces and cover with Rum for half hour. Mix milk, honey and vanilla, bring to simmer, then let it cool.

Mince the almonds and keep them aside.

Whisk the eggs with the sugar and dilute with the milk now cold. Pour the mixture in the icecream maker. When the icecream is ready, transfer it in a bowl and add the candied fruit and the chopped almonds.

Remember to use high-quality almonds such as Avola or the "hand-picked Bari" variety. To prepare sugared almonds, put them in a saucepan, cover them with sugar, add a tbsp of water and a tsp of cinnamon. Cook over a very low fire, stirring constantly, until the sugar becomes shiny.

Gelato di fragole
(Strawberry ice cream)

1+ ½ cup strawberry - ¾ cup sugar - 1 egg -
½ cup whipped cream - ¾ cup milk - 1 tsp
vanilla -the rind of half lemon

Wash the lemon, cut the rind of half of it. Warm the milk with the rind and the vanilla. Once it starts to simmer, remove from fire and let it cool. In the meanwhile wash the strawberries. Whisk the egg with sugar until stiff. Add strawberries, the whipped cream and the milk now cold, after removing the rind. Transfer the mixture in the icecream maker.

Gelo di melone
(Watermelon ice)

1 +1/2 cup nice and red watermelon pulp - 1 tbsp
jasmine flowers - ¾ cup sugar - 1 lemon - ¾ cup
whipped cream - 3 ½ oz squares unsweetened
chocolate for decoration and more jasmine
blossoms - ¼ cup shelled pistachio nuts - 1 tsp
powdered cinnamon - 1 tsp vanilla

Watermelon ice is a summer dessert served in Palermo, enchanting for its oriental perfumes.

First of all, you have to find yourself some nice and fresh jasmine blossoms, preferably of the Arab type which are small, extremely fragrant, and sweet. The evening before you prepare this ice, put the jasmine flowers in a container with a little water. Cover with a saucer and refrigerate it until the following day.

Take the watermelon, remove all its seeds, and pass the pulp through a sieve or food mill. This operation alone does not suffice to make the pulp absolutely smooth and thin, so strain the fruit again through a linen cloth or a sieve. Add the lemon juice and the sugar and whisk all together these ingredients. Pour the whipped cream and keep whisking. Add the jasmine water and then transfer the mixture in the icecream maker.

When everything is nearly cold, add finely minced chocolate pieces which should resemble watermelon seeds. Pour everything into a loaf pan that has been moistened with water (or lightly greased with almond oil) or you can pour the icecream back into the emptied watermelon rind. Refrigerate for several hours.

To serve the watermelon ice, decorate it with powdered cinnamon, fresh jasmine blossoms, and pieces of pistachio nuts.

Le graffe o "Krapfen"
(Doughnuts)

*3 ½ cups flour - 1 lb potatoes - ¼ cup
butter - 4 eggs - 1 oz Brewer's yeast - ½
cup milk - 1 tsp salt - 1 tbsp sugar - oil for
frying
Seasoning: sugar - cinnamon*

Graffe, folded back upon themselves and gleaming with sugar, and bombe ("bombs," a sort of cream doughnut), which contain the fascinating silkiness of white pastry cream (or dark chocolate cream, as is customary in Agrigento in Sicily), are both rather ambiguous desserts, balanced between the world of sweet foods - because they're covered with sugar - and the world of salted foods - because their basic flavor is that of fried dough.

Boil the potatoes, peel them, and pass them through a food mill while they're still very hot.

Mound the flour on your work surface, make a well, and fill the well with the potato purée, the butter (the hot potatoes will melt it quickly), the yeast dissolved completely in the warm milk, the salt, the sugar, and, finally, the eggs.

Begin to mix everything, first with a fork, then with your hands, until you obtain a thoroughly blended, very soft dough.

Break off as many pieces as you want - this will depend on the size of the doughnuts you wish to make - and roll them with your hands into little sticks. Curve these back upon themselves in the shape of a ring, place them on a napkin, and put them in a sheltered spot to rise.

When the rings have almost doubled in volume, fry them at once in plenty of hot oil. After draining them on paper, roll them in a mixture of sugar and cinnamon in a bowl.

They taste sublime when lukewarm.

Mandorle pralinate
(Almond pralines)

1 lb almonds - 2 cups sugar - 1 ½ cups
water - 1 lemon zest - 1 tbsp cinnamon

Pour the water into a high-sided copper pot and add the unpeeled almonds and the sugar. Cook, stirring constantly, until the almonds begin to crackle and the sugar to harden and become grainy. This should take about 15 minutes. Now, slowly, add the cinnamon, stir, remove the pot from the heat, and pour the almonds onto a marble slab moistened with water. Add the fragrance of a grated lemon peel. Before the almonds cool completely, separate those that are stuck together helping yourself with a lemon as they are hot.

Put them into an hermetically sealed glass jar.

They're exceptionally good!

Melanzane con la cioccolata di Sorrento
(Eggplant with chocolate, Sorrento-style)

6 Italian eggplants, about 1/3 lb each - 1 tbsp salt - 2 tbsp butter - 7 oz ricotta - ½ cup sugar - 3 oz squares unsweetened chocolate - ¼ cup candied citron peel - ¼ cup almonds - cinnamon - 1 shotglass Strega liqueur or Rum
For the meringue: 1 egg white - 2 drops lemon juice - 1 tbsp sugar

The story of an impossible love between working-class eggplants and noble chocolate. When we're children, it's easy to want everything; there's nothing that's impossible. As we grow up, we begin to notice that there's always something that's not allowed. The combination (many would say "clash") of ingredients in this recipe never fails to cause astonishment.

The result, however, is particularly delicious and certainly unexpected: a union of contradictions.

This dessert has its origins in the old village of Piano di Sorrento. You arrive there along a winding road which follows the coast, and your dazzled gaze takes in the sea, the little port and Mt.Vesuvius.

Boil the eggplants in salted water for 5 minutes. Remove them. When they're cool, cut them in half, use a sharp knife to remove the pulp carefully; leave the skins intact. Mince the pulp finely and sauté it in a skillet with a bit of butter to get rid of its moisture. While waiting for the eggplant to cool, you can prepare the other ingredients.

Crush the almonds, blanch them for 1 minute, dry them in an oven (very low heat) for 5 minutes, and then mince them. Chop the candied citron peel very tiny - it should almost disappear - and pass the ricotta through a sieve together with the sugar.

Grate the chocolate.

Now stir all the other ingredients together with the minced eggplant pulp. Add a small glass of liquor and 1 tbsp cinnamon and you'll get a marvellously creamy, fragrant mixture. Butter a bakingpan and dust it with a uniform mixture of fine flour and sugar.

Line up the eggplant shells, filled with the eggplant mix, in the baking-pan. Cook at 350° F for half hour. Remove from the oven (don't turn it off) and cover with a light meringue made by beating egg white with lemon juice and sugar.

Put the eggplants back into the oven for 10 more minutes and then leave them to cool.

These are wonderful served cold.

Migliaccio dolce
(Sweet cake)

3 cups milk - 5 tbsp butter - 2/3 cup semolina flour - 1 cup sugar - 5 eggs - 1 grated lemon peel - 1 tsp vanilla - 1 tbsp Cognac

This dessert, native to Sorrento, has the advantage of being rather simple to prepare and evoking great joy in children. It makes an ideal, delicious, nutritious snack. The sugar has a beneficial effect, not only thanks to its direct action in your bloodstream, but also to the pleasure it causes. Everything that produces pleasure enhances our muscular activity and greatly improves its efficiency.

Pour the milk into a saucepan, add the butter, and bring to a boil. When the milk is to the boiling point, add the semolina flour slowly and cook it over low heat, stirring constantly.

When the semolina is cooked, let it cool, then add the sugar, the grated lemon peel, the vanilla, the cognac, the egg yolks, and finally, the stiffly-beaten egg whites.

Butter a soufflé pan, dust it with flour and sugar, and pour the mixture into it. Cook in a moderate oven for about 40 minutes.

Millefoglie
(Millefeuille or "Thousand leaves")

*French-style puff pastry (p287) - custard cream
pastry filling (p288) - sour cherries - Pan di
Spagna (p.291) - Rum syrup (1 pt water, 1 tbsp
sugar, 1 lemon peel, ½ cup Rum) - confectioners'
sugar*

Another "miracle" born from the triple union of French-style puff pastry,
pastry cream, and sour cherries.
To your first layer of baked puff pastry add a rich, thick coating of pastry
cream. Next, add a layer of pan di Spagna soaked in the same syrup as that
described in the recipe for Diplomatici (see p.308), followed by sour cherries.
Puff pastry again, cream, cherries; then one final layer of puff pastry. Powder
with confectioners sugar.

Mousse au chocolat

*3 oz bitter baking chocolate, chopped - 2 tbsp
instant coffee - 2 tbsp Rum - 2 tbsp water - 4 eggs
separated - ½ cup sugar - 1 ½ cup heavy cream,
cold - ½ tsp vanilla extract - whipped cream and
chocolate shavings, for garnish*

Place the chocolate and water in a heatproof bowl and place over a saucepan
containing barely simmering water (or use a double boiler).
Melt the chocolate and stir with a wooden spoon until smooth. Add the egg
yolks to the chocolate, one by one, beating with a whisk until incorporated.
Remove from heat and cool slightly. Set aside.
Add coffee and Rum.
In another bowl, beat the egg whites until foamy.
Gradually whisk in the sugar and continue beating until stiff peaks form.
Beat heavy cream in a chilled bowl until it begins to foam and thicken up.
Add the vanilla. Continue to whip the cream until it holds soft peaks.

Gradually and gently fold the egg whites into the chocolate mixture to lighten it. Then, delicately fold in the whipped cream, taking care not to overwork the mousse.

Divide mousse into 4 or 6 individual glasses. Cover and chill for several hours.

Garnish with whipped cream and chocolate shavings before serving.

Orzata o latte di mandorle
(Almond milk)

2 cups almonds - 3 cups water - 4 cups sugar - 1 tsp vanilla - 1 lemon peel

To begin, you need to peel the almonds. To do this, pour some water into a saucepan, add the almonds, and heat. As soon as boiling point is reached, remove from heat. You'll be able to slip off the softened peels quickly.

After peeling the almonds, mince them very finely and place them in a coarse cloth or cheese-cloth. Wrap up the cloth like a little bundle, immerse it in lukewarm water, and squeeze it, so that it exudes a white, milky liquid. To this almond milk you add the sugar, the vanilla, and the thinly-sliced lemon peel. At this point, put the container onto the heat, but don't allow its contents to boil at any time.

A light froth will form; gentle stirring with a wooden spoon will dissipate this. The milk will attain a very thick consistency. It makes an excellent beverage, diluted with cold water as desired.

Pane di ricotta
(Ricotta cake)

2/3 lb very fresh, soft, moist ricotta cheese – less than a cup sugar - 2/3 cup milk - 3 egg whites - 1 tbsp baking powder - 2 tbsp butter - wheat (or potato) flour as desired - cinnamon - vanilla

Blend the ricotta and the milk in a large bowl. Then add the sugar, flavor with cinnamon and vanilla, pour in the melted butter, and fold in the well-beaten egg whites.

Finally sprinkle in, a little at a time, enough flour to make a rather soft mixture that you can work with a fork. When it is well blended, add the self raising powder. Butter a baking-pan, pour in the mixture, and bake it.

At least 1 hour before serving, you can make a topping for the cake. Crush some strawberries slightly in Rum or Cognac and sprinkle with powdered sugar.

Pane di sapa
(Sapa bread)

*2 cups sapa (cooked wine) - 1 oz Brewer's yeast -
1 tbsp cinnamon - 1 orange peel - 1 cup raisins -
½ cup sugar - ½ cup almonds - ½ cup shelled
walnuts - 5 cups flour - 1 egg*

Sapa is a sweetening agent made in Sardinia from the must of black grapes, spiced with cloves, cinnamon, and lemon peel, and reduced by boiling to a syrupy thickness. It can be preserved in hermetically sealed, darkglass bottles. *Pane di sapa*, a typical dessert for All Saints' Day and Christmas, is still widely used today, all over the island. Dissolve the yeast in lukewarm water, blend it with half of the flour into a dough (adding water as necessary), and let this sponge rise for a few hours.

When it has doubled in volume, knead the rest of the flour into it, along with the sapa (which it will absorb), the finely ground or minced cinnamon, the orange peel, the minced almonds and walnuts, the raisins, and the egg.

Work this dough vigorously so that all the ingredients are perfectly amalgamated, cover it with a warm cloth, and let it rise a second time. Then break it up into little loaves, arrange them on a greased cookie-sheet, and bake them in an oven at low temperature.

When they're baked, place them (still hot) on a platter and pour some cold sapa over them.

Let them dry and wrap them in silver foil.

Panettone all'Anice
(Sweet bread with Anise)

3 ½ cups flour - 1 scant cup sugar - 1 tbsp baking powder - 4 eggs - 7 tbsp butter - 1 grated lemon peel - ½ cup milk - ½ cup Anise liqueur

Cream the egg yolks with the sugar in a bowl, then slowly add the sifted flour, stirring constantly.

Next add the baking powder, dissolved in the milk, the butter, melted in a double boiler, the grated peel of a very fresh lemon, the Anise, a pinch of salt, and, lastly, the egg whites, beaten into soft peaks. Pour this mixture into a heatresistant soufflé pan, previously greased with butter and sprinkled with flour and sugar.

Put the dessert into a moderate oven and bake it for about 30 minutes.

Panettone nero con le noci
(Black sweet bread with walnuts)

3 ½ cups flour - 1 cup butter - 1+ 1/3 cups sugar - 4 tbsp cocoa powder - 2 oz squares unsweetened chocolate - 1+ ¼ cup milk - 30 walnuts - 4 eggs - 1 shot-glass Marsala - 1 tbsp baking powder

Shell the walnuts and chop them coarsely, place them in a bowl, and add to them the flour, the sugar, the egg yolks, the butter (barely melted over very low heat), the chocolate dissolved in warm milk, the cocoa, the Marsala, and the baking powder. You'll obtain a rather dense mixture, not soft at all. Beat the egg whites into soft peaks and fold them into the other ingredients. Butter a loaf-pan or mold, sprinkle it with some flour and a pinch of sugar, and shake off the excess flour from the pan. Now pour the mixture into it and bake in a 400 F oven for 25 minutes.

When the mixture has cooled, pass the loaf-pan over a flame for a few seconds; this will make it easier for you to detach the bread from the pan.

Turn the pan upside-down onto a pretty plate, slide the dessert out gently, and sprinkle it with powdered sugar.

Papassini
(All Saints' cakes)

*3 ½ cups flour - 1 tbsp baking powder - 7 oz butter -
¾ cup sugar - 3 eggs - 1 cup peeled almonds - 2/3
cup sultana raisins - 1 cup walnuts - 1 grated lemon
peel - 1 shot-glass Anise liqueur
For the icing: 1 egg white - 1 cup sugar - ½ cup
water - decorative sugar crystals*

Papassini are sweet cookies baked in Sardinia as part of the observation of All Saints' Day. If its true that desserts aren't foods just for gluttons and epicureans, but that they evoke *nostalgia* in us all. These bright, tender, homey-smelling little cookies contain many of the elements required to call up fond memories in us.

Blanch the almonds in boiling water, peel them, and dry them well in a moderate oven. Mince them finely and pass them through a food mill. Plump the raisins in the Anise liqueur. Blend together the flour, the eggs, the butter, the granulated sugar, and the grated lemon peel. Gradually, as you're working this dough, incorporate the almonds, the raisins, and the baking powder into it. Roll out the dough to a thickness of about 1 centimetre (a bit less than ½ inch), then cut out small rhombus-shaped pieces from it, place them on a buttered, floured cookie sheet, and bake them in a moderate oven.

Meanwhile, prepare the icing. Pour the sugar into a pan, cover it with the water, and cook for about 15 minutes until a drop of this mixture, when transferred to a marble slab or other non-porous surface, crystallizes instantly. Turn off the flame. Beat the egg white until it stands in soft peaks; while still beating, pour the sugar syrup in slowly. The result is the Italian meringue. Let it cool and thicken. Then, using a brush, spread it on the baked *papassini* as soon as you remove them from the oven. Sprinkle some decorative sugars crystals onto them as a finishing touch.

Pastiera napoletana
(Neapolitan Easter cake)

*1 lb wheat kernels (available in health food stores) -
1 ½ cups milk - salt - 2 tbsp butter - 4 lemons - 3
tbsp + 2 cups sugar - 2 lbs ricotta - 4 tsp vanilla - 1
tbsp cinnamon - 1 shot-glass Strega liqueur - 1+ 1/3
cups candied citron peel - 6 eggs - 2 oranges -
confectioners' sugar
For the custard cream: 1 cup sugar - ½ cup flour - 6
egg yolks - 1 qt milk - 1 lemon peel
For the short pastry: 4 cups flour - 1+ 1/3 cups
sugar - 1 ½ cup butter - 3 eggs - grated peel of 1
lemon*

This cake, traditional at Easter-time, a prelude to spring, can be (like the novel by Pirandello) one, no one, and a hundred thousand. Every family has its own recipe- There are a great many ingredients, and all you have to do is change the proportions of one of them for the taste to be different. Easter Cake requires a special element that's not always easy to find right away, and that must be prepared in advance: soft wheat kernels.

Clean the kernels and put them in a bath of cold water overnight. In the morning drain the wheat kernels and put them in a saucepan with fresh water. The surface of the water should be about 2 inches higher than the wheat kernels. Cook it for half hour. When cool, cook it again for 15 minutes with the milk and the butter. Add 3 tbsp sugar and salt.

The individual wheat grains should open gradually and release the starch they contain, forming a creamy mixture. Should the mixture reduce too much and become excessively dry, you can add more water, which you should keep handy and on the boil nearby.

It's a good rule to complete this operation the day before, so that the wheat, thus cooked, can rest an entire night and have time to swell up slightly.

When the cooking's over, the total weight of the wheat mixture will be about 3 pounds. The next day, you can proceed to the composition of this dessert, which might better be called a symphony.

Rub the ricotta and 2 cups sugar through a sieve into a bowl, then add the grated peels of 4 lemons, a brimming shot-glass of Strega liqueur, a pinch of cinnamon, the candied citron peel chopped into tiny pieces, the vanilla, the wheat kernels, and the egg yolks. Stir slowly. Complete this mixture with the pastry cream, along with the egg whites. These should be beaten until they stand in stiff peaks and then folded in with great care. At the very end, add the juice of the oranges.

Previously, you will have prepared the short pastry as follows. Mound the flour on your marble slab or other work surface. Rapidly blend in the sugar, the butter (this should be at room temperature), the eggs, and the grated peel of ½ lemon. The way to make short pastry is to mix the ingredients quickly without too much ado, because you don't want them to develop inconvenient stickiness or stiffness. Before using the short pastry dough, let it rest for about 10 minutes. With a rolling-pin, roll out a portion of the dough into a rather thin disc.

Use this disc to line the inside of a baking pan. Pour in the other mixed ingredients, spreading the mixture lightly and evenly with a knife-blade. Roll out another sheet of dough, cut it into thin strips, and arrange these into a kind of lattice or grill on top of the cake. Brush with a beaten egg. We should mention that the indicated quantities will make about 4 tarts.

Bake these in a moderate oven for about an hour. The filling should become firm, and the short pastry golden.

Easter Cake becomes even better if allowed to wait one day before being cut. But before slicing it, at whatever time, sprinkle it with powdered sugar and try to restrain yourself from licking your fingers, despite the character in Shakespeare (Romeo and Juliet, Act IV) who declares, *" It is an ill cook who cannot lick his own fingers."*

Pere Kaiser al forno
(Baked pears)

2 ¼ lbs Bosc or Comice pears - 1 cup sugar - ½ cup
honey - 1 shot-glass Cognac - 1 lemon – cinnamon

Select pears that are firm and not completely ripe. Peel the pears in such a way that you leave a bit of peel around the stem.Try to give this remaining peel the shape of two small leaves. Don't core the pears. Boil them for 10 minutes in water with 1 lemon peel and a pinch of cinnamon. Meanwhile, prepare a mixture of sugar, honey, and cognac or other liquor of your choice. Now arrange the pears in a baking-pan, pour the sweet sauce over them, cover the pan with foil, and bake in a moderate oven for about 2 hours. When this period is almost up, remove the foil for the final few minutes of baking.

Pere "mastantuono" farcite
(Stuffed pears)

1 lb ricotta - 1 heaped cup sugar - 4 lbs
"mastantuono" pears (Seckels or Bartletts will
do) - 1 ½ cups custard cream (pag.288) - 7 oz Pan
di Spagna (pag. 291) - cinnamon - 2 tsp vanilla -
½ cup candied citron peel

This dessert has its origins in Massa Lubrense, an enchanting spot on the Sorrentine coast, but is probably the result of other historical exchanges and cultural cross-breeding. The ricotta, the candied fruit, and the aromatic essences are surely Arab-Eastern in provenance, and the pan di Spagna ("Spanish Bread") adds softness to softness in this recipe.

For the preparation of this special dessert, a rather long and involved process, we must first of all procure some "mastantuono" pears: small, rather hard fruits that can be found only 15 days a year, and more specifically during the second half of the month of August. Wash the pears, cut off their tops (save them to cover the pears when you bake them later), and remove the cores from the pears with a demitasse spoon.

You'll fill the pears with a mixture prepared as follows.

Rub the ricotta and sugar through a sieve, add the pastry cream, the crumbled pan di Spagna, a little cinnamon, the vanilla, and the citron peel chopped as small as possible.

Fill the hollow pears with this mixture, replace their tops snugly, line them up in a baking-pan, and pour in a very little water. Bake the pears in a hot oven. During the first hour of baking, the pears should be covered with silver foil; for the second and final hour, remove the foil and reduce the heat to a moderate level.

"Petits fours"
(Petits fours)

For the short pastry: 3 ½ cups flour - 7 oz butter
- 1 cup sugar - 2 eggs - 1 tsp grated lemon peel -
1 tsp baking powder
For the filling: sweets of various kinds(follow
imagination)

Light, elegant, frivolous, eloquent tidbits, these petits *riens* are tiny, sweet mouthfuls that may be defined as the exhibitionists of the kitchen. They're graceful, attractive, miniaturized, and refined, delicious delicacies worthy of dancing across a luxurious 18th-century to caress genteel mouths and voluptuous palates.

Inevitably, the preparation of *petits fours* requires a good deal of time, patience, and attention. The short pastry is particularly soft and therefore more buttery, a very thin layer used to line tiny *moules* (oven molds), whose baking must be kept under constant surveillance.

Once these little receptacles of delight are unmolded, they can be filled with the most diverse kinds of sweets: a thin layer of mandarin orange marmalade, almond paste with minced almonds, cherry jam, chocolate melted in a double boiler with a few drops of milk and Strega liqueur, little strawberries, pastry cream sprinkled with grated lemon peel, a touch of sweetened ricotta with melted chocolate and crushed, toasted hazelnuts, candied cherries.

We could go on. But we'll allow each readers imagination the freedom to make up his or her own personalized *"mignardises"*.

Raffaioli
(Iced cookies)

5 eggs - 1/3 cup sugar - 1 ½ cups flour - ½ lemon
For the icing: 1 cup sugar - 7 tbsp water - 1
lemon

The procedure here is identical to the one followed in making Pan di Spagna. The only difference is in the quantity of flour, which is doubled for the raffaioli. To bake these, use a baking-pan that's completely covered with flour and arrange the dough in it, divided into little mounds about 4 inches long. Cover them with more flour, and bake them in a low to moderate oven for 45 minutes. It's absolutely essential never to open the oven door until the baking period is over.

Remove the cookies from the oven, brush away the flour that's covering them, and coat them with a thin layer of icing. This icing, or glaze, or topping, however you may wish to call it, is one of those things where a little secret has the power to alter a situation and give that particular touch that will determine the success of your dessert.

To produce the icing, boil the sugar with the water in a small saucepan until a pinch of the liquid feels a bit sticky between your fingers without necessarily forming a thread. The mixture will stop fuming at this point and small, more compact bubbles will agitate the surface. Now remove the saucepan from the fire and place it in cool water, stirring constantly.

When you see that the surface of the mixture is becoming opaque, add the juice of ¼ lemon and stir vigorously so that the icing becomes white as snow. You'll obtain a rather thick cream, which you'll spread over the cookies. Put these back into the oven for only 2 or 3 minutes, and you'll see that the topping will begin to look smooth, hard, and bright.

Riso dolce infanzia
(Sweet rice pudding)

*1 qt milk - ¾ cup rice - salt - 4 tbsp sugar –
cinnamon*

This dish comes from the region of Sannio in south central Italy, where it is traditionally prepared for the feast of the Ascension. It's an extraordinarily simple dessert, but its purity evokes sweet memories and innocent flavors.
Pour the milk into a saucepan. Bring to a boil, then pour in the rice with a pinch of salt. Let the rice cook until done, stirring often. When the rice is cooked, add the sugar, pour the mixture into a bowl, and sprinkle with cinnamon.
Delicious when cold.

Roccocò
(Roccoco cookies)

*3 ½ cups flour - 2 cups sugar - grated citrus peels
(2 mandarins, 1 orange, 1 lemon) - 1 ½ cups mixed
almonds and hazelnuts - ¾ cup   water - 1 tsp
ground cinnamon - 1 tsp baking powder - 1 egg
white*

These are Christmas sweets. Once again, the citrus aromas call to mind the Mediterranean coast and the gardens of Capri and Sorrento.
Impenetrable, hard, dry, yet somehow winsome in their doughnut shape: they're the little cookies called roccocò.
Sift the flour. Pour the sugar into it, and add the grated, aromatic citrus rinds, the peeled, minced almonds and hazelnuts, the water, the cinnamon, and the baking powder.
Amalgamate everything; you'll obtain a rather stiff dough. Make little rings out of the dough, flatten them a bit, brush them with egg white, and bake them in a hot oven for about 20 minutes.

Saint Honoré
(St. Honoré tarts)

French-Style Puff Pastry (p287) - Custard Cream (p. 288) – Cream Puffs (p.297) - Pan di Spagna (Sponge Cake, p.291) - Rum syrup (2 cups water, 1 tbsp sugar, 1 lemon peel, ½ cup Rum & Strega liqueur)

Another French invader in Naples!

The St. Honoré tart is a composite, opulent dessert, a masterpiece of decorative art, a voluptuous architectural alternation of soft and crunchy layers, gracefully adorned, a sugary *concerto* of airy delicacy topped with whipped cream.

The first layer consists of the puff pastry, already baked. Spread a layer of pastry cream on the pastry, followed by concentric circles of choux (cream puffs) filled with whipped cream. Leave an empty space in the center of the tart, and fill this with pan di Spagna moistened with a syrup or punch containing both Rum and Strega liqueur.

Another layer of custard cream pastry filling completes the dessert, and, as a final, delightful touch, close up the gaps in the structure with decorative whipped cream.

La Santa Rosa
(Santa Rosa turnovers)

Add to the ingredients for sfogliatella heavy cream, custard cream and sour cherries.

The *Santa Rosa* turnover is a more voluptuous ancestress of *sfogliatella*, having her origin, by force of circumstances, precisely in the convent of the nuns of Santa Rosa, situated sheer above the Amalfi Coast between Furore and Conca dei Marini. At a certain point, almost in the center, one of the enclosing little strips will open and a flood of crème chantilly will surge out, its flavor interestingly enhanced by the sourness of the cherries.

The procedure is identical to that followed for *sfogliatella*. The only difference is that the already voluptuous flavors are enriched by a final addition of crème *chantilly* that is injected into the center of the upper portion of the pastry with a pastry-maker's syringe. Arrange 2 or 3 sour cherries on top of the cream and the result is a pleasant surprise.

To prepare the crème *chantilly*, add to a given amount of Custard Cream Pastry Filling half of the amount by weight of heavy cream, whipped with an electric beater until it's airy and soft. Don't whip the cream past the correct point; otherwise, it'll turn yellow and become butter.

Sapienze o "susamielli"
(Honey-nut cookies)

1 heaped cup sugar - 4 cups flour - 2 cups. honey - fresh citrus rinds (2 mandarins, 1 orange, 1 lemon) - 1 ½ lbs mixed hazelnuts and almonds, toasted and minced - 1 egg

These are typical Neapolitan Christmas cookies, which, usually, are made in the shape of an "S" in honor of their place of origin: once again, a convent, the *Monastero della Sapienza* ("Convent of Wisdom"), where nuns used to prepare these traditional little cookies, making them fragrant with flowers, honey, and citrus fruits. They're also called *susamielli* because formerly they were covered with sesame seeds.

In a saucepan, liquefy and boil the sugar with the honey, the hazelnuts, the almonds, and the aromatic, grated citrus rinds. When everything has cooled, pour the sifted flour into the saucepan. Turn the mixture out onto your work surface and shape the little cookies. Bake them in a hot oven for about ½ hour after brushing them with the beaten egg.

"Scazzettine" al caffè
(Coffee pastries)

For the short pastry: 1 1/3 cups flour - ½ cup sugar - 7 tbsp butter - 1 egg - 1 tsp baking powder
For the filling: 4 tbsp butter - 5 tbsp custard cream (p.285) - 2 tsp instant coffee
For the glaze: ½ cup confectioners' sugar - 1 tbsp strong espresso coffee - coffee beans as needed

Convents and monasteries were veritable repositories of the most delicious delicacies, and their recipes were treasures of love and gluttony. As proof, we offer these exceptionally delicate little pastries, or *scazzettine*. In the Neapolitan dialect, *scazzettine* is the word for the small head coverings that bishops wear and that lend their name to these most elegant bundles of sweetness, wherein the aroma of coffee, judiciously measured, caresses the taste buds and uplifts the spirit.

Prepare the short pastry as usual and line the molds with it; you should use molds that are rather small. Prick the dough with a fork and bake the molds in the oven.

Now prepare a buttery cream as follows. Dice the butter and let it soften at room temperature. Whip the butter with an electric beater. When the butter is frothy, add it to the cream and the instant coffee. Fill up the short pastry molds with this buttery cream and top with a coffee glaze.

For the glaze, dissolve the sugar in the strong coffee at room temperature. Spread this mixture over the flat surface of the little desserts and place a coffee bean in the center of each. The sugar will set quickly.

Seadas
(Sweet cheese fritters)

3 ½ cups flour - 1 cup milk - 7 tbsp olive oil - 1 lb fresh, unripened cheese - ½ grated lemon peel - 1 pinch salt - 1 ½ cups honey - 1 grated orange peel - frying oil - Strega liqueur

Henry Gault, the gastronomical journalist who dissociated himself from Millau and his *Nouvelle Cuisine*, then founder of the gastronomical movement known as *"Modern Cuisine"* (which is the result, he asserts, of a proper balance between traditional ways and the new rules about lighter eating, embracing the innumerable regional peculiarities of traditional cuisine), while sampling various traditional dishes in Sardinia, cried out, *"but this is the kind of cooking to put your interest on"* . He was certainly tasting *seadas*, a dessert that underlines the Sardinians' attachment to their native earth by a happy contrast between fresh cheese (preferably from ewe's milk) and honey (a very important ingredient in Sardinian Cuisine).

In a bowl, add the grated peel of ½ lemon to the cheese, cut into thin little strips. Then pour the flour in a mound onto your work surface and sprinkle with salt. Add first the milk and then the olive oil; blend the ingredients together as you do so. Work the mixture well and you will produce a lovely, smooth, elastic dough, full-bodied but not soft.

Heat an empty pot for a minute on the stove, then overturn it upon the dough so that the latter is completely covered. Let it rest for 20 minutes. Then take it in hand again, break off little balls of it, and roll these out one by one with a rolling-pin to form so many little discs. Place a small quantity of the cheese, flavored with the lemon peel, on half of the discs. Cover these with the remaining discs, using light pressure from your fingers to close the edges. Continue this process until you run out of both cheese and dough-discs. Use the scalloped wheel of a pastry-cutter to trim and seal the edges of the discs.

Fry the seadas in hot oil. Let them turn golden on both sides, drain them, and pour over them an aromatic mixture of the liquefied honey, a little Strega, and the grated orange peel.

The honey used in Sardinia for many preparations is the bitter one, known as early as Roman times; it's produced by wild bees who suck the nectar from the flowers of the *Strawberry Tree*, what in Italian is called *corbezzolo*.

Semifreddo con arance
(Orange ice)

1 cup sugar - ½ cup milk - 4 egg yolks - 2 cups of heavy cream - 3 ripe oranges - 1 shot-glass Grand Marnier

Boil the milk and dissolve all but 3 tbsp of the sugar in it.
Beat the egg yolks and add them to the sugared milk, beating all the while. Let the mixture cool and refrigerate it. Meanwhile, whip the cream (which should be quite cold) in a bowl. When the milk, sugar, and egg mixture is cold, add it to the whipped cream. Pour everything into little porcelain or crystal cups and place these in the freezer at once. At the moment of serving this ice, peel the oranges, trim the threads from the individual wedges with a sharp knife, and place the orange wedges in a hot skillet where you have already flambéed the remaining 3 tbsp sugar in a shot-glass of Grand Marnier.
Let the oranges caramelize slightly, then pour them over the ices. Serve at once.

Sfogliatella sorrentina
(Delicate Neapolitan clam-shaped pastry)

For the dough: 7 cups flour - 1 ½ cups water - 1 ½ cup lard - salt
For the filling (in the Sorrentine version) 1 qt milk - 1 cup sugar - 1 cup flour - 6 eggs - the zest of 1 lemon - ½ cup candied fruit - 2 tsp vanilla

An enveloping spiral made up of a thousand paper-thin strips, crunchy on the outside and soft on the inside with its delicious filling (based on ricotta, semolina flour, and candied fruit in the Neapolitan version, but on delicate pastry cream and candied fruit in the Sorrentine version), the *sfogliatella* was probably invented in a religious house (as were, for that matter, very many gustatory marvels) towards the end of the 18th century. In Naples, in the early years of the 19th century, the cavalier Pintauro acted on a happy intuition and made the *sfogliatella* his own. To eat one hot is a sublime experience. These turnovers are not only somewhat difficult to prepare, it's not even easy to describe the process. With a bit of patience, however, both preparation and description are possible.

Let's first point out that a successful *sfogliatella* requires the use of high-quality, very finely-milled flour (a good pastry flour, for example) and special, white, cold-processed lard (the kind of lard that pastry-makers use). Work the cold water, a very little at a time, into the flour, and you'll get innumerable little hard flakes. Press the flour strongly with the palms of your hands, pound and roll it with the rolling-pin, working vigorously for a while, until at last you obtain a smooth dough.

Let this rest for ½ hour or more.

At the end of this period of time, roll out the dough into a rather long, thin sheet, and paint this with the lard, which should be liquefied but not hot.

The indicated quantities of flour, water, and lard are intended as guidelines; your own good culinary sense will tell you when you've used sufficient amounts. This assertion stands to reason, since anyone who's setting about to make a *sfogliatella* must unquestionably be a dedicated cook.

Spread on the lard with your hands so that it penetrates into the pores of the dough and begins to set. Then begin to roll up the dough very tightly, using its elasticity to draw and pull it snug. Roll this cylinder out flat with the rolling-pin once again; the dough should be reduced to minimum thickness. Then roll it back upon itself, cover it with a napkin or waxed paper, and let it stand in the refrigerator for 24 hours.

Remove the dough from the refrigerator and cut it into circular slices about an inch in diameter. Moisten these with more liquefied lard and refrigerate overnight once again so that the lard resolidifies and the dough becomes softer.

Flatten out each disc - they'll resemble spirals - first with your hands, then with the rolling-pin, uniformly and symmetrically, so that you obtain very thin little discs as precisely circular as possible. Don't, however, apply too much pressure, because you may jeopardize the desired separation of the individual layers of dough during the baking. With the help of the rolling-pin, turn each disc of dough bottom side up. Place a portion of filling on half of the surface of each disc. Then close up each disc upon itself so that you have a stuffed halfmoon. Lightly brush the edges of the dough with lard and press them together with your fingertips.

Lightly grease a cookie sheet and arrange the turnovers on it. Bake them at a high temperature for a few (10 or 15) minutes.

For the turnover filling, prepare a white cream as follows. Pour a small portion of the milk that you're going to use for this cream into a saucepan with the sugar and the flour. Mix carefully, dissolving the sugar, so that you obtain a thick, very smooth cream without lumps.

Now add, a little at a time, the rest of the milk and the lemon peel (all white and stringy parts must be ruthlessly removed), and put the saucepan on a very low heat. Stir constantly until the cream begins to give signs of boiling, murmuring happily. Then remove the cream from the heat. After it has cooled, add the eggs, one at a time, until the cream seems to be about to "exit," as the pastry-cooks say, that is, to move beyond the borders of the container it's in.

Then add the candied fruit, chopped into tiny pieces, and the vanilla, and use this mixture as a filling for the turnovers, which you will bake in the oven.

During the baking period, all the little layers of the pastry will rise and separate, becoming flaky and crunchy on the outside, while the cream will moisten the interior of the pastry, leaving it soft and scrumptious.

Ripieno per la sfogliatella napoletana
(Filling for Neapolitan-style turnovers)

1 qt water - 1 pinch salt - 1 ½ cups semolina flour - 2/3 lb ricotta - 1 cup sugar - 2 eggs - ½ cup candied fruit - 2 drops cinnamon oil

Put the water in a saucepan with a pinch of salt and the semolina flour and bring to boil, stirring constantly for 5 minutes until the mixture is solid.

Let it cool. Now rub the ricotta through a sieve with the sugar, and add these ingredients together with the eggs, the candied fruit minced as small as possible, and the 2 drops of cinnamon oil.

Sorbetto di frutta
(Fruit sorbet)

2/3 cup sugar - 1 ½ cup water - 2 cups fruit juice
- 1 lemon - 2 tbsp Gin

Even more than ice cream, sorbets are the summer dessert *par excellence*. Fresh and light, they draw the secret essences - the aromas, the perfumes - out of ripe fruit and enhance the vigor of its taste.
To make a successful sorbet, it's important to find the right balance between the sugar and the fruit; otherwise, you risk incurring the disappointment of producing a granita or ice because you haven't used enough sugar, or, if you've used too much, of turning out a sticky mush incapable of bringing out the delicate flavor of the fruit.
Prepare a syrup by dissolving the sugar in the water over low heat. When the syrup has cooled, add to it the fruit juice, 2 tbsp of lemon juice and the Gin. Place the mixture in the freezer for a few hours, being sure to stir it well whenever it begins to harden. Repeat this operation 6 or 7 times at 15 minute intervals.

Sorbetto di gelsomini
(Jasmine sorbet)

1 cup jasmine flowers - 1 cup sugar - 1 cup water -
1 orange - 1 lemon

The origin of the sorbet is simple and quite old: snow from Mt. Etna, honey, and fruit, with some added spices. Xenophon of Ephesus mentions it, and therefore it was already being enjoyed at the patrician tables of Imperial Rome. But the term itself is probably Arabic, from *sharbah*, to drink; it's something that one can sip (*sorbire* in italian).

Originally, in fact, sorbet was very similar to our granita or ice: fruit syrup and snow.

It was in the 16th century that the Florentine artist Bernardo Buontalenti discovered that the addition of egg whites to the ingredients just named succeeded in transforming their granular texture into a soft, velvety cream: *gelato.*

Caterina de' Medici, wife of King Henry II of France, introduced ice cream to the Parisian court. It was also in Paris, in 1650, that a Sicilian, one Procopio Coltelli, opened the Caffè Procope, which served exclusively ice cream made according to Italian recipes.

The Sicilians have a real talent for sorbets and ice cream, but certainly the most fragrant of all is Jasmine Sorbet.

The most seductive jasmine comes from India. *Jasminum sambac* (called also *Mogorium goaense*) arrived in Florence from Goa in 1688, a gift from the sovereign of Portugal to the melancholy Grand Duke Cosimo, lord of Tuscany. So enamored was he of this plant that he caused it to be guarded jealously. Only at the end of the 18th century, thanks to Pietro Leopoldo, were transplants allowed, and at last the peerless scent of Indian jasmine was able to delight other nostrils. Melt the sugar in a cup of water. Add the jasmine flowers for 2 minutes. Turn off the heat and let the flowers steep in the syrup for an hour. Then strain the syrup and add to it the juices (likewise strained) of 1 lemon and 1 orange. Pour this into the ice cream maker. Serve the sorbet garnished with jasmine petals and accompanied by thin cookies or wafers.

Sospiri
(Sighs)

*1 ½ cups sweet almonds - 1 heaped cup sugar -
grated peels of 1 lemon and 1 orange - 1 tsp
vanilla - 2 egg whites, beaten into soft peaks
For the glaze: 2 cups sugar - 1 cup water - 2 egg
whites*

This refined Sardinian dessert, lighter than the softest sigh, a puff of fragrance and discreet flavors, able to arouse the most jaded taste buds, furnishes an exciting, sugared concert of delicacy and tenderness before which even the firmest resolve is doomed to collapse.

Blanch the almonds, peel them, and dry them in a lukewarm oven to eliminate any trace of moisture. Mince them very finely, pass them through a food mill, and add the sugar, the grated citrus peels, the vanilla, and the beaten egg whites. Stir well. Shape the mixture into little balls and place them on a baking-sheet. Keep a little distance between them. Bake the sospiri at a very moderate temperature (210°F) for 10 or 15 minutes. They should take on a light golden color and remain soft. Let them cool, then brush them with the glaze that you will prepare as follows. Put the sugar and the water into a saucepan and boil for about 10 minutes, until the water has just about disappeared and the sugar begins to form threads. You can verify that the exact cooking point has been reached by moistening your thumb and forefinger in water and taking a pinch of the sugar between them; if it gives no indication of forming a thread, or if a drop placed on a marble slab crystallizes, the sugar is cooked properly. Extinguish the flame and incorporate the sugar and the very stiffly beaten egg whites.

Stir this mixture carefully. Then brush (or pour) the glaze onto the sospiri and let it dry.

Wrap up each little sweet, first in a bit of foil, then in transparent paper of various colors.

Soufflé al limone
(Lemon soufflé)

3 ½ tbsp butter - 5 tbsp flour - 2 cups milk - 1 pinch salt - 1 scant cup sugar - 3 lemons - 6 eggs

The virgin Parthenope (an ancient name for Naples) has been violated by Romans, Normans, Swedes, Angevins, Spaniards, Austrians, French, Piedmontese, Germans, and Americans.

The city of the sun, the conquerors'desire, has always managed to effect a particular liaison between those who are passionately devoted to it and its own resources.

We have made this French dessert our own, because, thanks to the superiority of our lemons, we can't help getting better results.

Make a rather thick béchamel sauce with the butter, the milk, and the flour, as follows. Melt the butter over low heat avoiding it to foam. Remove it from the flame and add the flour to it. Blend very well, then little by little add the milk, continuing to stir so that there won't be any lumps. Add a pinch of salt, return to the heat, and cook to boiling point, stirring all the while. Now turn off the heat and add the sugar and the grated peels of the lemons.

Prepare some little soufflé molds by greasing them with a bit of butter and sprinkling them all over with a mixture of flour and sugar. Shake off the excess. Now add to the bechamel mixture the juice of 1 lemon and the egg yolks; then, lastly, fold in the egg whites after beating them until they stand in soft peaks. Amalgamate everything very well, but very gently. Pour the mixture into the molds so that it takes up ¾ of their volume. Place these at once in a hot oven (350° F) for about ½ hour and serve them immediately, as soon as they begin to look puffy and irresistible.

Spuma di riso al latte
(Rice Mousse with Milk)

2 ¼ cups rice - 3 ½ tbsp butter - 2 qts milk - 1 cup heavy cream - 6 eggs - 2/3 cup sugar - cinnamon - grated breadcrumbs

Toast the rice in the butter, then pour in the milk. Let the mixture cook and thicken. Refrigerate it after it cools. When the rice is cold, add to it the cream, whipped stiff, with the egg yolks, the sugar, and the cinnamon.

At the end, add the egg whites, beaten until they stand in peaks. Butter a baking-pan and sprinkle it with grated breadcrumbs.

Pour in the mixture and cook it in a hot oven for about ½ hour.

"Struffoli"
(Neapolitan honey sweets)

For the dough: 3 ½ cups flour - 5 eggs - 2 tbsp
vegetable oil - 3 tbsp sugar - ½ tsp baking powder
- 1 shotglass Anise liqueur - salt - vegetable oil
for frying
For the coating: 1 cup honey - 2 tbsp sugar - 1
lemon peel - 1 orange peel - 2 mandarin peels
For the "crunch": 1 lb almonds - 2 ¼ cups sugar
- 1 ½ tbsp butter - 1 lemon

Hundreds of little balls of fried dough, simple and cheerful, welded together with honey: *struffoli* probably originated in the Middle East, but perhaps in ancient Greece. In the richer versions - during the Christmas holidays, for example - the sweet is served in crunchy little containers.

Sift and mound the flour, make a well in the center, and into this well put all the other ingredients. Prepare a good, consistent, elastic dough, at first with the aid of a fork, and then with your hands, working the dough vigorously. Cover the dough with a napkin and let it stand for about an hour. Then take small quantities of the dough, roll it between your fingers into the shape of tiny, thin tubes, and cut these into little balls that you'll arrange on a napkin. When this operation is finished, it will be time for you to fry all the little balls in plenty of hot oil. When they're pretty, golden, shiny, and crunchy, use an appropriate tool to remove them from the heat. Let the oil drain off and place them on paper towels so that as much of the oil as possible is absorbed.

Now, make the coating by liquefying the honey with the sugar in a saucepan. Add 2 tbsp. water and the grated, fragrant citrus peels. As soon as a light foam begins to form on the surface, the coating will be ready to receive the struffoli. Pour them in and stir them around a bit; they will shine brilliantly. You can either arrange them nicely on a pretty serving-platter, or, better yet, serve them in the crunchy containers we mentioned earlier.

To prepare these, preferably use almonds; if almonds aren't available, small hazelnuts will serve. Toast the almonds in the oven for a few minutes. Once they have become golden, chop them into small pieces and cook them in a skillet with the sugar and 1 1/2 tbsp. butter, stirring constantly for about 10/15 minutes.

Now you can use either one single mold or various small wheelshaped molds. Butter them lightly. While the almonds are still hot, press them into the molds so that they form a lining about 1/2 inch thick. You can add more fragrance and greater complexity by using an entire lemon (instead of a spoon) to pack the almond mixture so that it adheres perfectly to the sides of the mold or molds that you've chosen. After about 1/2 hour, when the almonds have completely cooled, unmold them. You will then have the crunchy containers you want. Fill them with the struffoli you've already prepared, and decorate them, if you wish, with strips of candied orange peel cut into the tiniest pieces possible.

Timballetti dolci alla crema
(Sweet rice pastry with cream)

1 qt. milk - 1 heaped cup rice - 1 tsp. vanilla - 1 pinch cinnamon - confectioners'sugar
For the custard cream: 1/4 cup sugar 2 tbsps. flour - 1 egg yolk - 1 cup milk
For the short pastry: 4 cups flour - 1 cup sugar – 7 oz. butter - 2 eggs

Boil the milk with the rice and the spices (vanilla and cinnamon). Reduce the milk completely over a slow heat so that you obtain a solid mass. Let this cool, then stir in the pastry cream.

Separately prepare some little baking molds by greasing them with butter and sprinkling them with a little flour and sugar. Line them with a thin layer of short pastry and fill them with the prepared rice mixture. Finally, bake them in a moderate oven. Unmold them, sprinkle them with powdered sugar, and serve them cold.

Torrone della nonna
(Grandmother's Nougat)

1 lb. hazelnuts - 1 cup sugar - 1 grated lemon peel

This stupendous torrone doesn't embarrass you as you eat it (as often happens with other crunchy desserts) because every single hazelnut, friable and obedient to the law of desire, graciously detaches itself from its neighbor and enters your mouth, where aroused salivary glands are waiting to dissolve it.

To prepare a good torrone of this type, it's essential to use an old copper (not tin-plated) skillet as the basic tool of your trade.

Put the hazelnuts and the sugar into a saucepan over lively heat and stir constantly with a wooden spoon until the sugar liquefies and then caramelizes. This process should take 15 minutes.

Now wet your marble surface with a little water, turn out the hazelnuts onto it, grate the peel of one lemon, and with the help of the lemon crush the hazelnuts so that you obtain a single layer. When this has cooled, you can easily break off pieces of it and preserve them in a glass jar - or eat them on the spot.

Torta all'arancia
(Orange cake)

1 large orange – 3 cups flour - 5 tbsp. sugar - 4 tbsp. oil - 9 tbsp. milk - 1 tsp. baking soda - 1 tsp. cream of tartar - confectioners' sugar

Grate the entire peel of 1 large or 2 small oranges and squeeze out all their juice. Add to the grated peel and the juice the flour, the sugar, the oil, and the milk. Stir at length and with attention. Then add the baking soda and the cream of tartar. Amalgamate everything quickly and thoroughly. Pour into a copper pan greased with butter and powdered with confectioners' sugar and flour and bake in a 350° F oven.

When the mixture begins to make little bubbles, lower the heat to 300° F and bake for 20 minutes more.

At the end, sprinkle the cake with vanilla sugar.

Torta alla crema della nonna
(Grandmother's cream pie)

For the dough: 1 ½ cups flour – ½ cup sugar - 7 tbsp. butter - 1 egg – 1 tsp. baking powder
For the cream: ½ cup flour – ½ cup sugar - 3 egg yolks – 2 ½ cups milk - 1 lemon peel, cut into a spiral - 2 oz. almonds

For this classic pie, which is relatively simple and very light, you need good short pastry and custard cream.

Pour in the custard cream, perfumed with the peel of a very fresh lemon. Place another layer of short pastry on the cream, and paint the upper surface of this layer with a beaten egg until it gleams. Garnish with peeled almonds. Bake in a 400° F oven for 1/2 hour. If eaten lukewarm, the tart will caress your palate with the full range of its flavors.

Torta al riso
(Rice cake)

1 qt. milk – 1 ½ cups rice – 1 1/3 cups sugar - 5 eggs - 1 lemon peel - 1 tsp. vanilla - 10 amaretti (Italian macaroons) - 1 scant cup custard cream custard filling (see p.278.) - salt
For the amaretti: 1/3 cup bitter almonds – 3 cups sweet almonds - 2 heaped cups sugar - 3 eggs whites

This excellent Sardinian dessert requires among its ingredients real amaretti, the kind that are still homemade according to the old recipe from Oristano on the west coast of Sardinia. Peel and grind the almonds and amalgamate them with the sugar and the egg whites, beaten into peaks.

The resulting dough should be soft but not too soft. Make little balls of it about the size of a walnut. Put these into a lightly buttered and floured baking-pan. Bake in an oven at a very low heat. These are homemade amaretti; if you're short of time, you can also use the ones that are available commercially.

Cook the rice in the milk for 12 minutes together with a fragrant lemon peel and a pinch of salt. When the rice is cooked, add the sugar. Let the rice mixture cool, then add the pastry cream, the finelyground amaretti, the vanilla, and the eggs (first the yolks, then the whites, beaten into peaks). Pour this mixture into a baking-pan and cook the cake in a 350° F oven for 40 minutes.

Torta Caprese
(Capri cake)

2 1/3 cups almonds - 1 heaped cup sugar - 5 oz.
squares unsweetened chocolate - 7 oz. butter - 5
eggs - 1 level tbsp. flour – 1/2 tsp. baking powder

The amount of Capri Cake consumed around Sorrento, Capri, Positano, Amalfi, and all along the coast that goes from Castellammare to Salerno can hardly be imagined. It's a dessert that's both simple and extraordinary.

Grate the chocolate into a crockery bowl, add the sugar, the 5 egg yolks, and the softened butter, and beat all this together until you have a soft, airy mixture. Peel, mince, and add the almonds, along with the flour and the baking powder. Lastly, fold in the egg whites, beaten into peaks with a pinch of salt. Turn the mixture into a buttered, floured baking-pan and bake in a moderate oven for about 1/2 hour.

Torta di castagne
(Chestnut tart)

*1 lb. chestnuts - 1 lb. ricotta - 3 cups sugar - 1
tbsp. cocoa powder - 1 shot-glass rum - vanilla -
1/3 cup candied fruit - 1/3 cup minced glazed
almonds*

Chestnut tart is a mélange of simple elements that produces a most flavorful result.
You have to boil the chestnuts, remove their shells and skin, and rub them through a food mill. They'll make a sort of cream, to which you then add the ricotta and the sugar, which you have passed through the food mill together. Next, blend in the cocoa, the rum, a few drops of vanilla, the candied fruit chopped into minuscule pieces, and the minced glazed almonds.
To prepare the glazed almonds, proceed as follows. Put the almonds in a small saucepan and cover them with sugar. Add 1 tbsp. water and a pinch of cinnamon. Set the saucepan on an extremely low heat and stir constantly until the sugar becomes shiny. Pour the almonds onto your work surface and mince them. The whole mixture, including the chestnut cream first described, is used as a filling between two layers of short pastry. Bake this marvelous pie in a 350° F oven for about 40 minutes.

Torta di crema massese
(Cream pie)

*For the short pastry: 2 cups flour - 7 tbsp. sugar -
7 tbsp. butter - 1 egg - 1 tsp. baking powder
For the custard cream: 8 tbsp. flour –1 cup sugar
- 6 egg yolks - a little more than 1 qt. milk –
1 lemon peel, cut into a spiral
For the cocoa mixture:4 tbsp. cocoa powder and
1/3 cup milk*

*1 cup Pan di Spagna (p.291) or Savoy Bread -
cinnamon - confectioners' sugar - sour cherries
(optional) - liquors: Anise liqueur, Strega, Rum*

For chocolate lovers, mixing cocoa, cinnamon, rum, and the gentle fragrance of lemon arouses powerful sensations. The attraction of chocolate flavored with jasmine must have appeared similarly irresistible to noses and taste buds when the fashion for the so-called "Indian brew" or the art of making chocolate, was all the rage in the second half of the 17th century. The illustrious preachers of the Society of Jesus fell head over heels in love with this delicate, precious beverage and were transported to visions ot eternal happiness through the enjoyment of its heavenly charms: "...tea, coffee, and chocolate are consumed in an intimate, private atmosphere, inside a confined area (the bedroom, the boudoir), at the breakfasts that accompany the lever or the ritual of rising, or at unofficial dinners in informal, confidential company."

According to Piero Camporesi's relation in *Il brodo indiano* ("The Indian Brew"), this is how the use of the new beverage in the 18th century could be described.

In the following recipe, we use the marvellous flavor of cacao to permeate half of the pale, carefully measured custard cream. After you prepare the pastry cream with the usual ingredients - flour, sugar, milk, egg yolks, and lemon peel - dissolve 4 tbsp. cocoa in a saucepan with 1/2 cup hot milk.

Add to this thick mixture half of the pastry cream together with 1 shot-glass rum. Meanwhile, you will have made the short pastry in the approved manner, and you'll have ready to hand some pan di Spagna (Sponge cake) or Savoy bread, which is like pan di Spagna or maybe even better: long cookies that are as yellow as gold, and broad, soft, spongy and light; one imagines that they have been prepared by virginal hands. We're thankful to Savoy for sending us such outstanding sweet delights.

This most worthy Cream Torte, like many such delicious delicacies, was part of the patrimony of mouth-watering, loving recipes from a religious house in Massa Lubrense, an enchanted, ancient spot on the Sorrentine peninsula.

Convents and monasteries have always been storehouses of the most appetizing delights, and precisely for this reason many *bon vivants* bitterly regret their disappearance. Line a baking-pan with a layer of short pastry, and cover this with a layer of fragrant pastry cream. Next comes a layer of crumbled pan di Spagna or Savoy bread, soaked in generous quantities of anise liqueur and Strega liqueur; then add a pinch or two of cinnamon and, if you wish, a garnish of sour cherries. This is followed by the chocolate cream, aromatized with a shot of rum and spread in one homogeneous layer. Sprinkle a bit more cinnamon on this, and, finally, cover with another sheet of short pastry. Brush the top with egg white before baking for about 1/2 hour in a 400° F oven. This dessert is eaten cold. At the moment of serving, sprinkle it with powdered sugar.

Torta di fragole
(Strawberry sponge cake)

Pan di Spagna (p.291) - Custard cream (p.278) - strawberries – rum - Strega liqueur – orange - lemon – sugar

In a fragment spared by the flames that destroyed the library in Alexandria, there's a description of an excellent method of preparing strawberries: they are steeped in the juice of a sweet orange (one of the "golden apples of the Hesperides"), together with the orange peel and some sugar.
Strawberries prepared in this way were surely served even at the banquets on Mt. Ida.
Let's take this advice, but we'll add lemon juice to the marinade for our strawberries. Then we'll use them as a filling for a flavorful, fragrant cake, a real springtime treat, prepared with the pan di Spagna described on page 291. Cut the pan di Spagna in half horizontally. Moisten the lower half with a little rum, Strega, and strawberry syrup. Cover this layer with the pastry cream, then with the strawberries. Next, place the other half of the pan di Spagna on top of the strawberries. Pour a little strawberry syrup onto this. Add one more thin layer of pastry cream, then make a final layer of strawberries, gracefully arranged. This cake gets even better if allowed to stand for 1 or 2 hours before being eaten.

Torta di mandorle
(Almond cake)

*1 cup almonds – 1 cup sugar - 2 eggs – 2 cups
custard cream (p.278.) - 1 tsp. vanilla
For the short pastry: 2 cups flour - 7 tbsp. butter -
7tbsp. sugar - 1 egg - 1 pinch baking powder*

If you've prepared a light dinner, you can permit yourself this imaginative, elegant Sorrentine dessert. With every mouthful, the unmistakable taste of almonds, enhanced by the fragrance of the lemon in the pastry cream, offers itself to your palate and gives you the sensation of an extraordinary dessert.
Plunge the almonds into boiling water, remove them quickly, and place them on a cloth napkin. It will then be easy to peel them. Next, pound them well with the sugar, reducing them to a fine mush. Add the pastry cream while it's still hot, so that it blends with the almonds in a marvellous, aromatic whole. Lastly, incorporate the eggs (first the yolks, then the whites, beaten until they stand in peaks). You can underline the flavors by adding a few drops of vanilla.
Line a buttered baking-pan with short pastry and fill it with the almondcream mixture. Cover this with another sheet of pastry, brush this with a little beaten egg, and bake in a hot oven for about 1/2 hour.
This is a delicious cake for anyone who loves almonds.

Torta di nocciole
(Hazelnut tart)

*For the filling: 1/3 lb. shelled hazelnuts - 1 cup
powdered sugar - 1 cup grated chocolate - 1 cup
milk - 2 eggs - vanilla
For the dough: 1 1/2 cups flour - 2 eggs - 2 tbsp.
olive oil - 2 tbsp. sugar - salt - rum*

Toast the hazelnuts and grind them finely together with half of the sugar. Separately, over a very low heat, dissolve the chocolate and the remaining

sugar in the milk. Then pour the ground hazelnuts and the chocolate mixture into a crockery bowl and stir them together well. Add a few drops of vanilla and the eggs, first the yolks, and then the beaten whites. The next operation is to prepare the puff pastry dough. Mix the flour with the eggs (1 whole egg plus 1 yolk), about a tablespoon of rum, 2 tbsp. olive oil, 2 tbsp. sugar, and a pinch of salt. Knead this dough on your work surface, adding flour if necessary until you can shape a rather soft loaf. Roll this out with a rolling-pin and use it to line a baking-pan (previously greased with oil or butter) about 3/4 inch deep. Then pour in the cream and cover this with some of the same dough, cut into strips and laid so as to form a grill. If you wish, you can garnish the cake with some raw hazelnuts chopped into small pieces.
Bake in the oven.

Torta di nocciole o noci
(Hazelnut or walnut cake)

2 cups flour - 2 cups confectioners' sugar - 7 oz.
butter - 2/3 lb. hazelnuts or walnuts - 6 eggs - 3
tsp. baking powder - 1 drop lemon juice

This Sorrentine dessert is particularly welcome during the winter season and is, moreover, a surefire success.
Cream the confectioners' sugar with the butter, stirring thoroughly to obtain a soft, creamy mixture. Add to this, first, the egg yolks, then the sifted flour, the minced nuts, the baking powder, and, lastly, the egg whites, beaten with a drop of lemon juice until they stand in very stiff peaks.
Pour this mixture into a baking-pan that has been buttered and sprinkled with flour and sugar. Bake the cake in a 400° F oven for about 1/2 hour.

Torta di ricotta
(Ricotta cheesecake)

1 lb. very fresh ricotta - 2 cups confectioners'
sugar - 1 cup mixed candied citron and orange
peel - 2/3 cup candied cherries - 4 oz. squares

unsweetened chocolate – 3 1/2 oz. savoiardi
(Italian ladyfingers) - strong liqueur - 4 eggs

Dice all the candied fruit and chop the chocolate into small pieces. Rub the ricotta through a sieve and into a small tureen. Stir with a wooden spoon, adding the sugar a little at a time, then the egg yolks, one by one. Next, stir in 2 shot-glasses of liquor and all the candied fruit, then the chocolate, and lastly the egg whites, beaten into soft peaks.
Soak the ladyfingers in the liquor (not too long). Line a rather high-sided pie-pan with waxed paper, arrange the soaked savoiardi in it, and pour the ricotta mixture over them. Make sure the surface is level, then place the pan in the refrigerator and leave it there for several hours. When you're ready to serve the cheesecake, turn the pie-pan upside down on a serving-platter, remove the paper, decorate with candied cherries, and bring your dessert to the table.

Torta di semolino
(Semolina flour cake)

1 pt. milk - 1 1/3 cups semolina flour - 2 tbsp.
butter - 1 pinch salt – 2 cups sugar – 1 lb.
ricotta - 5 eggs - peel and juice of 1 lemon -
distilled orange water - 1/3 cup candied citron
– vanilla

This flavorful and extremely delicate cake offers the advantage of possible presentation in two different versions: you can serve it after simply mixing and baking the above ingredients, or you can serve it between top and bottom layers of short pastry.
This recipe comes from the towns around Mt. Vesuvius. Pour the milk into a saucepan and heat it. When it's hot, sprinkle in the *semolina*, stirring all the while with a wooden spoon. Continue cooking for 6 or 7 minutes. Then add the butter, the salt, and half the sugar. Rub the ricotta with the other half of the sugar through a sieve and into the semolina mixture.
Now add all the other ingredients: first the egg yolks, then the flavorings (only a few drops of lemon juice and 2 drops of distilled orange water, along

with the candied citron and a little vanilla). Lastly, add the egg whites, beaten into soft peaks.

Grease a baking-dish with butter and powder it with a pinch of flour, turning it in your hands so that the flour is evenly distributed over its surface. Pour the semolina mixture into the baking-dish and bake the cake in a hot oven. After about 40 minutes, the cake should be set and golden-brown.

Torta di zia Lucia
(Aunt Lucy's pie)

1 lb. ricotta - 1 1/2 cups sugar - 6 eggs –
3 1/2 tbsp. butter -4 tbsp. flour - 1/2 cup
milk - 1 orange - 1 tsp. vanilla - 1 shot-
glass rum – 3 1/2 oz. pan di Spagna
(p.291) or savoiardi (Italian ladyfingers)
For the short pastry: 2 cups flour - 7
tbsp. butter - 7 tbsp. sugar - 1 egg -
grated lemon peel

Here's another sweet based on ricotta and related to cassata, cannoli, and Easter Cake.

First of all, prepare the short pastry as described in other recipes and set aside. Meanwhile, rub the ricotta through a sieve with the sugar. Stir 7 tbsp. flour into the milk. Beat 3 whole eggs plus 3 egg yolks. Mix all these ingredients with the vanilla, the grated peel of 1 orange, and its juice. Then divide the short pastry into 2 parts and roll out a thin sheet from each with a rolling-pin. Line a baking-dish with a disc of short pastry. Press the dough down firmly and cover it with the pan di Spagna or the lady-fingers. Moisten with the rum. At this point, pour in the ricotta mixture, which should be very soft.

Cover with another disc of short pastry dough, brush this with a bit of egg white, and bake in a 400° F. oven for about 1/2 hour or until the pie is golden-brown on every side.

Torta margherita
(White cake)

1 3/4 cups very finely-milled pastry flour - 1 cup
sugar - 4 eggs - 1 tbsp. cream of tartar - 1 tsp.
baking soda - juice of one lemon, strained

Beat the egg yolks with the sugar in a bowl until you get a very light, frothy mixture. Quite slowly, a little at a time, add the sifted flour, stirring all the while with a wooden spoon. If the mixture seems to you to be getting too stiff, soften it by slowly adding the strained lemon juice; in this way it will absorb all the flour magnificently.
Stir in the cream of tartar and the soda. Beat the egg whites with a whisk until they stand in firm peaks; fold them into the mixture so that it absorbs them slowly. Butter a baking-pan and powder it with a combination of sugar and flour.
Pour in the filling mixture and bake in a preheated, moderate (340° F) oven for about 1/2 hour.

Torta soffice al limone
(Soft lemon pie)

For the filling: 1 1/3 lbs. ricotta - 1 cup sugar - 2
lemons - 2 eggs - 1 shot-glass Strega liqueur
For the short pastry: 2 cups flour - 7 tbsp. sugar -
7 tbsp. butter - 1 egg - 1 pinch baking powder

As it's true that desserts aren't at all mere objects of gluttony, but elements of nostalgia, this particular dessert is indeed a moment in memory. A consistent texture of ricotta, which evokes a magnificent dessert (Pastiera napoletana) worthy of all respect; a crunchy exterior of short pastry, a bewitching hint of Strega, the unique fragrance of just-harvested lemons from the land of lemons (*das Land, wo die Zitronen blühn*, as Goethe says), all unite to produce a tart that's light as a breath, fresh, and most delightful.

Prepare the short pastry with the sifted flour, the softened butter, the sugar, and the egg. Mix all these ingredients without working the dough too much. Let it rest while you prepare the filling for this dessert.

Rub the ricotta with the sugar through a fine sieve and into a bowl. Add the grated peels of 3 very fresh lemons - still somewhat greenish, if possible - being careful to avoid the white pith below the rind.

Moisten everything with a good shot-glass of Strega liqueur and with the egg yolks. Lastly, beat the egg whites into soft peaks and add them. Roll out a thin sheet of short pastry and line a baking-pan with it.

Pour into it the lovely, soft, frothy ricotta filling, and cover this with another sheet of short pastry dough. Brush the top with a beaten egg. Bake the tart in a hot oven until golden. Serve cold, sprinkled with confectioners'sugar.

Overwhelmed by Villa Tritone's beauty, by Mariano's virile and civil charm, by Rita's refined and very civil cuisine, which with her lemon cake reminded me of the ancient scents from the gardens in Sorrento.

Franco Zeffirelli

Tortelli di ricotta o il colpo dello Strega
(Ricotta fritters or the stroke of the Strega)

For the dough: 4 cups flour - 7 tbsp. olive oil –
1 cups milk - 1 pinch salt - 1 shot-glass rum
For the filling: 1 lb. ricotta - 1 cup sugar - 2
yolks - 1 good shot of Strega liqueur - 1 grated
orange peel - vegetable oil for deep frying

Here's another marvel that seems to straddle the dividing line between sweet dessert-type dishes and the savoury dishes usually eaten as part of the earlier courses of the meal. These tortelli result from the marriage of crunchy baked dough with a fragrant, voluptuous cream.

To prepare the dough, pour the flour onto your work surface, and blend the milk into it, a little at a time, using a fork in one hand and the fingertips of the other. Then add the salt a little rum, and the oil. Work the dough well and roll it out into rather thin sheets. Lightly mark the dough with a circular ravioli cutter to indicate the outline of each of the tortelli. Rub the ricotta through a sie with the sugar, flavor it with the grated peel of 1 orange and a shot-glass of Strega liqueur. Bind these ingredients with the egg yolks. Now, using a teaspoon, place a little of the ricotta mixture in the center of each circle as marked on the dough. Place a second thin sheet of dough over the first so that the tortelli, with their filling, are completely covered. Cut out the tortelli. Press the dough down around each little mound of filling in order to make sure that the two discs of dough adhere perfectly around the perimeter of each tortello. Arrange them in an orderly fashion on plates covered with napkins.

Refrigerate them for 1 or 2 hours. Just before serving them, fry them in plenty of hot vegetable oil, drain them on absorbent paper, sprinkle them with sugar, and bring them to the table.

Zeppole di pasta bollita
(Doughnuts or pastry rings)

*5 cups flour - 5 cups water - salt - lemon peel - 2
tbsp. lard - 1 shot-glass anise liqueur - 1 1/3 cups
honey - oil for frying*

Bring the water to boil, having added the salt and lard.
As soon as it begins to boil, remove it from the heat and pour in the flour all at once. Stir vigorously. Put the saucepan back on the heat and continue to work its contents with a wooden spoon for about 5 minutes until the dough comes away from the walls of the pan.
At this point, remove the pan from the fire and turn out the dough onto a lightly oiled marble slab. Keep working the dough, rolling and pounding it with a rolling-pin. As soon as the temperature of the dough allows it, start working it with your hands until it becomes soft and smooth. Then break off small pieces of the dough, shape little sticks or cylinders out of it, form them into rings by joining their ends, and fry in plenty of hot oil. Take them out of the oil and let them drain on paper towels. Melt the honey over a very weak flame and flavor it with the lemon peel and a small glass of the liquor. Roll

the drained doughnuts in the honey. They're good whether you serve them hot or cold. Perfect lukewarm!

Zeppole di Natale (Christmas doughnuts)

1 lb. potatoes – 5 cups flour – 1 oz. brewer's yeast - oil for frying - 1 lb. honey - 1 tbsp. rum - 1 tbsp. Anise liqueur – salt

Boil the potatoes in salted water, peel them, and rub them through a food mill to obtain a thin purée. Add the flour, stirring and blending painstakingly.
Dissolve the yeast with a pinch or two of salt in a little lukewarm water and add that.
Work the dough at length until its surface looks polished and its texture is very soft. Let it rise in a tranquil spot away from air currents for about an hour. Moisten your hands with a little oil. Break off pieces af dough, shape them into little rings, and fry them in abundant, extremely hot oil.
Liquefy the honey with 1 tbsp. rum and 1 tbsp. anise liqueur over very low heat, and roll the doughnuts in this mixture to coat them completely.

Zeppole di San Giuseppe
(St. Joseph's doughnuts)

3 1/2 tbsp. butter - 1 cup water - 1 pinch salt - 1 tsp. vanilla - grated peel of 1 lemon - 1 1/5 cups flour - 5 eggs - custard cream (p.278) - sour cherries

The origin of this dessert goes back a long way. From around 500 B.C., the Romans used to celebrate the Liberalia, the feast of the god Liber (dispenser of wine and grain), on March 17th. In honor of Silenus, companion of carousers and "tutor" of Bacchus, the celebrants drank rivers of red nectar and fried fragrant fritters made from wheat flour. Nowadays - on nearly the same day, March 19th - the feast of St. Joseph is the occasion for repeating the ceremony of the fritters.

The dough for St. Joseph's Doughnuts is prepared in a way similar to that used in making Cream Puffs (p.290), also known as choux. The difference lies in the smaller quantity of butter and the method of cooking; these doughnuts are in fact fried, while cream puffs are baked in an oven.

In a saucepan, heat the water with the salt and the butter until the latter melts. Then bring to boil and remove from the heat. Add the sifted flour all at once and stir vigorously. Return the saucepan to the heat and continue to stir for half a minute over a low flame.

Lightly oil your marble slab and turn out the mixture onto it. Let the mixture cool.

After the flour mixture has cooled, incorporate the eggs, one at a time, first the yolks and then the whites. Add the vanilla and the grated peel of 1 lemon.

To fry the doughnuts, prepare two skillets with plenty of vegetable oil. Place one on low heat and the other on lively heat. Since the dough will be very soft, it will be difficult to fry without resorting to a little trick. Take a sheet of waxed paper and punch holes in it. Put the dough, a little at a time, into an appropriate syringe or cookie-press (preferably one with a star-shaped opening). Pressing down on the plunger, squeeze out the dough directly onto the waxed paper. Shape the dough into rings or doughnuts. Then immerse the sheet of waxed paper with the doughnuts in the sizzling oil. Air will pass through the holes in the paper and allow the *zeppole* to detach themselves from it easily. Remove them from this skillet and plunge them into the other, hotter skillet so that they cook perfectly and become golden-brown. Drain the zeppole on absorbent paper as you do for all fried foods. Then arrange them on a platter and garnish each with a tablespoon of pastry filling topped with a pair of sour cherries.

Zeppoline con l'uvetta sultanina
(Little sultana raisin doughnuts)

4 cups flour - salt – 1 oz. brewer's yeast - 3 cups milk - 1 1/2 cups sultana raisins - 1 1/3 cups honey - 1 lemon peel - 1 shot-glass anise liqueur or rum or Strega - peanut oil for frying

In Naples, the ultimate origin of zeppole (China, perhaps?) has been lost in the mists of the centuries.

There was a time when, on St. Joseph's Day, zeppole were fried on street corners and eaten hot. Simple doughnuts made with raisins, fried, and sweetened with sugar and cinnamon or with honey, they are always delicious, especially if you eat them while they're still warm.

This is one of the tastiest recipes. It requires great care, especially in the frying, which should take place in plenty of hot (but not smoking) oil.

Pour the flour into a bowl with a pinch of salt. Dissolve the yeast and about 1 tsp. salt in the lukewarm milk, then add this to the flour, a little at a time. Mix continuously with a fork to avoid the formation of unattractive lumps. Keep working the dough until it becomes smooth and very soft and little bubbles begin to form on its surface. Then let it rest and rise in a warm spot, away from air currents, for about 1/2 hour.

During this time you should wash the sultanas and put them in a bowl to soak in whatever liquor you're using. When the dough has risen, incorporate the raisins into it and begin the frying process. Be sure to stir the dough from time to time so the sultanas don't all settle to the bottom of the bowl.

The oil should be abundant, hot but not fuming, and you should fry the dough in tiny portions, using a teaspoon to transfer the dough to the oil. Quickly turn the zeppoline over in the oil. When they're looking pretty and golden - remove them and drain them on absorbent paper. Then prepare the honey, heating it with a lemon peel in a small skillet over a very weak flame. Add a shot-glass of liquor if you wish, arrange the doughnuts on a handsome platter, and pour the honey over them immediately.

PRESERVES AND LIQUEURS

Amarene al sole
(Sun Cherries)

2 lbs. sour cherries - 3 rounded cups sugar

Here's a sublime melody of crystallized cherries. To prepare these sour cherries, the basic ingredients are patience, love, and soft summery heat. When the sour cherries are ready to be picked around the middle of June, you can set about preparing them according to this old Sorrentine recipe for preserving them in glass jars. Then you can enjoy them at your leisure as they are, delicious straight from the jar, or use them to garnish ices, puddings, or little short pastry cookies.

First of all, pit the cherries. Try not to break them. Arrange them on an enameled earthenware platter, cover them with the required sugar, and set them outdoors in the sun. They should be brought inside only at sunset, and this operation should be repeated for 20 days. Be careful to keep your sunset appointment with the cherries, because if you wait much longer you're liable to be preceded by other greedy little creatures: ants. After 20 days have passed, you can store the cherries and their nectar in glass jars and seal them hermetically.

Amarene in confettura per crostata
(Cherry jam for tarts)

2 lbs. sour cherries - 3 rounded cups sugar - juice of 2 lemons

The washed, pitted cherries are allowed to macerate in the sugar for one day only. On the following day, add the juice of 2 lemons and cook over a very low fire for about 2 hours. During the cooking period, a thick scum will rise to the surface from the cherries; conscientiously remove all traces of it. When you have thus obtained well-cooked cherries and a rather thick syrup, you can be certain that your efforts have been successful.

You can make sure you've got the desired results by pouring a few drops of this jam onto a saucer; if they slide slowly across the surface, that's the sign that you're looking for.

Heat some glass jars in the oven (this avoids subjecting the cherries to sudden temperature changes) and pour the cherry jam into them for safe keeping. Close up the jars immediately and place them in the pantry, ready te be used in future tarts.

Amarene ubriache
(Inebriated cherries)

*2 lbs. sour cherries - 1 cup grain alcohol - 3
cups anise liqueur - 4 cups sugar*

Wash the cherries well and dry them with a napkin. Don't remove their stems. Leave them out in the open air until you're sure that they're perfectly dry.

Place them in glass jars that are equally dry and perfectly clean, alternating sugar, alcohol, and anise liqueur with the cherries. Close the containers hermetically and leave them outdoors, exposed to sunshine and darkness, to changes of temperature and light, for about 40 days.

After this period of time has passed, transfer the jars to your pantry, but don't fail to wait at least 3 months before tasting the cherries, in order to give them enough time to be completely impregnated with the alcohol.

Bucce di arance candite
(Candied orange peels)

*1 lb. orange peels – 1 cup. honey – 2 cup almonds -
3 tbsp. sugar - decorative sugar crystals*

Remove the orange peels, being careful to exclude any white pulp or fibers. Cut the peel into very thin slices and let them dry for a few hours. Then soak the sliced peel in water to soften it for 24 hours. When this operation is concluded, put a copper pot on the fire with a little more than a pound of honey; when this is good and hot, pour in the drained slices of orange peel.

Stir constantly until the peel slices take on a handsome golden color. Peel the almonds, chop them into small slices, and add them to the hot honey.

Keep stirring all the while. Add 3 tbsp. sugar in order to give the mixture more consistency.

Finally, remove the mixture from the heat and transfer to a rectangular baking-pan.

The depth of the mixture should be approximately equivalent to the width of a finger. Cut this hard candy into small rectangles. Sprinkle some decorative sugar crystals over them. Store the candied orange peels in tightly-sealed glass jars.

Conserva di violette (Violet preserve)

1 1/3 cups sugar - 1 cup water - 1/2 lemon –
1/2 cup fresh violets

This is an old remedy used as a cough suppressant. Put the sugar into a crockery pot along with the water and the juice of 1/2 lemon. Simmer this briefly, add a few fresh, fragrant violet flowers (first remove their stems and sepals), minced and ground finely. Stir as you continue to cook the mixture over low heat until the liquid begins to turn white.

Pour into a glass jar and cover with waxed paper.

Cotognata (Quince candy)

4 1/2 lbs. quinces - 5 cups sugar - 2 lemons - 1/2
cup water

The memory of tastes from the past, of children's games enlivened by little square pieces of dense candy that would melt between your tongue and your palate and release a comforting sweetness.

Peel the quinces. While you're coring them, let them stand in water acidulated with the juice of one lemon so that they don't begin to darken.

When you've finished this operation, drain the quinces well and put them in a saucepan with 1/2 cup water and the juice and rind of another lemon. Bring this to boil and let it cook for a while, stirring from time to time.

When the quinces are cooked, rub them through a food mill and return them to the saucepan. Heat the sugar in the oven; add to the quince purée. Bring this back to boil, stirring and skimming until you have a mixture with the proper thickness and a very smooth appearance. While the concoction is still hot, turn it onto a very lightly oiled cookie sheet.

Spread the quince mixture out to a uniform thickness of about 1 inch. When it's cold, cut into squares and preserve these in closed, dry boxes or jars.

Fichi della nonna (Grandmother's figs)

*2 1/4 lbs. dried figs - 1 lb. walnuts - 5 lemons - 2
cups white wine – 2 cups water - 1 heaped cup
sugar - 1 shot-glass brandy - 1 shot-glass anise
liqueur*

This incomparable delight causes sensory confusion: it's a provocative combination of alcohol and crunchy walnuts, while the voluptuous flesh of the figs invites the tongue to envelop it as it clings to the palate, and the fragrance of the lemons inebriates the olfactory nerves.

Wash the dried figs carefully, first in plenty of water, then in white wine. Divide them in half, but don't separate them entirely; leave them joined at the stem. Insert half a walnut into each, then close them again. Place them close to one another on a cookie sheet and bake them for about 10 minutes. Meanwhile, prepare a syrup with the sugar and the juice of the 5 lemons. Bring this just to boiling point. Turn off the heat and let the syrup cool before adding to it the brandy and the anise liqueur. Put the figs into a glass jar. Pack them in closely, arranging them in layers. Pour some of the prepared syrup over each layer. When the jar is full, make sure that the figs are completely covered by the syrup. Close the jar and keep it in a dry, dark place. These figs can also be eaten right after the preparation described.

"Folarielli" (Stuffed Fig Leaves)

2 qts. must - 2 heaped cups sugar - 2 1/4 lbs. uva regina (large, sweet, crunchy, golden-yellow grapes) - salt - 1 cup white wine - 3 mandarin oranges - 3 lemons - 1 shot-glass anise liqueur - 1 shot-glass cognac - fig leaves - lemon leaves

This method of preparation is very old and guintessentially Sorrentine. *Folarielli* (from the Latin folium, "leaf") represent a renewal of the genteel custom, part of the way of life along this blessed coast, of offering one's guests tasty delicacies, prepared with love and presented most attractively.
The ritual of preparing folarielli begins at grapeharvest time, continues around the middle of November, and concludes gloriously on Christmas day. There's not a Christmas table that doesn't offer this delicious treat.
Set aside 2 qts. of grape must. Cook this with 2 heaped cups of sugar for about 3 hours, or until the volume of the mixture is reduced by half. Store this in a large bottle in the cellar. The mixture will be used later in preparing the folarielli.
Uva regina are also available during this same time of the year. In Sorrento, such grapes are called *uva pane*, "bread grapes." They're a little hollow in the center. Heat plenty of water and add to it several pinches of salt. When the water boils, plunge the grapes into it two or three times for several seconds. Put the grapes into a box and expose them to the heat of the sun for a week.
Next, arrange the grapes in a baking-dish and bake them in a moderate oven for 1 hour. Then bathe them with the white wine and put them back in the oven for 10 minutes. The dried grapes are now ready to be set aside in plates covered with napkins or parchment paper.
Towards the middle of November, when the mandarins are still rather greenish, the ceremony of preparation continues. Soak the dried grapes in the

must for 2 days, together with the very finely-chopped mandarin and lemon peels, a shot-glass of anise liqueur, and a shotglass of cognac.

Now get yourself some fig leaves with the stems still attached. Fold each leaf into a cone shape, place 2 lemon leaves in the center, and then spoon in a tablespoon or so of the grapes, now completely impregnated with wonderful flavors.

The stem of the fig leaf can be whittled to a point with a sharp knife, folded over, and pinned to the other side of the leaf to close the little package.

Put the stuffed leaves into a moderate oven for 20 minutes. Your "little leaves" are, at last, ready to be eaten.

Limoncino (lemon Liqueur)

1 qt. grain alcohol - 6 garden lemons, still a little green - 2 cups white sugar - 6 small leaves of lemon verbena – 3 cups water

The art of making liqueurs owes a great deal to Louis XIV of France, who sometimes suffered from spells of weakness and experienced those difficulties of ordinary living that often manifest themselves in one's seventh decade. The king's specialists in such matters would mix together brandy, sugar, and aromatic herbs to rejuvenate his spirits, and these beverages became known as "cordials".

And so here is the *limoncino*; a strong liquor that's been sugared and aromatized, and that is satisfying to both taste and smell. As the personal cook to Her Majesty Catherine in St. Petersburg wrote, felicitous combinations of liquors "can shed much light on the physics of aromas and flavors."

Remove the outer portion of the lemon peels with a very sharp knife, leaving behind the mesocarp (the white internal portion). Place the peels with the leaves of lemon verbena (also known as Luisa or vervain) in the alcohol in a covered jar. Leave these ingredients in infusion for seven days. At the end of this time, filter the infused liquid through an old cloth. Prepare a light syrup by boiling the water with the sugar for five minutes.

After this has cooled, pour it into a jar with the alcohol.

Let this stand for another week, then strain again through a very finely-woven cloth so that the liquor becomes limpid and clear. *Limoncino* is generally served in small liqueur glasses. It has a pleasant taste and promotes the digestive functions.

Liquore di fragole (Strawberry Liqueur)

1 1/2 lbs. strawberries - 3 cups sugar - 3 cups grain alcohol – 1 1/2 cups water - 2 tsp. vanilla

Select your strawberries, wash them, and let them dry. Then put them into a glass jar that can be hermetically sealed, add equal amounts of sugar and alcohol, the water, and the vanilla. Leave the strawberries in this infusion for 20 days. Shake the jar three or four times a day to ensure that the sugar dissolves in the alcohol and water. At the end of the 20 days, strain the liquor through a paper filter and pour it into a bottle. You can store the strawberries that remain in a glass jar, cover them with some more alcohol, and use the result as a topping for fresh fruit salads or as a garnish for desserts.

Marmellata di arance amare
(Bitter orange marmalade)

5 lb. bitter oranges - 2 1/2 lb. sweet oranges - 2 lemons - 1 qt. + 1 pint water + enough water for the seeds - 6 1/2 cup sugar

Peel the bitter oranges very finely and cut the orange peel "a julienne", that is in very fine strips. Cut the oranges in half and collect all the seeds. Squeeze the bitter oranges and the sweet oranges.
Work the lemons as you did the bitter oranges. In a saucepan collect the juice of all the citrus fruits. Add the peels and the water.
Place all the seeds in a bowl and cover them with water. After 24 hours put the saucepan on the heat. In the meanwhile the seeds will have produced the pectin which we will need to thicken the marmalade. Filter the liquid through a cheesecloth, close the bundle and add it in the saucepan. Let cook until the

juice is reduced to less than half (about 2 hours). Warm the sugar in a stainless steel bowl in the oven and add it in the saucepan trying not to reduce the boiling. After 4 minutes turn off the heat.

Warm the absolutely clean glass jars in the oven. Pour the marmalade in them when it is still warm and liquid. Close the jars hermetically.

Marmellata di fichi (Fig marmalade)

2 1/4 lbs. figs - 1 3/4 cups sugar

Remove the skin from the ends of the figs only; leave the central part of the skins intact. Put the figs in a saucepan and cook them for about an hour. Heat the sugar in the oven, add this to the saucepan, and stir slowly. After about 10 minutes, the marmalade will be ready to be poured into the glass jars which you will have warmed in the oven. Seal the jars hermetically.

Marmellate di fragole (Strawberry jam)

4 1/2 lbs. strawberries - 2 lemons - 3 cups sugar

The addition of lemon juice helps increase the acidity and the pectin of those fruits, such as cherries, peaches, strawberries, and pears, which contain low levels of jelling agents.

Wash the strawberries, place them in a large pot with the lemon juice, and cook them for about an hour until all the water has evaporated. Heat the sugar in the oven, stir the warm sugar into the strawberries, and let the mixture simmer for about 20 more minutes. Turn off the heat and let the strawberries cool for 10 minutes. Meanwhile, wash the glass containers to be used - they must be heat-resistant - and dry them upside down in a hot oven so that they're well sterilized and free from microorganisms. Pour the marmalade into these small jars, clean their rims, seal them with plastic film, screw on the lids and label them.

Marmellata di mandarini
(Mandarin Orange Marmelade)

11 lbs. mandarin oranges - 5 lemons – 2 1/2 qts. water – 5 lbs. (11 cups) sugar

Citrus fruits, Arabian in origin, have for centuries now occupied an important position in the Mediterranean diet, where they are eaten fresh and used in the preparation of ices, sorbets, and desserts. Our country can be considered as virtually a giant factory for the production of ascorbic acid or vitamin C, which is found principally in citrus fruits but also in grains and green, yellow, and orange vegetables, which provide vitamins A and E as well.

These are the "anticancer" vitamins, which play an important role in the prevention of that disease, as proved by the studies of the Nobel Prize laureate Dulbecco, who was the first to determine the close correlation between the development of pathological tumors and vitamin deficiencies.

Although the present recipe for this delicious marmalade is British in origin, it qualifies for mention here because we thought it wouldn't be amiss to include it in view of the significant part that citrus fruits play in our diet here in Italy. Slice the mandarins and the lemons in half. Collect as many of the seeds as you can in a bowl. (They're rich in pectin, a water-soluble, gelatinizing substance that will be responsible for giving the marmalade the proper consistency.) Cover the seeds with water - about 1 cup should be enough. Transfer to a saucepan the juices from the citrus fruits as well as their peels. These should be cut off with a sharp knife, trimmed of all traces of white rind and fibers, and chopped rather fine. Add the water and let these ingredients steep for 24 hours. At the end of this time, you can begin the cooking process, which should take about 3 hours. But first, be careful to strain the liquid from the bowl; contact with the seeds will have made it become a bit gelatinous. Add this liquid to the saucepan and place the seeds in an old cloth. Tie this into a tight little bundle and drop it into the saucepan. Light the stove. As soon as the liquid begins to boil, lower the heat, and let simmer for about 3 hours until a good part of the liquid has evaporated and the chopped peels seem close to touching the bottom of the saucepan. At this point, warm the sugar thoroughly in the oven and add. (Warming the sugar removes all its moisture and at the same time makes certain that the marmalade won't be subjected to a sudden drop in temperature.) Let the marmalade cook for 20 minutes longer, then turn off the heat. You can tell you've reached the point that's exactly right in cooking the marmalade by putting a teaspoon of it onto a saucer and cooling it rapidly in the freezer. Then use the side of a knifeblade to lift it off the saucer; if the mixture detaches itself slowly in one single thread, it's properly cooked. After about an hour, heat some small, perfectly clean glass jars in the oven to prevent any traumatic experiences for the marmalade. Use a small ladle to fill the jars. Cover with a disc of plastic film and screw the lids onto the jars.

Marmellata di pesche
(Peach jam)

4 1/4 lbs. (fresh weight) peaches - 4 cups sugar - 2 lemons
Fruit contains (in its peel, seeds, and core, for the most part) a gelatinizing agent, pectin, which can nonetheless be reduced or eliminated by cooking for a long period of time. This is why it's preferable to produce marmalades in small quantities that cook more rapidly. To prepare this marmalade, wash the peaches and remove their peels, stems, pits, and any damaged parts. Chop the fruit into pieces and place them in a rather large, uncovered saucepan with the juice of the two lemons. Cook for about an hour, until the fruit has eliminated almost all the water it contains. In the oven, warm the sugar, then take it out and add it slowly to the peaches. Stir until the boiling point is reached again. Keep cooking for another 15-20 minutes, until the mixture starts to gel. Remove from heat and allow to cool for 10 minutes.
Pour the marmalade into hot, sterilized jars, clean the rims well, seal with film, and cover the jars. Keep in a cool, dry place for a maximum period of one year.

Nocino (Walnut cordial)

1 qt. grain alcohol - 13 walnuts - 13 raw coffee beans - 13 toasted coffee beans - 3 cloves - 1 tsp. cinnamon - 3 tbsp. sugar - 1 nutmeg – 1 cup water

...We call it David and Goliath: a little one and you are stoned!

Nunc est bibendum ("It's time to drink") sings Horace, in an ode composed on the occasion of the victory at Actium.

Wine had been drunk for centuries and centuries before anyone imagined that it was possible to extract its spiritous essence, the cause of every heightening of flavor that gives such special excitement to wine-tasting. It was Paracelsus who, in the 16th century, succeeded in isolating the most subtle, quintessential ingredient of wine and called it alcohol vini. Alcohol exalts one's state of mind; the various elixirs that contain it cause joy and arouse energy, although it can of course also be a formidable weapon, because going beyond certain limits in its use can cause confusion and destruction.

A fitting conclusion to a good meal is this aromatic little cordial, fragrant with the past and prepared from the excellent walnuts of Sorrento, the fruit of the *Juglans regia*, a tree of the family *Juglandaceae*.

Between St. John's Day and St. Paul's Day, absolutely not before nor after the period from June 24th to June 29th, when the moon is favorable to such an operation as this magic ritual, collect the walnuts.

Given the time of year, they will still be enclosed in their shells, not yet fully mature. You should use 13 walnuts for every quart of alcohol. Cut each nut into four pieces and add them to the alcohol together with the raw coffee beans and the toasted coffee beans, a slightly crushed nutmeg kernel, the cloves, and the finely- minced cinnamon. Let this infusion stand inside a large, wide-mouthed, hermetically closed bottle. You should place it somewhere out of doors, in the sun and in the open air.

After 40 days have passed, strain the alcohol and free it from all the ingredients that were in infusion. Set the strained liqueur aside.

Prepare a solution of about 1 cup water and 3 tbsp. sugar. Bring this to boil and make sure the sugar is completely dissolved. Leave to cool. When the solution is cold, add it to the alcohol and let this stand as before for 40 days. At the end of this time, strain the nocino again.

Now you can begin to serve it in tiny glasses as a tonic and digestive beverage. If you can manage to keep some of it in the cellar, in a cool spot, for a few more months, it will reach an even higher level of aroma and taste.

I kept a bottle of nocino for ten years and I can assure you it is sublime!

OIL-PACKED FOODS

Carciofini
(Artichokes in Oil)

2 lbs. small artichokes - 4 lemons - 2 qts. white
vinegar - salt - olive oil - 4 cloves garlic - wild
oregano - hot pepper

Remove all the tough outer leaves from the artichokes, slice off their tips, and cut them into wedges (you must remove the choke); or, if you succeed in finding those tiny artichokes that can be obtained only on a few days of the year, the last days of May, use them whole. Keep them for two days in fresh water and the juice of 2 lemons. When you're ready to prepare them, wash them, drain them, and put them in a saucepan with the vinegar, several pinches of salt, and 2 peeled lemons, cut into pieces. Turn on the heat and bring to boil. After 2 minutes of boiling, remove the artichokes with a slotted spoon. Drain them and place them on a white napkin to dry for 2 hours. Then store them in a glass jar, alternating layers of artichokes with some thinly-sliced garlic, hot pepper, and wild oregano, and pour in enough olive oil to cover the contents of the jar.

Involtini di melanzane
(Stuffed eggplant rolls in olive oil)

2 lbs. Italian eggplants - 6 salted anchovies - 4
cloves garlic - 2 hot peppers - 1/2 cup capers -
oregano - plenty of olive oil - vinegar – salt

When high summer has arrived and our garden begins to produce an amount of eggplants that exceeds our ability to consume them, we find it a good idea to preserve some of them for use when it begins to get cold, as a remembrance of summer days, of *a stagione*, "the season," a Neapolitan figure of speech for the summer. Peel the eggplants and cut them lengthwise into thin slices. Leave them in a solution of vinegar and salt for 2 days.

Now we'll prepare a rather thick mixture with the salted anchovy fillets (cut into small pieces), the garlic cloves (chopped fine), the hot pepper (not mild), the oregano, and the capers. Cover everything with pure olive oil. Gently squeeze the eggplant slices to eliminate excess vinegar. Use a teaspoon to place a little of the mixture described above on the center of each eggplant slice. Roll up the slices to form little bundles (*involtini*) and place them in an orderly manner, one next to the other, layer upon layer, in a glass jar. Then cover them with the purest extra-virgin olive oil and close the glass container with a cover.

We can commence "hostilities" at once and eat these freshly prepared, or, calm and disciplined, store them in the pantry for all the long winter months.

Olive verdi schiacciate
(Crushed green olives in oil)

Fresh green olives - garlic - hot pepper -
oregano - fennel seeds - salt - olive oil

Crush the fresh green olives one by one. Eliminate their pits and put them in a large glass jar. Cover with water.

After about 24 hours, change the water; repeat this operation every 12 hours, morning and evening, for 15 days. When this preliminary phase is over, the olives will be purified having lost any bitter taste. Drain them and press them so that all the water they contain is eliminated. Put them in the glass jar again, sprinkling every layer with pieces of crushed garlic, hot pepper, oregano, fennel seeds, salt, and olive oil.

Apply pressure on each layer to pack the olives well. When the jar is full, cover the olives with plenty of olive oil, close the jar, and place it in the pantry.

Tonno (Tuna in Oil)

2 lbs. tuna - 1 qt. water - 4-5 tbsp. salt - olive oil
- vegetable oil

The goal of the art of preserving foods is to be able to offer at any time of the year the various items that are particular to each season. When summer is nearing its end, small tuna fish venture into the southern Mediterranean. Much effort is expended to catch these fish, members of the order Perciformes, which have blue backs and silver sides. And so it's become the custom along our coasts to preserve tuna, as well as albacore, a fish that is closely related to the tuna and whose flesh is even more highly prized.

The preparation goes like this. Cut the tuna (or albacore) into large pieces, about 1/2 lb. each. Put these pieces into old dishtowels and tie them into tight little bundles. Immerse these bundles in cold, salted water, making sure that the fish are well covered. If you need to, you can add more water.

Always figure on a bit more than 1/4 salt for every quart of water.

Calculate a cooking period of two hours from the moment when the water begins to boil.

Then remove the little bundles from the water, open them, and spread the fish out on cloth napkins or paper towels. Remove any dark portions and skin. After this operation is completed, arrange the cleaned fish pieces in a jar with an hermetic closure. Cover them completely with oil, using equal parts of olive oil and vegetable oil. Seal the jars and immerse them in a large pot of water. Bring this to boil and keep the jars boiling for more than an hour.

Bibliography

Jaucourt, article *Cuisine*, from l'Encyclopèdie, Paris 1752, vol II.(1752)
Alexandre Dumas father, *Le Grand Dictionnaire de la cuisine* (1850)
Lewis Carroll, *Alice's Adventures in Wonderland* (1865)
Guillaume Apollinaire, *Le poète assassinè* (1910)
Ludwig Feuerbach, *Philosophical Scripts* (1844)
Marcel Proust, *A la recherche du temp perdu (Swann's Way)* (1913)
Jean Baudrillard, *L'autre par lui-meme* (1988).
Anthelme Brillat-Savarin, *Physiology du gout* (1855)
Roland Barthes, *Myth Today* (1962)
Pellegrino Artusi, *Science in the Kitchen and the Art of Eating Weel* (1891)
Petronio Arbitro, *Satyricon* (I sec. A.C.)
Piero Camporesi, *Il pane selvaggio* (1980)
Piero Camporesi, *I balsami di Venere* (1989)
Piero Camporesi, *La miniera del mondo* (1990)
Piero camporesi, *Il brodo indiano*1990)
Claude Lèvi-Strauss, *The raw and the Cooked* (1966).
Diogenes Laertius, *Lives of the Philosophers* (III sec. A.C.)
Michel Onfray, *Le ventre des philosophes* (1991).
Guido Gozzano, *Poems* (1907)
Quintus Horatio Flaccus, *Ars Poetica* (I sec. B.C.)
Jean-Jacques Rousseau, *Emile* (1750)
Georges Bernier, *Antonin Carême - sensualitè gourmande en Europe* (1989)
Plinius Secundus Maior, *Historia naturalis* (V chapt.) (I sec. A.C.)
Wolfgang Goethe,*Italianische Reise (Italian Journey)*. (1826)
Giovanni Boccaccio, *Decameron* (1351)
Nello Oliviero, *Storie e curiosità del mangiare napoletano* (1983)
Folco Portinari, *Il piacere della gola* (1986)
Matilde Serao, *Il ventre di Napoli,* Delfino, Napoli, 1973. (1880)
Giulio Cesare Croce, *Le sottilissime astuzie di Bertoldo* (1978)
Michel Foucault, *L'usage des plasir* (1985)
Francois Rebelais, *Gargantua e Pantagruel* (1550)
Gualtiero Marchesi, *Oltre il fornello* (1986)
Fabrizio Mangoni, *Dolcipersone* (1986)
Giuseppe Tomasi di Lampedusa, *Il gattopardo* (1958)
Italo Calvino, *Italian folktales* (1956)
Benedetto Croce, *Storie e leggende napoletane* (1892)
Jean Clausel, *Venise exquise* (1990)
Alberto Savino, *Capri* (1920)
Marcus Gavius Apicius *De re coquinaria* (I sec. A.C.)

Ovidius,, *Metamorphes* (I sec. A.C.)

Lorenzo Da Ponte, *Don Giovanni,* (atto I scena nona). (1787)

Giuseppe Marotta, *L'oro di Napoli*, 1(948)

Ippolito Cavalcanti, *La cucina Teorico Pratica,* (1847)

Carlo Goldoni, *Donna di garbo*, (1743)

William Shakespeare, *Romeo and Juliet*, (act IV scene II). (1595)

English index

Italian index

Zuppa primavera (Springtime soup) 81

Main index

Printed in the United Kingdom
by Lightning Source UK Ltd.
128242UK00001B/6/A